ENTERPRISING WOMEN

Other books by *Caroline Bird*

THE INVISIBLE SCAR
BORN FEMALE
THE CROWDING SYNDROME
EVERYTHING A WOMAN NEEDS TO KNOW
    TO GET PAID WHAT SHE'S WORTH
THE CASE AGAINST COLLEGE

ENTERPRISING

Caroline

WOMEN

Bird

A BICENTENNIAL PROJECT OF THE BUSINESS AND
PROFESSIONAL WOMEN'S FOUNDATION

W · W · NORTON & COMPANY · INC · NEW YORK

Library of Congress Catologing in Publication Data

Bird, Caroline.
    Enterprising women.

    "A Bicentennial project of the Business and Pro-
fessional Women's Foundation."
    Includes bibliograghical references and index.
    1. Women—United States—History.   2. Women in
business—History.   I. Title.
HQ1410.B52   1976   331.4'0973   75–33662
ISBN 0–393–08724–7

DESIGN BY M FRANKLIN–PLYMPTON

PRINTED IN THE UNITED STATES OF AMERICA
4 5 6 7 8 9

To the memory of my great-grandmother,
Louisa Brayton Sawin, first schoolteacher in Madison,
Wisconsin

CONTENTS

PROLOGUE

If you believe what you read in history books, the prosperity of America is strictly man made. Very few female names appear in the index of any standard economic history of the United States, and if the word "women" occurs in the index at all, it refers to some parenthetical remark on the growing employment of women outside the home, or the impact of their "emancipation" on the birthrate.

Economic historians readily concede that the work of women has always been essential to the economy, but they have never thought that they had to pay special attention to it.

This book challenges that convention. The changing home duties of women have been an important influence on the development of the economy at every stage of our history. In addition, there have always been some women who have stepped outside the assigned limits to work in business or the professions, or to shape economic affairs in a nontraditional way.

A woman printed the signed copy of the Declaration of Independence, and since then there have always been American women making money or exercising economic power. Enterprising women have always been on the scene, but generally in the background. Their contemporaries shrugged them off as anomalies, and because they belied convenient assumptions, historians have short-changed them for the sake of conceptual tidiness.

The women in this book are a sample chosen to illustrate the variety of economic scenes in which women have played starring roles at various periods of our history. Some were included because we found their stories provocative in themselves; others, because their influence on the direction of the economy deserves more thought than it often receives. As we hunted for them in the corners of history, we found ourselves cheering for their gallantry in coping with the unpromising circumstances which forced so many of them into earning their own living. We marveled at the ingenuity with which they discovered or created opportunities overlooked by men, or found loopholes in the conventions which limited them as women. Their patience sometimes put us to shame, even though we suspected the high price they paid for it. Most of them are worth knowing as people because of their constructive response to the economic conditions facing them.

Some achievers have been forgotten because their work left no permanent trace. Susan King made money in the mid-nineteenth century by speculation in New York City real estate, but she sank out of sight as far as history is concerned. A little later, Maggie Walker responded to the exclusion of emancipated blacks from early insurance coverage by building an insurance company just for them. Segregated insurance is happily an industry of the past. But we thought you would like to know how a determined black woman built a stable business in an insurance market that the big companies of her time couldn't or wouldn't serve.

Other women from earlier times have influenced the economy of 1976 in ways that historians have failed to recognize. The present is based on ideas that were new in the past, and not all of the new ideas sprang from the minds of men. The innovations of women have been ignored because they are not usually mechanical inventions which can be credited to a single individual. Women seldom invent the sort of thing that can be drawn, described, and filed in the patent office.

Just after the Civil War, for instance, William Demorest

patented a tucking attachment for the sewing machine he had invented, but it never occurred to him to patent the idea on which he and his wife built a successful business. Nell Demorest had realized that paper patterns, which women had made for themselves as a guide in cutting material for a dress, could be mass produced, and also used to sell fashionable designs.

We've included some of the women who initiated concepts that created new kinds of work or affected the rules of the economic game. Catharine Beecher does not appear in economic histories, but it is hard to overestimate the economic impact of her argument that women are better than men at teaching little children—and ought to do it at less pay.

Traditionally, the achievements of women have been defined in other than economic terms whenever it is possible. Only 42 women were listed, for instance, as "entrepreneurs" among the 1359 included in *Notable American Women*, the three-volume dictionary of biography from colonial days to 1950 published in 1971 under the auspices of Radcliffe College.

It is a mistake, however, to assume that entrepreneurs are the only ones who contribute to the economy. Economists themselves are the first to tell us that some of the most substantial contributions cannot be reckoned in money at all. When Ellen Richards founded the profession of home economics, she improved the productivity of the unpaid work women do at home. Alice Lakey, although she made no money herself, made every American family budget stretch farther by securing public regulation of foods and drugs. The casework method of administering welfare developed by Mary Richmond is now the basis on which billions of dollars have been transferred from taxpayers to the poor.

We think of these women as social reformers, but they are economic heroines as well. None of them created the social invention we've credited to her singlehandedly. We've chosen to write about them as representatives of a large group of likeminded women because the conditions women have had to overcome can best be illustrated in terms of individual careers.

Some of the women innovators we have selected, however, have profoundly influenced the economy and the status of women for the worse. Sarah Hale's assertion that women have a special "sphere"—one requiring the interpretation of lady "editresses" like herself—created career opportunities for women to serve other women at the expense of perpetuating an auxiliary, dependent status for *all* women. Her insistence that women are "above" financial concerns was an understandable defensive response to their exclusion from financial policy making, but it also justified lower pay for women in any occupation that could be interpreted as womanly.

We have made no attempt, therefore, to set up role models for other women to follow. Enterprising men are often ingenious and perceptive rather than noble, and enterprising women have a right to be the same. We could not resist including, for instance, the brilliant economic *tour de force* of the Everleigh sisters, who put prostitution on a sound businesslike basis at a time when the existence of a market for a product or service was regarded as justification for supplying it. They extracted money from a sexist society by making men pay for what they expected to get at home for nothing, whether their wives were willing or not.

Others we included were personally and ideologically less attractive than the Everleighs. Frances Leigh defended slavery. But all of their stories shed light on the economic opportunities and contributions of women in relatively unexplored corners of history.

Like them or not—and there is no reason why anyone has to like them all—enterprising women have always been part of the American scene. As we follow their achievements, we can see that they have been as consistent a force in American economic history as blacks, Jews, immigrants, intellectuals, Catholics, labor, and other groups that historians identify and analyze.

During the women's equality movement of the 1970s, many individual women have made the reassuring discovery that they are not alone among women of their time in questioning the traditional role society has assigned to them. Now we have learned that this questioning is not just a contemporary phenomenon. As we searched for enterprising women through two hundred years of American history, we were delighted, and even chagrined, to find our counterparts in crinolines observing truths we thought we had been the first to perceive.

Readers who take comfort in the support women are now giving each other will be reassured to find that from Eliza Pinckney, our earliest example, to Eleanor Holmes Norton, our most recent, enterprising women have been sisters under the skin.

This book was undertaken at the suggestion of the Business and Professional Women's Foundation, whose encouragement and financial support made the research for it possible. Margaret Hickey, Chairperson of the BPW Research Committee, was especially helpful.

Emily Wheeler, Radcliffe '75, and Ellen Schreier, Vassar '75, both history majors, helped me make a feasibility study of the project in the summer of 1974. Ellen devoted a substantial portion of her time to the effort until its completion and at the same time earned election to Phi Beta Kappa and the 1975 Vassar history prize. She contributed criticism and concepts as well as important research and my principal intellectual debt in writing this book is to her.

I am specially indebted to Dr. Elsa Dixler, who taught Vassar's course "Women in American History," for her historical insights. Others who shared their special historical knowledge included Drs. Jeffrey Barach, Tulane University; Betty Daniels, Norman Hodges, and Leslie Koempel, Vassar College; Ward L. Miner, Youngstown State University; Muriel W. Pumphrey, University of Missouri, St. Louis; and Leonard Sayles, Columbia University; also Franklin R. Bruns of the Smithsonian Institution, and Arthur Hecht of the National Archives.

Helpful with research also were Stephen Booke, Jane Chapman, Bob Chase, Elizabeth Colclough, Lenora R. Cross, Marjorie Godfrey, Bonnie Herndon, John Jones, Betty Jane and Thomas Kelley, Barbara Lyon, Nancy E. MacKenzie, Marty Madory, Harold Mandelbaum, Tom Mahoney, Barbara Pierce, Ishbel Ross, and Timothy Wheeler.

Elizabeth Bennett, State University of New York, Albany, MLS '73, procured and returned the hundreds of volumes we consulted. Jane McGarvey of Adriance Memorial Library, Poughkeepsie, obtained many of these through the interlibrary loan services of Mid-Hudson Libraries and the Southeastern New York Library Resources Council. Special librarians who did research for us include Jenrose Felmley, BPW librarian; Patricia King, Schlesinger Library, Radcliffe College; Catherine Kennedy, Enoch Pratt Free Library of Baltimore; and most importantly, Frances Goudy, Shirley Maul, and Joan Murphy of the Vassar College Library.

As she has done on previous books, Helene Mandelbaum served as architect: she not only defended the track of the book, but frequently rediscovered it in the swamp of interesting and irrelevant data. Her editorial judgment has been invaluable.

Marjorie Godfrey kept accounts, researched and interviewed resources, and checked facts. Esther Vail cheerfully typed draft after draft of the manuscript as did Angela Abbate, Olga Carmel, and Ann Marie Hampson.

My husband, Tom Mahoney, who is an authority on business history, read, researched, and did whatever needed to be done at any time.

Caroline Bird

July, 1975
Poughkeepsie, N.Y.

ENTERPRISING WOMEN

1

THE DECLARATION
OF INDEPENDENCE
Mary Goddard
and the Early Printers

Very few people know that the official Declaration of Independence—the version containing the authenticated names of the signers that was circulated to all the colonies—was printed by a woman.

Because the Declaration was "conceived out of a decent respect to the Opinions of Mankind," its purpose could only be achieved by publication. Although this incendiary document had been approved on the fourth of July, 1776, it wasn't until August that some of the founding fathers dared to sign their names to it, and Congress didn't muster the courage to order it printed and distributed until January 18, 1777, when the approach of the British forced the legislators to flee from Philadelphia to Baltimore.

The job of printing the Declaration went to a woman because as publisher of the leading newspaper in town, she had the facilities to do it. We know who she was because printers sign their work, and the printer on this job must have realized that she was making history. Instead of using her initials as she often did, she spelled her name out in full. She was Mary Katherine Goddard (1738–1816), and she had learned the trade from her brother, William Goddard.

In the Revolutionary era, and well into the early years of the republic, a man with skills practiced his trade or craft at home, relying on the help of the women in his family. If the business thrived to support apprentices, servants, slaves, and journeymen, the women in the family became managers, charged with the care, feeding, training, health, and encouragement of these additions to the household. Apprentices were always underfoot—extras to be fed, nursed in illness, guided, and taught like the master's children.

In addition to caring for this extended household, the women in the family were expected to take charge whenever the master was away or unable to function. Mary Katherine Goddard was often left in charge of her brother's print shop, and she had learned what was called "the Mystick Art of Printing" by helping him out. As a young woman, she had hung around William Goddard's shop in Providence, Rhode Island, learning how to set type, inking the forms with leather balls, and feeding paper into the small presses.

This was no more than all women did in a family business, and most remained anonymous helpers behind the scenes.

Mary Goddard appears as a footnote to history because of the symbolic importance of one of her printing jobs. But she interests us for other reasons. Her story is a splendid illustration of what one woman could do with the opportunities that came her way because of the circumstances of her own life, and because of the economic setting in which she worked.

Mary acquired an exceptional education for a woman of her time, much of it from her mother, Sarah, who had enjoyed extraordinary educational advantages before her. Sarah Goddard (c. 1700–1770) enjoyed "acquaintance with several branches of useful and polite learning," according to Isaiah Thomas, the chronicler of early printers. She had learned these "branches" the only way a colonial lady could have learned them, by hitchhiking on the education of a male relative.

Sarah's father was affluent enough to import a French tutor for his sons, and according to contemporary calculations it therefore cost nothing to let the daughters sit in on the lessons. The eulogy printed at Sarah's death, an unusual honor even for an eminent woman, mentions her "uncommon attainments in literature," but hastens to add that these were "the least valuable parts of her character." The valuable parts were her cheerfulness, her piety, and her unfailing service to her family. One of these services was teaching her children, and we can assume that she passed her own learning on to them.

In addition to her education, she gave her daughter an unusual example of female enterprise. As so often happened in colonial families, Sarah was left as a widow with full responsibility for preserving the family property. She inherited an estate from her husband, a prosperous physician, while her son William was still a printer's apprentice. In 1762, she lent him 300 pounds, with which he founded his first newspaper, the *Providence Gazette.*

Two years later, William was berating Rhode Island authorities because he felt they had not given him an adequate share of the public printing business. By 1765, he had lost interest in the paper, and had taken up the campaign against the British Stamp Act that was restricting the trade of the colonies. While Sarah supervised the apprentices and journeymen, Mary rolled up her sleeves, put on a big apron, and set type in her brother's place. It was only the first of several times that Sarah and Mary would take over so that William could move on to another project. And though Sarah Goddard continued to dole out money when William needed it, she did not deed him the remainder of his father's estate, in exchange for regular support, until she was nearing 70.

But Sarah was much more than a source of money and labor for her son. She and her daughter Mary contributed humorous tidbits to the *Gazette*, enlivening the long-winded political essays of the period, and they culled British books and publications for material they thought would appeal to their readers. One choice that William might not have made was the letters of Lady Mary Wortley Montagu, the famous

English intellectual who is regarded as the first feminist. The first North American printing of these letters was a 204-page volume published by Sarah in 1766.

In addition to suggestions for material to reprint, Sarah bombarded her son with admonitions to keep out of fruitless quarrels. It was not unwarranted advice. In Philadelphia, where he was running the *Pennsylvania Chronicle,* he fought openly not only with the competing paper, the *Pennsylvania Journal,* but with his own partners. In 1767, he told the world about his grievances by writing and selling an account entitled *The Partnership.* During the following year, William persuaded his mother to invest in the new paper and move to Philadelphia with Mary to watch over the shop. Money was always short. In 1771, William actually spent some time in debtor's prison.

By 1773, William had lost interest in Philadelphia and was busy founding Baltimore's first newspaper, the *Maryland Journal.* Disgusted with the official British post riders between Philadelphia and Baltimore, William paid his own riders to keep his two papers in touch. That gave him an idea. In 1774, he closed the Philadelphia paper and turned the Baltimore paper over to his sister so that he could spend all his time promoting his ambitious "Scheme for Colony Post Riders," a postal service for the rebelling colonies that would secure their communications from the secret agents of the British controlled mails.

A truly American postal system was an idea whose time had come. Local patriots in every colony rallied around William Goddard's "scheme." Within a year, his riders had supplanted the British almost everywhere. In 1775, Congress adopted the new system but entrusted it to Benjamin Franklin, who had long run the colonial mail service for the British crown.

William was miffed at the slight. When he turned down the postmastership of Baltimore, a logical job for the publisher of the local paper, Franklin gave the job to Mary Katherine, making her the new republic's first postmistress, and appointed William to be surveyor, or traveling inspector, of the whole system. The surveyorship sounded better, and it suited

William's wandering habits, but he quarreled with his superior. After a year, during which his performance was rated "careless, slovenly," William Goddard was out of work with nothing better to do than hang around the *Maryland Journal*, which Mary had grown accustomed to managing her own way. She was in charge when the Continental Congress employed the *Journal* printshop to print the "authenticated" copy of the Declaration of Independence with the names of all the signers.

Meanwhile, William brooded and picked fights. In 1777, the superpatriot Whig Club of Baltimore missed the irony of an article he wrote and tried to run him physically out of town. In 1778, a good friend talked him out of a public attack on Benjamin Franklin. A year later, Continental Army officers were mobbing him for printing the complaint of an officer courtmartialed for misconduct.

The inevitable break with Mary Katherine came in 1784. During the ten years of her management, Mary Katherine had built the *Maryland Journal* into a thriving enterprise which William's quarrels threatened. In order to have a project of his own, William considered setting up a "noncompeting" press, but Mary objected both privately and, at least once, in the pages of the *Journal* itself. In 1784, he bought her out on terms which she resented so deeply that she retired from publishing and refused to have anything to do with him ever again.

William Goddard sounded off a great deal in public. From his letters, broadsides, editorials, and essays, he emerges as a typical American promoter, a man of large and shifting schemes, a touchy man, quick to take offense, a creator of brawls both verbal and physical. He was a master of the eighteenth-century art of political invective, and seems to have made enemies for the sheer joy of telling them off.

The record of William's life also suggests that he was dependent on women at every stage of his career. He relied on Sarah and Mary to make each of his projects earn enough money to fund the next one. He did not marry until two years after his break with Mary Katherine, and the wife he finally took, at 45, was an heiress. Shortly after his marriage to Abigail Angell, he sold the Baltimore paper to her younger brother and retired to her home in Providence.

So much for William. We know much less about the women who supported him at every turn, and next to nothing about Mary Katherine. While quite capable, especially in her later years, of defending her own interests—when she fell out with William she brought five lawsuits against him in a single day—she never expressed her own opinion on the political issues which she reported as an editor, and she left no letters. Her character must be reconstructed from oblique references in other documents.

The reports in which she is mentioned provide provocative glimpses of an efficient and respected businesswoman. Her brother testified that she was "an expert and correct compositor of types." Unlike the publishers of other revolutionary newspapers, Mary always met her deadline, whether William was at home, away, or in jail. While he was galloping up and down the colonies on wild goose chases, Mary exploited the controversies of the day by printing the fulminations of both sides. Her brother's friend, General Charles Lee, gave Mary as well as William a power of attorney to act for him in selling his plantation. Did he know that Mary would do the actual work her brother undertook? Or did he feel safer knowing she would be watching over the transaction? The contemporary verdict on Mary was "a woman of extraordinary judgment, energy, nerve, and strong good sense," and there is evidence that her hard work paid off in a comfortable income. We have, for instance, an advertisement in which she offered a reward for the return of a trunk full of guineas, dollars, and Portuguese half-johans, apparently stolen from her in 1783. At the Census of 1790 her household counted four slaves and one free person.

In addition to being a successful newspaper publisher and printer, Mary Katherine Goddard was the new nation's first, and for many years our only, woman postmaster. She was equally respected in that position. Thomas Jefferson is said to have praised her efficiency. The postmaster general wrote that her records were better kept than those of other postmasters, all of whom were male. More to the point, in his

eyes, she sent her receipts to him promptly, instead of leaving money "lying around" in her office.

Not that there was an excess of money anywhere in the
new system that her brother had initiated. In order to keep
the post riders on their rounds, Mary frequently dug down
into her own pocket to add "hard money" to the depreciated
Continental currency she had to accept as postage. Since
newspapers were major beneficiaries of the postal system,
the contribution was good business as well as good patriotism.

During the Revolution, the posts were a thankless task.
Publishers took on the job because they had a business stake
in keeping the mails moving. But in 1789, when there was
money to pay postmasters, and the job had become a political
plum, an emissary from the new postmaster general dropped
in to the Baltimore postoffice with a note ordering Mary to
turn the office over to one John White.

Baltimore was shocked. Hundreds of citizens signed a petition demanding that Mary Goddard be restored. When the
new postmaster general didn't answer their petition, Mary
Goddard herself wrote to President Washington. Washington insisted that the postmaster general answer, and the answer was that the job now required a man because the Baltimore postmaster was henceforth to be required to tour the
area on horseback, something a woman could not be expected to do. Mary appealed to the U.S. Senate, but her
complaint was tabled and no action was ever taken.

The end of her story would be reenacted again and again
in the long history of female enterprise. The male who replaced Mary Goddard never assumed any of the "unfeminine" duties cited as the reason why a woman could not do
the job. When she died, in 1816, alone and apparently forgotten, she freed Belinda Sterling, the slave woman who attended her last days, and left her all her property.

What was she like? The compressed lips of the portrait she
chose to have printed of herself in one of her publications
suggests that she was naturally as pugnacious as her brother,
but prided herself on keeping her temper under control. She
looks straight out of the picture, and everything we do know

about her confirms the impression of a formidable woman not to be trifled with. Mary's protests when she was forced from her job as postmistress tell us that the conscientious girl who picked up typesetting in her brother's shop, counseled him against picking quarrels, and shielded him from angry mobs, was quite capable of standing up for herself.

We know about Mary Goddard by accident, and she certainly isn't typical of the women of her time, but many of the circumstances which set her apart from other women will turn up again and again in the lives of the enterprising women as we follow them through the expanding American economy. They bear a family resemblance to each other in a number of ways.

First, enterprising women almost always started with the equivalent of the best education available to men of their time, even when they had to get it by looking over the shoulders of fathers, husbands, or brothers. Mary was the daughter of an unusually well educated woman, and both of them learned printing from William. There are exceptions, of course, but through the years self-made women have been rarer than self-made men.

Even more important has been some kind of encouragement to achieve beyond the normal role of women. Almost all enterprising women have been rewarded for being competent instead of merely pleasing. Mary Goddard had her mother as a model of enterprise, but we will make the acquaintance of many women who were the pets of educated and ambitious fathers; some of these daughters were expected to take the place of sons. Still other women were encouraged to enterprise by husbands, sponsors, or family friends.

Although Mary Goddard died a spinster, a majority of the enterprising women we will meet did become wives and mothers at some point in their lives. However, they tended to be childless and/or husbandfree during the years of their most intense career involvement. And for a number of reasons, of which late marriage is only one, they tended to achieve at older ages than comparable men. Mary Goddard never had a family, but it took her longer than her brother to get started on a career of her own. Enterprising women seem, however, to make up for their late start by remaining active longer than men. We will encounter quite a few who were still going strong in their eighties.

Finally, many of these women ascribed their enterprise to some unusual event or family crisis. They seemed to need an excuse for behaving in a nontraditional way, and the most acceptable excuse for a woman was that she was working for her family. Mary Goddard and her mother began working as helpers and replacements for William, but they became more assertive on their own when his erratic behavior threatened the family fortunes. Widowhood is the classic impetus. A great many women began their careers when their husbands died, and others were widowed while pregnant, a disaster that provided a most urgent excuse for enterprise before life insurance was commonly available.

But while enterprising women have been remarkably similar in the circumstances of their lives over the last 200 years, they have had to respond to a wide gamut of differing economic conditions.

In Mary Goddard's time, the printing industry offered unusual opportunities for women. The light but skilled work of setting type by hand for small presses, some of which could be set up in a bedroom, was not physically taxing. Moreover, early printers were not mere mechanics. All were involved in preparing the "copy" the typesetters followed, as well as in manipulating presses and paper.

Printing gave the women of the Revolution a window on the world which no other occupation of the time afforded either sex. The early printers were a closely knit clan, marrying and apprenticing into each other's families, buying each other's presses, and lending each other money. Those who did not yet have presses of their own wandered up and down the Atlantic seaboard as itinerant printers, stopping in with relatives or merely visiting with those locally established. They were one of the few links between the isolated colonies which united to form a nation.

Benjamin Franklin's central position in this loose, familial network of printers and publishers was the solid economic base of his political power in the colonies. His influence was moral and professional as well as economic. His former apprentices, junior partners, and debtors in the trade knew personally that he was a good businessman, so they respected his judgment in politics, too.

Women were indispensable in maintaining these links. Take, for instance, Ann Franklin (1696–1763), widow of James, Benjamin Franklin's older brother. She continued his press in Newport, where he had migrated after an early run-in with the British regime in Boston. Her intention was merely to hold the business for her son while he served his apprenticeship with Uncle Benjamin, then in Philadelphia. When the son died before her, she took in a male partner, Samuel Hall, and continued the business with her two daughters, whom she had taught to set type herself. A female servant did the heavy work of running the hand press.

Women maintained the succession of the *South Carolina Gazette*, set up by Lewis Timothy, one of Benjamin Franklin's many junior partners. When Timothy was accidentally killed in 1738, his widow Elizabeth put the *Gazette* out in the name of their 14-year-old son, Peter, without missing an issue. And a generation later when Peter died, his wife, Ann Timothy (c. 1727–1792), carried on as her mother-in-law had done.

Political and economic interests were intertwined. Newspapers raised the consciousness of the colonists over the injustices they suffered at the hands of the British, and the consciousness of injustice sold papers. During the long dialogue leading to the Revolution, newspapers were set up in communities formerly too small or sleepy to support them.

Colonial publishers developed some of the techniques of war propaganda which have been standard operating procedure in every conflict since. One of these was the atrocity story: publicity on the outrages committed by the hired Hessians was calculated to maintain the indignation required to keep a volunteer army in the field. Another was the development of catchy slogans, such as "taxation without representation is tyranny," coined by James Otis, one of the war propagandists. His sister, Mercy Otis Warren (1728–1814), furthered the cause by writing political satires in the form of plays, novels, and poems for Boston newspapers and publishers. Like Abigail Adams, wife of John Adams, one of the signers of the Declaration of Independence, Mercy was one of the many women who helped plan the strategy of propaganda because it was talked through at indignation meetings in their own homes.

We know a great deal about women in early printing because this craft left records at a time when records were rare, but we cannot assume that these women were exceptional. All women knew what the men in the family did to make a living and many of them learned the trade because they lived with it. In preindustrial craft enterprises, occupations passed down from father to son, but if the sons were not old enough to do the work when their father died, their mothers could and did put their hands to it. Advertisements in eighteenth-century newspapers tell us that widows continued family enterprises in such thoroughly male occupations as coach making, ship building, rigging, horse shoeing, painting and glazing, carpentry, and glass engraving, as well as the more traditionally feminine crafts of making pots and fish nets. Though we know nothing else about them, we can assume that these women learned their crafts by helping the men in their families and continued the business under their own names when the men died.

2

FAMILY BUSINESS
Nantucket Women,
Eliza Pinckney, Abigail Adams,
Sarah Astor

The early women of Nantucket are a laboratory example of the conditions which developed self-reliance in American women from the very beginning of our history.

The thirteen original colonies were strung out along a thousand miles of coastline, and were three thousand miles away from the ports of Europe. When their men were away trading, or on other business, women were often left in charge of formidable enterprises for long and uncertain periods.

Nantucket was often an island of women in the years of the Revolutionary period. Husbands were generally away at sea, either whaling, shipping, or trading in distant parts of the world. Unlike most American communities of the time, women outnumbered men four and sometimes five to one. Married women whose husbands were away on indefinite trips were thrown upon their own resources. Nantucket daughters couldn't expect to marry. And because Nantucket was an island, the women of Nantucket were forced to adapt to a society of women who were accustomed to making their own decisions.

The independence of Nantucket women impressed Hector Crevecoeur, a French consul during the first years of independence, who wrote extensively about his travels in America. Crevecoeur visited Nantucket in the 1770s. "As the sea excursions are often very long, their wives in their absence, are necessarily obliged to transact business, to settle accounts, and in short, to rule and provide for their families, . . ." he wrote of Nantucket ship owners. "The men at their return, weary with the fatigues of the sea, full of confidence and love, cheerfully give their consent to every transaction that has happened during their absence, and all is joy and peace. 'Wife thee hast done well' is the general approbation they receive for their application and industry."

Nantucket women demonstrated unusual enterprise when their island was blockaded by the British. They kept the island population decently clothed with wool (available from the island's thousands of sheep) and the flax they grew, and their initiative in trade gave rise to legends of blockade running that may well have been based on facts we can no longer verify. A heroine—some would say an anti-heroine—of the Revolution on Nantucket was Keziah Coffin (1723–1790), who seems to have played both sides in a single-minded pursuit of profit. Keziah's husband was away whaling when the blockade was declared. Posing as a Tory, she wrote the British commander of the squadron patroling Nantucket and wangled permission to use her own ships to supply the "loyal" subjects of King George on the island. Having secured a monopoly of all trade with the mainland, she proceeded to sell necessities such as firewood and fish at prices as high as the traffic would bear. When desperate neighbors couldn't pay, she calmly took mortgages on their property. Such high-handedness could not go unpunished, and after the blockade was broken, Keziah lost her ill-gotten fortune.

Nineteenth-century writers were fascinated with the legends of early Nantucket women who traded in dry goods and provisions and fitted out vessels for merchant service. Although most of the names of the originals have been lost,

Eliza Barney, a Nantucket woman writing in the 1880s, says that fifty years earlier, "all the dry goods and groceries were kept by women, who went to Boston semi-annually to renew their stock." She adds that she could recall the names of nearly 70 women who since that time had "successfully engaged in commerce, brought up and educated large families, and retired with a competence." Eventually, competition from big merchants on the mainland drove them out of business.

The initiative of Nantucket women was not, however, solely the product of isolation and a lopsided sex ratio. An accident of history added another important variable. Nantucket was settled by Quakers, who early asserted the worth of women. The result was a small, self-contained laboratory for several of the conditions that favor the development of enterprising women: an encouraging sponsor, in this case the Society of Friends; freedom from the domestic care of husbands; protection from perpetual pregnancy; and responsibilities for the home-port aspects of the family enterprises which took their menfolk to sea. In addition, the women had access to the considerable capital that successful whaling, trading, and shipping could accumulate.

Nantucket provided a supportive environment for enterprising women available nowhere else on the North American continent. Many early American women had to cope alone without the help of a well-ordered community. The lively letters of two of the most distinguished women of the Revolutionary period show how those who rose to the challenge were strengthened by the experience.

Neither Eliza Pinckney of South Carolina nor Abigail Adams of Massachusetts was brought up for business, but both managed family property left in their keeping so well that their menfolk were financially able to devote themselves to public service.

Eliza Pinckney (1722–1793) enjoyed an unusually good education, even for an upper-class woman of her time, and an unusually stimulating relationship with her father, George Lucas, a British Army colonel stationed for years in the West Indies. She had the run of her father's library and his encouragement to read widely in it. He did not approve of the usual "fancy work" with which most young ladies of Eliza's background whiled away their time. Her mother was an invalid, and when military duty called Colonel Lucas away from the South Carolina plantation he bought for his family, he left young Eliza in charge. On her own, she was conscientious to a fault.

"In general," she once wrote, "I rise at five o'Clock in the morning, read till Seven, then take a walk in the garden or field, see that the Servants are at their respective business, then to breakfast. The first hour after breakfast is spent at my musick, the next is constantly employed in recolecting something I have learned for want of practise it should be quite lost, such as French and shorthand. After that I devote the rest of the time till I dress for dinner to our little Polly [her younger sister] and two black girls who I teach to read, and if I have my papa's approbation (my Mama's I have got) I intend [them] for school mistres's for the rest of the Negro children. . . ."

Eliza responded to the confidence placed in her with an assertion of independence unusual for dutiful daughters. Firmly, and ever so politely, she turned down first one and then a second older man her father suggested as a husband for her. They were rich, but she found them unappealing, and she wrote him that "a single life is my only Choice and if it were not as I am yet but Eighteen, I hope you will [put] aside the thoughts of my marrying yet these two or three years at least."

When her father was away, which was most of the time, she learned to cope with complex personnel, marketing, financial, and legal problems.

"I have the business of three plantations to transact, which requires much writing and more business and fatigue of other sorts than you can imagine," she wrote when she was 17 to the woman in whose house she had lived while attending school in England. As a Southerner, she also had responsibility for feeding, clothing, nursing, and training the black slaves. In addition to direct operation of the 600-acre Wappoo Creek plantation with its 20 slaves, she had to supervise the 1500-acre Garden Hill plantation, whose products were pitch, tar, and pork, and 3000 scattered acres of rice along the Waccamaw River. Her letterbook gives us glimpses of the broad range of the "business and fatigue" involved:

> November 11, 1741. Wrote to Mr. Murry [an over-seer] to send down [to Charlestown] a boat load of white oak Staves, bacon and salted beef for the West Indies. Sent up at the same time a barrel salt, 1/2 weight salt peter, some brown Sugar for the bacon, and 6 weight sugar and a couple bottles wine for Mrs. Murry. And desire he will send down all the butter and hogs' lard.

> January 1741/2. Wrote my father a letter consisting of 7 sides of paper—about the Exchange with Colo. Heron, the purchasing his house at Georgia, the Tyranical Government at Georgia. . . .

> March 1742. I have planted a large figg orchard with design to dry and export them. I have reckoned my expence and the prophets to arise from these figgs. . . .

> June 1742. We have some in this Neighborhood who have a little land and few slaves and Cattle to give their children that never think of making a will till they come upon a sick bed and find it too expensive to send to town for a Lawyer. If you will not laugh too imoderately at me I'll Trust you with a secret; I have made two wills already. I know I have done no harm for I coned my lesson very perfect and know how to convey by will Estates real and personal. . . .

> 1742 The crop at Garden Hill turned out ill, but a hundred and sixty bar[ls] [of rice] and at Wappoo only forty-three, the price is so low as thirty shillings pr hundred, we have sent very little to town yet, for that reason.

The major problem facing American Colonial planters was earning money to buy goods from Europe. Eliza loved the "vegitable world extremely" and tried ginger, cotton, lucerne (alfalfa), and other potential export crops to supplement rice. She was intrigued by the possibilities of growing indigo in South Carolina in order to break the dependence of Britain on dye cakes made from indigo grown in the French Caribbean islands.

Eliza succeeded in growing the indigo plants from seeds her father sent from the West Indies, but the technician who came along to process the leaves into dye cakes turned out to be a problem. "He made a great mistery of the process," Eliza wrote, "said he repented coming as he should ruin his own Country (the French island of Montserrat) by it . . . and threw in so large a quantity of Lime water as to spoil the colour." Although not yet 20, Eliza arranged to have him replaced. Her indigo cakes were a great success. In 1744, Wappoo sent 17 pounds to London, where it was pronounced as good as the French product. To insure against a crop failure that would have made South Carolina dependent on importing more seeds from the West Indies, she gave most of the rest of the 1744 crop "in small quantities to a great number of people." A few years later, the French made exportation of indigo seed from their islands a capital crime, but thanks to Eliza's gift of seeds to her neighbors, the embargo was ineffective. In 1747, South Carolina exported 135,000 pounds of indigo cakes.

At 21, after she had established indigo as a profitable American crop, Eliza married an older man who has been described as "perhaps the most distinguished Charlestonian of his time." He was Charles Pinckney, a lawyer who was the widower of her best friend. They spent 14 idyllic years together, mostly in London. Her sons, Charles and Thomas, attended British public schools. When Pinckney died unexpectedly on a trip back to South Carolina, she moved back there and restored the neglected family holdings. As a side activity, she was superintendent for a time of "a little small pox hospital" and boasted that only one of 15 patients died.

Eliza did not see her sons for ten years, but supervised their English education via the transatlantic mails, writing warm and thoughtful letters to them and to their teachers. She succeeded in the difficult task of influencing the character of her sons by remote control. On February 7, 1761, for instance, she wrote Charles: "[I] recommend to you to be very careful of what acquaintances you make and what friendships you contract, for much depends on the example and advice of those we are fond off." Both sons became leaders in the new nation. The Pinckney Treaty with Spain, which insured the new republic the use of the Mississippi River, was negotiated by Thomas when he was U.S. envoy to Spain. Charles was one of the first planters to grow the long-staple, sea-island cotton which eventually replaced indigo as the main source of foreign exchange for South Carolina. When Eliza Pinckney died in 1793, President George Washington requested, and was granted, the honor of serving as one of her pallbearers.

Abigail Adams was a New England counterpart of Eliza Pinckney. Both women came from exceptionally well educated families, a critical advantage at a time when, to quote Abigail Adams herself, "the only chance for much intellectual improvement in the female sex was to be found in the families of the educated class and in occasional intercourse with the learned of the day." As Eliza had the run of her father's "little library," so Abigail grew up in a parsonage where the talk was lively and books were plentiful.

Like Eliza Pinckney, Abigail Adams had an unusually happy marriage, but relatively few years of normal married life. In 1764, when she had been married 12 years, Abigail lamented, "I believe we have not lived together more than six." Separation and widowhood very probably spared both women the perpetual pregnancy which sapped the energy of most wives of their day. As it was, Abigail reared four of the five children she bore, Eliza three of the four—a good record at a time when mothers were accustomed to losing many of their children as infants.

Abigail became a "farmeress," as she put it, by default when her husband's public service took him away from home. Young John Adams was trained in the law, but like all colonial Americans, he looked to his lands for his major support. When he took Abigail to live on the Adams farm at Braintree, Massachusetts, she had a slave to help around the house, and he supervised hired men in outdoor work, but they both expected to make their living largely with their own hands. Legal fees were a welcome extra.

From the very beginning, however, John Adams was away from home often, riding circuit or taking law cases arising a few days' ride from Braintree. In 1774 he went to Philadelphia as a delegate to the Continental Congress. During the ten years of almost constant separation which followed, Abigail reared four young children while buying farm stock, hiring help, coping with tenants, buying land, paying bills, borrowing money, supervising the construction of buildings, laying in provisions, and at all times practising "ridgid oeconomy" so that "I might always have it in my power to answer the first demand of a Creditor."

This was not easy because of wartime inflation and the scarcity of hired help of any kind. In 1778 she wrote John:

> Labour is much more exorbitant than it was when you left us. The most indifferent Farmer is not to be procured under 10 and 12 pounds per month. I know you will give me joy when I tell you that I have wrought almost a miracle. I have removed H(ayde)n out of the house, or rather hired him to remove and have put in a couple of Industerous young Fellows, to whom I let the Farm to the Halves. This I found absolutely necessary to do as I could see no way for me to get through the Labour and Rates so that I have reduced my Family from 13 or 14 to 7.

Abigail accompanied John to Europe while he was negotiating a treaty of peace and commerce with Great Britain and serving as minister to The Hague. She continued to coax money out of the farm to send the boys to Harvard and manage the rising taxes in Massachusetts. She cut down her "Family" of farm workers, and made her own and the children's clothes. Yet she managed to buy a piece of land John had always wanted in 1782, and five years later she arranged for the purchase of the big mansion which still stands as a tourist attraction in Quincy, Massachusetts.

By 1790, she learned to compare farming with alternative ways of earning a living and concluded, long before the economists, that the return on farm land was generally exaggerated. In a letter to her sister, the immediate problem discussed is what to do with the farm while she was away in New York serving as the nation's second First Lady:

> With regard to our House, I should have no objection to a carefull person living in the kitchin to take care of it, but as to letting it I cannot consent unless any person offers to take House and furniture all together. There is the other part of the House in which Bass lives that might be let, but then I should be loth that a shoe makers shop should be made of either of the Rooms. In short, I do not know of any persons property so unproductive as ours is. I do not believe that it yields us one pr cent pr Annum.

Husband John has been away from home so long, she writes, that she "cannot get him to think enough upon his domestick affairs." He had not been looking at the farm as a business, but as a way of life or an investment to hold for the rise in land prices. Her letter to her sister continues:

> I never desired so much Land unless we could have lived upon it. The money paid for useless land would have purchase[d] publick securities. The interest of which, poorly as it is funded, would have been less troublesome to take charge of then land, and much more productive. But in these ideas I have been so unfortunate as to differ from my partner, who thinks he never saved anything but what he vested in land.

There is some evidence that she took advantage of John's frequent absences to stash some family money away in the investment she preferred. According to Page Smith, who compiled a history of the Adams family, Abigail bought securities surreptitiously through Dr. Cotton Tufts, who served as unofficial steward for the family, and the interest gave Abigail and John some comforts the farm could never have provided.

When John was at home, he tended to go overboard buying for the farm. "We have for my comfort, six cows without a single convenience for a dairy," Abigail wrote in the summer of 1788. "But you know there is no saying nay." While Abigail was away in Jamaica, New York, attending the birth of her daughter's baby, John bought 15 heifers, leaving the Adams family so short of cash that the faithful Dr. Tufts had to take the heifers in return for paying the bills of the Adams boys at Harvard.

Spring planting and the building of a new dairy kept Abigail from attending her husband's inauguration in New York as the nation's first vice president. When she fretted over finding good hands in which to leave the property, he wrote as impetuously as a young husband:

> My Dearest Friend—If you think it best, leave Thomas at college, but I pray you to come on with Charles, as soon as possible. As to the place, let my brother plough and plant as he will, as much as he will. He may send me my half of the butter, cheese, etc., here. As to money to bear your expenses, you must, if you can, borrow of some friend enough to bring you here. If you cannot borrow enough, you must sell horses, oxen, sheep, cows, anything at any rate rather than not come on. If no one will take the place, leave it to the birds of the air and beasts of the field, but at all events, break up that establishment and that household. . . .

Then came the presidency of the United States, in 1797, and it was a financial drain. The Washingtons had brought their own furniture to the first executive mansion in Philadelphia, and Abigail had to improvise housekeeping in the half-empty premises they left behind them. As usual, she set energetically to work making do. She wrote her sister for help:

> I wrote you in my last that I should want some stores, a couple pound Hyson Tea, ditto souchhong, Hundred Brown Sugar, several dozens Hard bread, half Hundred Coffe, Gallon of Brandy, Quarter pd.

Nutmegs, pd. cinnamon, Mustard, Pepper, 2 oz. Maize ((mace)), half pd. Cloves. . . . I think I must have a couple of Bedsteads. . . . I have Bedsteads enough out in the Grainary chamber, but they are such lumber that I do not know if anything could be done with them. If they could I should not regret their being cut for the purpose. They put up with screws which screws are in the store closset some of them & some of them over the Top of the Granary chamber window. . . . I also wish you to purchase me a peice of Russia sheeting and . . . a peice of the plain Russia towelling. The sheeting & towelling take a receipt for as thus, "for the use of the Household of the President of the U.S."—I also want some Tea pots & a coffee pot or two, some tea spoons for the kitchin. Any thing which you may think I want beside you will go so good as to provide. I inclose you a Bill of an Hundred dollars. . . .

Charles Francis Adams, Abigail's grandson, credits her "prudence through the years of the Revolution" with saving John and herself from an impoverished old age. There were, of course, no regular pensions for patriots who spent their working years attending to public rather than private business.

"Mr. Adams was never a man of large fortune," Charles Francis wrote almost smugly. "His profession, which had been a source of emolument, was now entirely taken away from him; and his only dependence for the support of his family was in the careful husbanding of the means in actual possession."

Abigail Adams and Eliza Pinckney were intelligent and articulate women who did not hesitate to make important decisions for their families. But neither of them would have openly challenged their fathers or husbands. In spite of Abigail's charge to John that he should "remember the ladies" when helping to frame the Constitution, she can hardly be described as a feminist within the modern meaning of that term. "Tho I am very willing to relieve him from every care in my power, yet I think it has too much the appearance of weilding instead of sharing the Sceptor," she wrote. She took responsibility in the name of her absent husband, but when she took the initiative on her own as she seems to have done in buying securities, she did it "surreptitiously."

The unique experience of building a new country fostered independence in some early American women, but it could not completely overcome the age-old relationship of man as master and wife as helpmeet. The labor of a wife might be part of his economic security, but it was all done in his name, and for his benefit. We know a little about one wife who followed this traditional pattern because she helped her husband found one of the great American fortunes, and for a brief period of time, she made a very special contribution to it.

Sarah Todd Astor (1762–1832) and her widowed mother were running a Manhattan boarding house at 81 Queen Street (later called Pearl in a post-Revolution elimination of royal names) when the first John Jacob Astor rented a room there soon after he arrived in New York to seek his fortune. He was 22 and she was perhaps a year older when they married September 19, 1785, in the German Reformed Church.

Young John Jacob had left his home in Germany at 17 to escape his father's odoriferous butcher shop and an unkind stepmother. He went first to London where an older brother, George, was making flutes and other musical instruments. In three years work for his brother, John Jacob learned to speak English and saved enough for a steerage passage to America. During the voyage a fellow passenger told him of fantastic profits to be made in the fur trade. With a spare suit, seven flutes, and $25, he landed at Baltimore in 1784 and came to New York where another older brother, Henry, had a meat stall in the Fulton Market. But butchering had no more attraction for him in New York than in Germany. John Jacob declined Henry's offer of a job, and after a brief stint in a Queen Street bakery, went to work at $2 a week for Robert Bowne, a furrier.

His first job was to beat dirt and bugs out of furs and put

them into bales. He then was sent alone into the wilds of upstate New York to trade cloth, liquor, or cheap jewelry to Indians for their pelts. He did so well that he was sent to London to sell furs and buy British goods for sale at a profit in New York.

John Jacob married Sarah, as he later told a grandchild, "because she was so pretty." According to a historian of the family, she was "a slender girl with great big eyes in a thin face," and had a temperament that was "a curious combination of pride and reserve, ambition and shyness." She had, in addition, more tangible assets.

Sarah was the only daughter and youngest child of Adam and Sarah (Cox) Todd, both of thrifty and enterprising Scottish ancestry. Her father had been married previously, and a daughter of one of her half-sisters had married Henry Brevoort, giving Sarah a connection with that famous pioneer Dutch family.

Sarah had a dowry of $300, which enabled John Jacob to go into business for himself. They opened a small store on Water Street, lived frugally over it, and worked as a team. In the store, they sold pianos and flutes from John Jacob's brother in England, and bought furs. The latter were often raw and stinking, and they shared the hard work of processing them. Sarah soon developed a better knowledge of fur quality than her husband, something which he freely conceded and utilized.

When John Jacob was away buying furs in upstate New York or Canada, Sarah had full charge of the growing business. While efficiently managing the shop downstairs, Sarah gave birth upstairs to eight children between 1788 and 1802. Five of them lived to adulthood.

As his wealth and his family grew, John Jacob bought a home at 233 Broadway. At Sarah's suggestion and with the help of the Brevoort relatives, he began to invest extensively in New York City real estate, which eventually became the bulk of the Astor fortune.

He continued, meanwhile, at intervals to ask Sarah to value furs, especially sea-otter skins and other fine items which his ships carried to China and exchanged for even more valuable cargoes of silks, tea, and spices. In view of his increasing income, she proposed that she be paid for this service. They decided that a rate of $500 an hour would be fair compensation for her consultations. He paid her bills promptly and she used the money for various church and religious activities in which she was interested.

John Jacob's dream of a fur monopoly was not realized, but the rising real-estate revenue more than offset declining fur profits. By the time Sarah died in 1832, the Astor fortune was probably the biggest in the country. John Jacob lived on until 1848, and when he died he was worth at least $20 million, according to some sources, and possibly as much as $30 million. Depending on their points of view, biographers have called him either robber baron or American hero, but all agree that in a career marked by extraordinary good luck, his marriage was his most fortunate decision.

Sarah Todd Astor brought her husband capital in the form of a dowry and profitable alliances with the business interests of her blood relations. This European model was not unusual in the early merchant enterprises of the Eastern seaboard, and especially among the Dutch families of New York, but New World conditions quickly modified it. Labor was so short in America that the physical work of wives was just as important as the capital or connections they could bring as dowries, and their work became even more important as the country expanded to settle the West.

3

COMMUNITY BUILDERS
Women of the Frontier

The work women did was essential to the settlement of the North American wilderness from Plymouth Rock to Oregon. The first colonists had had to make or grow virtually everything they needed. Trade with Europe and between American ports was difficult, even if farmers had been able to produce enough to pay for professionally crafted products. Labor was dear and land was cheap, so the New World had spread out, isolating settlements one from the other. American households, rich and poor, remained self-sufficient longer than did their European counterparts, and those on the moving frontier had to make their own long after those in the cities could buy what they needed. While the men in the family cleared the land and did the plowing, women took care of food and clothing, reared the children, and crafted whatever they could for comfort and convenience.

Women in early America were never idle. The activities noted in the 1775 diary of one Abigail Foote of Colchester, Connecticut, show some of the tasks that they faced. "Fixed gown for Prude, mended her mother's riding hood, spun short bread, carded tow, spun linen, worked on cheese basket, hatchel'd flax, pleated and ironed, read a sermon of Doddridge's, spooled a piece, milked the cows, made a broom of Guinea wheat straw, set a red dye, had two scholars from Mrs. Taylor's, carded two pounds of wool, spun harness twine, and scoured the pewter."

Women served their families and neighbors as unpaid mid-wives, ushering them into the world, and as unpaid under-takers, laying them out for burial. Rich men and poor depended on the women in their families for food and clothing. The suit in which George Washington was inaugurated first president of the United States was made from cloth woven in his own household, and as late as 1810, the Census estimated that more than 90 percent of the textile products made in the United States were manufactured by women in their own homes. Spinning was so universal a way for unmarried women to earn their keep that the term "spinster" entered the language as a synonym for "single woman," and all women spent so much of their time spinning that "distaff" still means "female." The ambitious and thrifty could live well, but it took a lot of doing.

Christopher Marshall, a prosperous Philadelphia Quaker, devoted a 1778 entry in his diary to praise for his energetic wife. He spoke not only of her care for a large house which was "a constant resort of comers and goers," but also of "her attendance in the orchard, cutting and drying apples of which several bushels have been procured, add to which her making of cider without tools, for the constant drink of the family, her seeing all our washing done, and her fine clothes and my shirts, the which are all smoothed by her; add to this, her making of twenty large cheeses, and that from one cow, and daily using with milk and cream, besides her sewing, knitting, &c."

When homes were workshops and the family was the economic unit, there was substance to the sometimes cruel American assumption that individuals received their just deserts in this world. Standards of living depended squarely on the ability of fathers, mothers, and children to invent, repair, construct, and pull together. At the time of the Revolution, the family farm was being glorified as morally virtuous, the only sound investment for a man of character. More than 70 percent of the Revolutionary colonists were farmers, and although the proportion of farmers has declined at every census, the ideal of the self-sufficient family farm has persisted through 200 years of industrial development, and challenges idealists to try it even in 1976.

In the new Republic, the land of opportunity, a self-sufficient family farm was more than a way for a hard-working people to keep themselves in food and clothing. On virgin land that cost nothing, people without money could convert their own labor, adults and children, into capital. From the very beginning, Americans were land speculators who expected to make their fortunes by improving wilderness real estate so that it could be sold at a profit.

When the stony farms of Massachusetts would no longer provide enough return on the investment of labor, settlers pushed West to find land worth developing. The pattern was repeated again and again, with amazing rapidity, and before the nineteenth century was over, the best land had been claimed and developed from coast to coast.

Few women really wanted to go West. Many a bride simply sat down and cried when she saw the shack or the clearing in the woods her husband had chosen for their home. Some were so lonely that they literally went out of their minds. They couldn't understand why their men had brought them into the wilderness to live.

The men were marching to a drum their women couldn't hear. Women wanted homes and families; men wanted to make money. Women were essential to this enterprise. They created the social capital of a settled community—a home rather than a hut, neighbors, a church, some sort of schooling for the children, shelter for a stranger in a land without hotels, help in sickness and bereavement. And women were expected to bear the children who could be put to work at an early age at the endless chores of farming new land.

In a home on the frontier, women had to practice skills no longer needed on the settled Eastern seaboard. A vivid account of how it felt to leave accustomed comforts behind comes down to us in the memoirs of Christiana Holmes, who married John Tillson in 1822 and immediately set out with him for Hillsboro, an outpost in Montgomery County in southern Illinois. Tillson represented buyers and sellers who were dealing in land that had been given to veterans between the Illinois and Mississippi Rivers, and he served as postmaster and storekeeper for the wilderness community.

The new bride soon discovered that she was expected to assist her husband in all of those roles. The overland trip took seven weeks and brought her face to face with situations for which a genteel upbringing in civilized Massachusetts had not prepared her, but she had little time for reflection. Almost immediately she was plunged into cooking for an indefinite number of visitors who came to see the new settlement, making household necessities that she formerly bought in the East, and doing it all while bearing and rearing children with only occasional and uncertain help.

Christiana also helped her husband with the extensive correspondence he had to maintain with the Eastern landowners who were his clients. "As I was a fast writer, it became my privilege to wield the pen in the evening," she recalled.

Her store work included "measuring cotton cloth and linsey, weighing coffee, indigo . . . and in exchange for which would be the weighing of butter, beeswax, honey, and counting of eggs."

She usually had "six hungry men to be fed three times a day" and sometimes unexpectedly many more. Fourteen arrived one day when she had the table set for eight. "When preparing breakfast," she recalled, "I never knew whether it was for my own family, or several more."

"We usually had a quarter of beef—nothing less—brought at a time; sometimes a whole animal," and since her husband knew nothing about cutting, she learned how to butcher "by the help of directions laid down in a cookery book and a little saw."

Some of the workloads recorded by women who went West with their husbands are staggering. Mary Richardson Walker, one of three brides who walked to Oregon with their husbands in 1836, put her hand to every kind of chore once they had made their cabin. She milked six cows morning and night, salted beef, cleaned tripe, wove carpets, churned butter, tried tallow, made clothes, repaired roofs and chimneys, and cared for a sick neighbor, Mrs. Eells. On one day she "cleaned Mrs. E's earthen ware. Cooked for both families," "sat up all night, dipping 24 dozen of candles," and "cut out eight pairs of shoes." Cheese making was a problem until she discovered that rennet from a deer worked just as well as the calves' rennet used at home. Pioneer husbands saw nothing wrong with a dirt floor. "Find it pleasant to have a floor to wash again," Mary wrote proudly when she succeeded in getting wooden boards installed.

When the land was developed and sold, a woman might justifiably feel that her labor had helped to make the profit. "Then Dan'l sold the farm—sold it for $10,000. I've often thought that a considerable part of that $10,000 surely belonged to me," Maria Foster Brown wrote of the farm where she and her husband brought up their family in Iowa during the 1850s. "We left it in a good state of cultivation. Those fourteen years seemed a long time to me, a big price to pay. We had buried there two children and our youth was gone." Grandmother Brown realized that in making a home in the wilderness she had increased the cash value of the land.

Most men did not realize just how much a wife was worth until they tried living without one. When gold was discovered in California in 1848, impatient young men who weren't willing to carve farms out of the wilderness rushed to the ultimate bonanza in the ultimate West. If you went as far across the continent as you could go, you could dig the money right out of the ground. The forty-niners were so sure that they would strike it rich in a few weeks or months that they left their women behind. In the spring of 1849, there were only 15 women in San Francisco, and when an official census of California was taken the following year, less than 8 percent of the inhabitants were female. Many mining towns had no woman of any age or kind at all. Well-off pioneers soon discovered that it was no use bringing domestic servants even when they were deliberately chosen for their ugliness or advanced age. Some womanless settler was sure to carry them off.

The price of laundry in those womanless communities is worth analysis. Before the automatic washing machine, washing was one of the most disagreeable occupations. It was a day-long, sometimes a two-day, enterprise, involving not only the hauling and heating of water, but sometimes the making of soft soap as well. "Today Oh! horrors how shall I express it, is the dreded [sic] washing day," a woman on the Rogue River in Oregon wrote in her journal one day in the 1850s.

Disagreeable or not, there had always been women desperate enough for cash to do washing at a reasonable wage. But in the mining towns, there were no women, and the men were so intent on mining gold that they were unwilling to stop long enough to wash their own underwear.

The few women willing to do washing for others were able to charge prices so high that it sometimes was cheaper to buy new underwear and shirts, even at inflated gold-rush prices, than to have the old ones washed. In 1849, the going price in San Francisco for washing was $20 a dozen pieces, regardless of size. Flush gamblers and miners found it cheaper to send their underwear and boiled shirts by clipper ship to Honolulu or Canton for proper washing, starching, ironing, and return —a round trip of three to six months. At these prices, prostitutes and even men went into "clothes refreshment," and by the spring of 1850, laundry prices were stabilized at $8, and then $5, a dozen.

Women who took in washing could roll up sizable nest eggs —and win a new respect from men. In 1851, Louise Clappe and her physician husband visited a saloon kept by a frail-looking little woman in Rich Bar, one of the mining towns. "Magnificent woman that, sir," a man said to Dr. Clappe, referring to the saloon keeper. "A wife of the right sort, *she* is. Why, she earnt her *old man* nine hundred dollars in nine weeks, clear of all expenses, by washing. Such women ain't common, I tell *you;* if they were, a man might marry, and make money by the operation." Louise Clappe recalls hanging her "diminished head" in shame, "particularly when I remembered the eight dollars a dozen, which I had been in the habit of paying for the washing of linen-cambric pocket-handkerchiefs while in San Francisco."

Women had been scarce at an earlier time in American history, and entrepreneurs had made money shipping potential brides to Virginia and Louisiana, there to be "bought" by men at a price that rewarded the enterpriser after the woman's passage money had been paid. High prices on the

West Coast for the work women usually did as wives now revived interest in women as a commodity of trade. Demand for wives was higher than the supply in California, but lower than the supply in New England. Not only was there a profit to be made in shipping the surplus New England women to the West, but some women believed it was "the right thing to do."

A trip to California convinced Eliza Farnham, a New York prison matron, that "the presence of women would be one of the surest checks upon many of the evils that are apprehended there." In 1849, she proposed taking a party of 130 respectable women "not under 25" to California to work at the high wages being offered; but as it turned out, only three who wanted to go could find the $250 passage money.

But the most successful speculation on the Western marriage market was organized by an enterprising Yankee bachelor by the name of Asa Mercer. The Washington territorial legislature was willing to support his venture, but the treasury was empty. Nonetheless, some eager men pledged enough financial support for him to go ahead. Mercer reached Seattle in 1864 with eleven mill girls probably laid off when the Civil War cut the supply of raw cotton to the North. Soon after their arrival, nine of the women settled down to teaching jobs and/or marriage. One left shortly after arriving and another died of a heart attack.

Pleased with his first success, Mercer attempted a more ambitious "female emigration" expedition in 1866. He contracted with several men in the Washington Territory to bring each of them "a suitable wife of good moral character and reputation" for a payment of $300, which would compensate the woman for her passage and Mercer's expenses.

The Eastern press ridiculed the Mercer expedition and the *New York Times* had a correspondent on the boat to cover the newsworthy event. "Proper" people on the West Coast thought no one on the boat could possibly be respectable. However, the young women who had been recruited by Mercer had very different notions about what they were going to do. None was specifically contracted to marry anyone, and Mercer had led them to believe that small fortunes were to be made in teaching and tailoring. Several planned to save their money and return to New England in style.

"Some of the young women no doubt expected to secure schools, and did so," recalled Flora Pearson Engle, who was accompanied on the second Mercer voyage by her mother and brother. "Others, I am sure, came for the express purpose of finding homes and husbands, and did so also."

The Mercer ventures remain something of a joke. But the economic implication of marriage did not escape a perspicacious economist writing later in the nineteenth century, whose sharp perceptions were ignored until the recent move for equality of the sexes. "The economic position of women in the world heretofore has been that of the domestic servant," Charlotte Perkins Gilman wrote crisply. "When a man marries a housemaid, makes a wife of his servant, he alters her social status, but if she continues in the same industry, he does not alter her economic status."

Most women—and men, too—blanched at Charlotte Gilman's uncompromising logic. "The labor of women in the house, certainly, enables men to produce more wealth than they otherwise could; and in this way women are economic factors in society," she conceded in *Women and Economics*, her major work. "But so are horses."

4

THE INDUSTRIAL REVOLUTION
Rebecca Lukens

The West was a powerful magnet, drawing ambitious young men and their reluctant brides deeper into the wilderness, filling in the blank spaces on the map with trading towns and people. In the first decades of the nineteenth century, the young country grew bigger and richer. There was more food from the new lands under cultivation, and more of the big families women bore survived infancy. But the country was growing so fast that there were never enough hands to make the shoes, the guns, the stoves, the barrels, the plows, and the other tools and goods that the expanding population required.

This was the setting for the Industrial Revolution in America. Before the century was over, it would put many of the old crafts out of business, create new industries, and change the way all work was done. A widow could no longer assume that she would be able to continue a business by doing what her husband had taught her. The existence of a nineteenth-century Mary Goddard became increasingly less likely as industrialization proceeded.

The change was most dramatic in the cotton textile industry. A number of inventions had converged to mechanize the manufacture of cotton cloth. The cotton gin lowered the cost and increased the quantity of cotton available for spinning. New spinning machines processed more of this cotton than could have been spun by hand. Cheaper and plentiful yarn made better weaving machinery profitable. All these improvements created a market for textile machinery.

Every new idea that succeeded created new wealth and the appetite for more. Enterprisers dreamed of fortunes to be made if they could get steamboats and locomotives to bring crops from the farms into the cities and take back more tools and luxuries.

It all depended on more and better metal, and the primitive iron industry was struggling to meet the demand when Rebecca Lukens inherited an iron mill on the Brandywine Creek in eastern Pennsylvania during the summer of 1825. Shortly before his death, Dr. Charles Lukens had won a contract to make boiler plate for the *U.S.S. Codorus,* the first metal-hull vessel to be constructed in the United States, but the conversion to this new work had been expensive, and the mill was way behind in its orders when his widow, Rebecca, had to take over.

"Then commenced my hard and weary struggle with life," Rebecca wrote later. "Dr. Lukens had just commenced the Boiler Plant Business . . . and he was sanguine in his hopes of success, and this was his dying request—he wished me to continue and I promised him to comply.

"The estate shewed an alarming deficiency when the books were examined. . . . There was difficulty and danger on every side. . . . Mother wanted me to leave Brandywine and said it would be folly for me to remain. Necessity is a stern taskmistress, and my every want gave me courage."

Though she and her mother had often been at odds, Rebecca Pennock Lukens (1794–1854) had been encouraged to take an interest in the family metal-working business by her father and her husband, both of whom were Quakers ideologically committed to respect for the intellectual potential of women. As a child, she had read widely and attended a school where she had been exposed to higher mathematics, botany, chemistry, and the study of static electricity in addition to "ornamental drawing" and French. She was the oldest surviving child, and her father's favorite. She had followed him around the mill, learning how iron rods were "slit" for sale to blacksmiths, who would then shape them on small hand forges into horseshoes and simple metal tools.

After she married, her husband abandoned the practice of medicine to lease the Brandywine Iron Works and Nail Factory from Rebecca's father, Isaac Pennock, who also owned another iron mill. Pennock had told Rebecca that on his death the Brandywine business would be hers. But when he died a year and a half before Charles Lukens, he left it to her mother "during her life, if she choose to hold it." It was not clear whether Mrs. Pennock was given absolute control, or whether she was holding the business in trust for her children.

Matters were further complicated because Dr. Lukens died intestate, with resources "insufficient for the payment of his debts," including the payments to his father-in-law's estate.

Rebecca's first task was to stave off bankruptcy. She put her brother-in-law, Solomon Lukens, in charge of the workmen, and undertook to unravel the paperwork herself. At the office by 7 every morning, she paid off bills, arranged credit, collected accounts receivable, and saw that orders were promptly delivered. Learning as she went along, she bought bituminous coal, watched costs, set piece rates and established prices that could yield a profit. She promised to pay all her husband's debts "as soon as practicable"—including the rental payments to her mother, who, Rebecca wrote, "thought as a female I was not fit to carry on such a concern." It was not until after the death of her mother 19 years later and after a number of lawsuits and large payments to other heirs that Rebecca became sole owner of the business.

Along the way, she had to battle outside opposition as well as her mother. The Brandywine Creek powered a number of small mechanical operations in the early days of the Industrial Revolution, including the DuPont gunpowder mills, various grist mills, and other iron mills. All these small operators had to share the flow of water. If one mill built a dam that held the water back, other mills were affected. When competitors complained that Rebecca had raised the level of Brandywine Creek, a Committee of the Orthodox Branch of the Society of Friends ordered her to lower her mill dam six inches.

She was not intimidated. "Men," she told them, "I have something to say to you. You have started out in business taking unfair advantage of your neighbor, and, mark my words, you will never prosper."

Rebecca did prosper. She continued her husband's expansion into iron plate rolling. A few months after she took charge, the *Codorus* was completed at York, Pennsylvania, sheathed in plate from her mill. Her boiler plate went into early locomotives and into Mississippi steamboats.

During the 22 years she managed the company, the iron industry grew from a small, local craft operation serving neighborhood blacksmiths to a large-scale national industry essential for factories and transportation. Rebecca Lukens was one of the few who rode the tide. Despite the scoffs of neighbors, she advocated and saw built a railroad bridge spanning the Brandywine. It enabled her to serve customers farther away than iron could be profitably hauled by wagon. Brandywine boiler plate attained a national reputation for quality. When Rebecca Lukens died in 1854, she left an estate of $100,000, a formidable fortune at that time.

Five years later, the name of the mill was changed from the Brandywine Iron Works to Lukens Iron Works, and it eventually became the Lukens Steel Company, which has remained one of the major independent enterprises in the competitive steel industry. It had sales of $283 million in 1974.

After the Industrial Revolution, family businesses became larger and more technologically complex, and were run less like families. A laboring class, made up primarily of immigrants, appeared, thus relieving wives and daughters of shopwork. As the nineteenth century progressed, the development of financial techniques for buying and selling shares in enterprises and the rise of a class of overseers, foremen, managers, and industrial specialists of various kinds provided alternatives for the widow who had no special aptitude for running the family business herself. Like Mary Goddard, Rebecca Lukens was succeeded by males. Because she had no living sons, she turned for help to sons-in-law. As good Victorian ladies, her daughters were protected from the ugly environment of the iron works, and the operations had in any case become so specialized that they could not have learned about them as easily as Rebecca had when she followed her father around the mill.

5

THE VOCATION OF WOMANHOOD

Sarah Hale

One of the attractions of America in the mid-nineteenth century was that sons didn't have to follow the trades of their fathers. The Industrial Revolution and the opening of the West which accompanied it gave men a wide range of choices. They could leave the family farmstead and their customary chores to build canals and railroads, open up stores, or take up new land in the West. Many, of course, went broke and came back. Risk was part of the game. But every occupation that beckoned a man away was more productive than the subsistence farm he left, and it usually paid off in cash money a man could spend as he pleased.

Unfortunately for women, the choice and the cash were labeled For Men Only. In the early years of the cotton textile industry, a few young farm women—who considered themselves lucky—escaped the home chores to work in the mills in Lowell, Massachusetts. It was an exciting social and intellectual adventure, and gave them a chance to live in dormitories with other women their own age, talk about books, and accumulate a nest egg. Like college, the experience was temporary, and the women expected to quit when they married.

In any case, factories were not important employers of either sex before the Civil War. As late as 1840, less than 9 percent of the labor force were employed in manufacturing, most of them men. When women were gainfully employed, they almost always worked in a home setting. They "took in" boarders, or sewing, or washing, or "worked out" as domestics in the homes of other women, and then only so long as they were single. Most women in America spent most of their lives in the traditional domestic work of baking bread, growing and preparing food, keeping chickens, making clothes, rearing children.

In economic terms, the worlds of men and women were drifting apart. Men monopolized the productive new work of retail trade, construction, and transportation, leaving women an economic step behind in the old subsistence economy. Women were consigned to the work of their mothers by the accident of their sex.

While the work of men was becoming specialized, tasks of women remained as various as the tasks that had always been assigned to them. What distinguished these tasks was not so much their function—rearing children, cooking, sewing— but the fact that they were *done by women.* A man could describe himself as a shoemaker, or an ironmonger or a carpenter, but a woman could describe herself only as a woman.

This was the economic reason why women eagerly embraced a set of assumptions and practices which made womanhood a vocation in itself. Under the new dispensation, all women were to find their highest fulfillment in marriage and motherhood. With an assist from Victorian sentimentality, popular philosophers glorified women on the basis of their sex. Barbara Welter, an associate professor of history at Hunter College, has labeled the new sex role "the Cult of True Womanhood." A century after Queen Victoria's heyday, the cult was still going strong. It was, of course, what Betty Friedan called, in her 1963 book of that title, "The Feminine Mystique."

It is best defined in the words of the woman who did more than anyone else to popularize it, Sarah Josepha Hale, the editor of *Godey's Lady's Book:*

All that is truly good and beautiful in society, we owe to women . . .

She [woman] was the *last work* of creation . . . the *last*, . . . and therefore the *best* in those qualities which raise human nature above animal life. She was not made to gratify [man's] sensual desires, but to refine his human affections, and elevate his moral feelings. Endowed with superior beauty of person, and a corresponding delicacy of mind, her soul was to "help" him where he was deficient,—namely, in his spiritual nature.

Woman's spiritual strength seems perfected in her physical weakness.

Is not moral power better than mechanical invention?

Woman is the appointed preserver of whatever is good and pure and true in humanity. She is the first teacher. Every human being is submitted to her influence at the period when impressions take root, and character receives its bias. Hence the condition of woman is the standard by which to estimate the true condition and character of the nation.

Every attempt to induce women to think they have a just right to participate in the public duties of government [is] injurious to their best interests and derogatory to their character. Our empire is purer, more excellent and spiritual.

Sarah Josepha Hale (1788–1879) became editor of *Godey's Lady's Book* in 1837, the year Queen Victoria succeeded to the throne of England. "Victoria's reign will be one of the longest in English annals," the new editor predicted in one of her first editorials. "She may so stamp her influence on the period in which she flourishes that history shall speak of it as her own. . . . Victoria we consider as a representative of the moral and intellectual influence of woman."

Sarah Hale and Queen Victoria were cut from the same cloth. Both women were sticklers for ceremony. Both cherished their status as widows, and after their husbands died, both dressed in elegant black for the rest of their lives. And while Americans had no queen to police their manners and morals, they had Sarah Hale, scolding them on some detail of public or private behavior through the pages of *Godey's*, during most of Queen Victoria's long reign over the British.

There were many others writing about the role of the sexes at this time, but during the 40 years that Sarah Hale edited women's magazines for a wide readership she helped to build the pedestal on which, for good or evil, American women have been segregated from her day to ours. Although her name is all but forgotten, it is hard to think of another individual of her time who exerted influence over so many areas for so many years.

Like other enterprising women, Sarah Hale managed to acquire an extraordinary education for a woman of her time, by hitchhiking on the schooling of the men in her family. Her own account shows that her model of the proper relationship between men and women was based on experience:

> To my brother I owe what knowledge I possess of the Latin, and the higher branches of mathematics, and of mental philosophy. He often lamented that I could not, like himself, have the privilege of a college education. To my husband I was yet more deeply indebted. He was a number of years my senior, and far more my superior in learning. We commenced, soon after our marriage, a system of study and reading which we pursued while he lived. The hours allowed were from eight o'clock in the evening till ten; two hours in the twenty-four: how I enjoyed those hours! In all our mental pursuits, it seemed the aim of my husband to enlighten my reason—strengthen my judgment, and give me confidence in my own powers of mind, which he estimated much higher than I. But this approbation which he bestowed on my talents has been of great encouragement to me in attempting the duties that have since become my portion. And if there is any just praise due to the works I have prepared, the

sweetest thought is—that *his name* bears the celeb-
rity.

Sarah had taught school before she was married, primarily
to help out when her father lost his money. During her marriage the role of wife was all absorbing, and before her husband's death she had no career ambitions of her own.

Two days after their ninth wedding anniversary, David
Hale died of pneumonia. He had been a rising and well-liked
young lawyer in Newport, New Hampshire, but he did not
leave enough property to support his widow and her five
small children. Sarah's fifth child was born four days after her
husband's death. Desolated, earnest and modest in her
becoming black gown, 35-year-old Sarah Hale was just the
kind of widow men loved to help. Her husband's brother
Masons rallied round to set her up in a millinery shop. When
she expressed an interest in writing, they helped her publish
her poems and introduced her to people who could launch
her on a literary career. According to one account, some of
the Masons backed the foundation of the new *Ladies Magazine* in Boston in order to provide her with a job.

Ladies was an instant success. Although it was not the first
woman's magazine of its kind, it was the first to survive as
long as five years.

Sarah Hale's magazine differed from the other, short-lived
woman's magazines which were then springing up by an-
nouncing its intention of "improving the reputation of the
sex," campaigning for specific reforms, and talking about
temperance, the abolition of slavery, women's education,
and religion. Instead of stealing editorial material, largely
from British authors, *Ladies Magazine* tried to publish original material by Americans, even when the "editress," as she
preferred to be called, had to write most of it herself.

Sarah wore her success gracefully. During her career, she
was remarkably free of literary vanity or relish for the personal recognition that came her way. She always knew she
was not working for herself. In the first issue of *Ladies Magazine,* she thanked her patrons in the name of her orphaned
children. Untried as she was—and the very idea of a woman

editor was new—she always put her children ahead of her job. At first she tried to edit *Ladies* from Newport, New Hampshire, and when she was finally forced to leave her children in order to earn their livelihood in Boston, she took the youngest along with her. To assure proper care for her five-year-old, she engaged a teacher and provided a room in her home for what must surely have been one of the first nursery schools on record. But she did so well at work in spite of motherhood that Louis A. Godey, then publishing a rival magazine, bought *Ladies Magazine* to acquire its editor. Sarah agreed to the merger of the two magazines, but she refused to leave Boston for the home office of *Godey's Lady's Book* in Philadelphia until her youngest son was safely graduated from Harvard.

The four of her children who survived her did well in life: Horatio became a professor, William a judge, Frances the wife of a physician, Josepha the proprietor of a school for girls.

Sarah Hale's long years of collaboration with Louis Godey were an elegant demonstration of her theory that the "spheres" of man and woman are separate and apart. Godey was marketer enough to recognize that Sarah Hale's high-mindedness was a trend, and snob enough to want some of her class for his own book. When he bought *Ladies Magazine* to merge into *Godey's Lady's Book*, a Boston editor lamented that "like many a better half, it assumed the name of a worse one."

Although, as we shall presently see, the editorial intuition of the "editress" accounted for at least half of the magazine's phenomenal success, she was not invited to a testimonial dinner given Godey on the twenty-fifth anniversary of the *Book*, and it appears that in keeping with the privacy accorded respectable women, her name was not even *mentioned*. To her dying day she opposed as immodest the appearance of women as public lecturers.

Godey and Hale made an impressive team. Godey was fascinated with the logistics of preparing the fashion plates which made his *Book* an early "coffee-table" magazine. He claims to have been the first American editor to send fashion artists to Paris, and he loved to boast, in print, about the rising number and cost of the pictorial "embellishments" which had to be hand-colored on each individual copy of editions that ran as high as 150,000 copies in 1860. Young women, paid piece rates, did the hand coloring in their homes.

Publisher and editor must have come to one of those quiet accommodations so often recommended to wives in the interest of marital harmony, in which a True Woman, secure in her moral superiority, formally submits without compromising her principles. If, as Godey wrote toward the end of his life, they had "never had in any one instance, a single serious disagreement," it was not because they always shared the same values. As she had done in *Ladies Magazine*, Sarah Hale continued in her own column, to oppose the slavish following of fashion, as well as tight lacing of the waist, while in a dramatic and public reversal of the "spheres," Godey covered fashion in *his* column and reminded readers that responsibility for the fashions in the *Book* was his alone. And although Godey himself was captured by the glamour of the foreign scene, *Godey's* continued the practice of Americanizing French fashion designs which Sarah Hale had begun in *Ladies*.

Godey's heart was in maximizing circulation, so he banished politics, religion, and any controversy that could have offended readers. Since the magazine was popular in the South, mention of slavery was taboo. Godey succeeded in publishing all through the Civil War with only oblique references, in fiction, to the existence of the conflict. Sarah Hale kept her views on slavery to herself, citing the doctrine of separate spheres. "We do not," she wrote, "admit disquisitions on politics or theology because we think other subjects are more important to our sex, and more proper for our sphere."

That women's sphere was not inferior to the sphere of men, Sarah Hale never tired of telling her readers. Women were not beneath men, but above them. They were pure, their moral sense uncontaminated by sensuality. Nowhere does Sarah subscribe more directly to the Cult of True

Womanhood than in her life-long campaign to hound the term "female" out of polite English usage on the ground that "the word applies equally to cows, she-asses, and any kind of animal" too. Thanks to her, Vassar Female College became plain Vassar College. She was not, however, pleased with that institution's androgynous curriculum. Women were not men, she scolded, and in their difference lay their real power. A True Woman did not scramble for money and power because she did not need them. She influenced those around her directly by her superior moral sense.

Almost as if in return for restraining her superior moral sense on the big divisive issues, Godey allowed his editress to pursue whatever noncontroversial reforms she pleased in her "Editor's Table," tucked in as a sort of appendix behind the glamorous embellishments and big print of the featured fiction. By using the smallest type size available in the font, she managed to pursue a staggering variety of causes.

Sarah Hale's batting average on causes is impressive. Though she succumbed to the claims of phrenology, the nineteenth-century craze for reading character from the bumps on a person's head, most of the causes she touted have either now been accepted or remain as sweetly reasonable in the 1970s as they were when she proposed them. All of them were "social and domestic," and many called for housekeeping improvements of public institutions—well within a True Woman's widening sphere.

Take, for instance, her campaign for playgrounds. "Can wise men have made such a regulation?" she wrote in August 1843, criticizing the park regulation that kept children off the grass. "That is a question we often ask ourself, when we see sickly, sad, discontented looking children and their weary attendants sitting on the hard seats of the gravel walks, in the public squares, as though they were doing penance for the privilege of seeing the green grass, which they are peremptorily forbidden to 'trespass upon,' as though it were a bed of tulips."

Sarah Hale took a lively interest in monuments, ceremonies, and symbolic detail. She nagged Abraham Lincoln into making Thanksgiving a national holiday, and Matthew Vas-

sar into hiring a "lady principal" for his new college for
women.

In *Ladies Magazine,* she publicized the campaign to complete the Bunker Hill monument. To raise money for it, she
organized a gigantic "woman's fair" to which women offered
their home-crafted products for sale. It was one of the first
and most spectacular of the familiar fundraising devices
through which women have been able to convert their unpaid home work into cash (for good causes only, of course).
Later, as editor of *Godey's,* she helped the Mount Vernon
Ladies Association buy and restore the home of George
Washington.

Sarah liked these projects because they encouraged
women to join together to make their influence felt. Even
the clubs created to sell subscriptions to *Godey's* at cut rates
could break the isolation which then kept proper ladies sepa-
rated from each other behind the curtains of their respective
drawing rooms. Joint effort was then so novel for women that
Sarah could claim that these "Ladies Clubs" were the first in
the country outside of churches.

In her wide-ranging column, she came out against pie for
breakfast, corporal punishment of children, airless sleeping
rooms, and feather mattresses. She favored home-baked
bread, swimming and horseback riding for girls, "pic-nics" in
the great outdoors, Saturday-night baths, and the polite
French word "lingerie" for a woman's invisible unmention-
ables. In 1853, she issued a call for inventors to submit designs
for a washing machine and publicized the most practical
entry, a hand-pumped device that sold for $40.

She campaigned for schools to teach immigrant women
how to be good domestic servants. She petitioned Congress
after Congress to set aside federal land to support normal
schools in which women could be trained as teachers, and
supported the campaign of the Ladies Education Association
to send young women teachers to serve in Western schools.
And although she didn't think government service fell into
woman's sphere, she urged that women ought to be elected
to school boards.

The doctrine of spheres enabled Louis Godey to make a

substantial amount of money, and Sarah Hale to "make females better acquainted with their duties and privileges as women." The magazine formula they hammered out became the model for all the other women's magazines that have followed it, and blazed a trail for the women who have edited magazines ever since. Sarah Hale's insistence on paying American authors and giving them by-lines helped to create the first genuine literary marketplace in this country.

Sarah Hale was also the first American woman to become a nationally recognized success in a business she built without family help. She herself did not make a fortune. Publisher and editor were so close-mouthed about their financial relations that Isabelle Webb Entrikin, Sarah's most painstaking biographer, was not able to unearth the salary Godey paid her. But in power, prestige, and progress towards her own self-assigned goal—"to do good, especially to and for our sex" —she must be counted a success.

She did it by following the classic formula that was making so many of her male contemporaries rich and famous: invent a new product that meets a felt need of millions of potential customers and then sell it to them. Her product was both message and medium. She marketed the notion that womanhood was a mystic vocation that had to be taught to humans who were born female, and she packaged the message in a magazine intended to teach it to them.

6

TEACHERS
Catharine Beecher

One of the most important contributions to American economic growth was made by a woman so "True"—in Barbara Welter's sense of the word—that she feared the liberal arts curriculum of Vassar College would distract women from their destined vocation of homemaking.

Catharine Beecher (1800–1878) was not opposed to education for women, but she wanted them educated for their natural business which, in her mind, included the teaching of small children. She spurned material concerns, and would have been insulted at the idea that her campaign to train women teachers was intended to make the country grow richer, but that's exactly what it did.

It is a generally recognized economic principle that workers who can read, write, and do arithmetic produce more than illiterates because they can follow instructions and understand new methods more readily. The phenomenal growth of the American economy in the nineteenth century has been attributed to the fact that the white labor force of the United States attained near universal literacy earlier than the labor force of any other country. But economists seldom add that we could not have achieved this educational level without women teachers willing to teach at less pay than would have been required to staff all the classrooms with men.

Elementary school teaching has since become so over-whelmingly a female monopoly that it is hard to realize that there was no real evidence to support Catharine Beecher's claim that women would be better as teachers than men. The women who were teaching school in the early nineteenth century were less well paid than male schoolmasters, but very few of them could be described as better. Most were sketchily educated young women in need of quick cash who knew little more than their young pupils. And there were not enough of them.

"In the whole nation, there are a million and a half children, and nearly as many adults without any means of instruction," Catharine Beecher wrote in 1835. "At the same time, thousands and thousands of degraded foreigners, and their ignorant families, are pouring into this nation at every avenue. All these ignorant native and foreign adults are now voters. . . . The terrific crisis is now before us." She estimated that 30,000 new teachers were needed at once to stave off national disaster, and she knew where to find them. "Because few men will enter a business that will not support a family . . . females must be trained and educated for this employment."

Catharine was born to enterprise because she was born a Beecher. She was the oldest of the 12 surviving children of her adored father, Lyman Beecher, the evangelical Presbyterian preacher. Her sister was Harriet Beecher Stowe, whose depiction of slave life in her novel *Uncle Tom's Cabin* was credited by Abraham Lincoln with starting the Civil War. One of the seven of her brothers who became ministers was the famous spellbinder Henry Ward Beecher.

In addition to being a Beecher, Catharine enjoyed the special advantages that mark the lives of so many enterprising women. She grew up in an intellectual household and was afforded practice in the arts of rhetoric and persuasion. According to family tradition, her mother Roxana tied books to her spinning wheel so that she could read while she worked. Roxana set her daughter a model of enterprise by teaching school and taking in boarders to supplement the family income.

Catharine's own account of her early life sounds like a psychiatrist's case history. When Roxana died, 16-year-old Catharine was called upon to take her mother's place, and she continued to manage her father's home even after he remarried and added more children to it. Her attachment to her father was so frank that as an adult she could say, "I can not hear him without its making my face burn and my heart beat." Her father returned her affection and indulged her neurasthenic ailments.

Both Catharine and her father seem to have enjoyed her role as executive director of his extended household. When Catharine's fiance was lost at sea, her father convinced her that God was telling her she was destined for service above and beyond the lot of ordinary women, and she readily agreed. Abandoning all thoughts of marriage, she planned a career appropriate to her concept of womanhood.

At 23, she opened a school for girls. Her father told her he would be ashamed of her if she ran a "commonplace, middling sort of school," and she did not disappoint him. From the outset, the school that later became the Hartford Female Seminary was run like a college, with a faculty of specialists, a board of trustees, and a fund-raising program to which Catharine, the good manager, devoted personal attention.

Money was not, of course, a proper concern for a True Woman, but no scruple deterred Catharine from what she perceived to be her duty. She took one or another of her numerous male relatives along on fund-raising speeches and trips, and manipulated them into cooperating. Her brother-in-law Calvin Stowe joined her crusade at the urging of men he respected, but he did not know that Catharine herself had asked them to plead her cause and not to tell Calvin that she had put them up to it.

Catharine really believed that women should stay behind the scenes. She disapproved of woman suffrage, and she did not agree with her sister Harriet that the abolition of slavery was a proper cause for women to pursue in public.

She would have been uncomfortable at being credited with creating a paid profession that enabled millions of respectable women to declare their economic independence of men. Her objective was to dignify women by professionalizing their God-given work of homemaking and teaching. She wrote textbooks to systematize the miscellany of skills required to run a home, and she did not take a narrow view of what she called domestic economy: plumbing, heating, and the design of homes and schools were all women's work. She extended woman's "sphere" to what she called a "pink and white tyranny" over the minds of men and spoke of implanting "durable and holy impressions" on the minds of little children. In cultivating that "tyranny" however, she was both inventive and indefatigable.

Catharine's school in Hartford was so well organized that it survived her frequent absences and a series of nervous breakdowns which interrupted her whirlwind campaigns. In 1831, when her father was called to head a theological seminary in Cincinnati, Catharine moved her own activities West, too.

On the frontier, the teacherless children of newly settled communities seemed to cry out to her for help, and she responded with characteristic enterprise. When the school she founded in Cincinnati failed, she took her cause to the country, lecturing, writing, and setting up organizations to promote what, in one of her pamphlets of that title, she called *The Duty of American Women to Their Country.* That duty was to go West, in spite of hardships and low pay, and teach the children who needed them.

Catharine needed money to sell this idea, and she earned it by writing and speaking about her crusade. Under a special arrangement with Harper & Brothers, her publisher, she kept half of the net profits on copies sold of her *Treatise on Domestic Economy* and *The Domestic Receipt Book.* When she lectured on education, she announced that "every woman who feels an interest in the effort [could] contribute at least a small sum" by buying one of her books. If she kept the money for her own use, it was merely because she came to regard herself as an embodiment of the noble cause she was promoting. At the age of 60, she could claim that she had spent every waking minute of her life in the service of others.

Consistency never cramped Catharine's style. Although

she believed that women should stay in the background and avoid competing with men, she obviously regarded herself as a legitimate exception to these rules. At the age of 70, for instance, she insisted on taking a course at Cornell, then a school for males, on the ground that the young men couldn't bother her because she was old enough to be their grandmother.

The actual projects that Catharine launched were not notably successful. Of the normal schools she started in many Western communities, only the forerunner of Milwaukee-Downer College survived for long. She set up organizations to find and send women to teach in the West, but most of the women promptly married or quit their teaching jobs.

By contrast, however, the success of the idea behind these projects was stunning. In the 1830s, when Catharine began her campaign, a majority of teachers were male. When she died in 1878, a majority were women.

The economic consequences were more important than even Catharine Beecher could have foreseen. Mobilizing women to teach doubled the available supply at wages communities could afford. If women had not moved into the schools, a great many children would not have been taught as well, or even at all. According to the *Dictionary of Modern Economics,* "the growth of human capital, *particularly* investment in education, is one of the largest sources of past and future economic growth" as well as "one of the distinctive features of the U.S. economic system."

The term "human capital" is new, but the economic argument for funding education was used in Catharine Beecher's day. Horace Mann told business leaders that they ought to be willing to support public schools because they would benefit from a stabler and more productive labor supply. Recent calculations indicate a very high rate of return on investment in primary schooling, and theoretically it might even have been profitable to pay wages high enough to staff the schoolrooms with men.

But there was no possible way enough American men could have been kept in classrooms at a time when the West beckoned with open-ended opportunities. In the sexist culture of the time, men who indulged humanitarian or even intellectual interests were suspected of being weaklings. A red-blooded male had to regard schoolteaching as a stopgap occupation.

A True Woman, on the other hand, suffered no cultural penalty for choosing to teach. Since a woman was always expected to help others, Catharine Beecher was able to portray teaching as an occupation that enhanced a woman's femininity. Her contribution was to extend one of the functions of a traditional mother beyond the home to paid employment. Imperialist by nature, she wanted the sphere of women to take in as large a territory as possible, and succeeded better than she knew. The rationale by which she claimed that teaching was "right" for women was eventually applied to social work, nursing, secretarial work, and even library work. Anything that can be interpreted as helping people has automatically become woman's work—and underpaid—because women are expected to work, in part at least, "for love."

7

FASHIONS
FOR EVERYONE
Ellen Demorest,
Margaret La Forge

A True Woman wasn't supposed to be concerned with money, but she had to have a rich husband to dress like a *Godey's* lady. The dilemma did not worry the theorists of the Cult of True Womanhood. According to the conventional wisdom of mid-nineteenth-century America, men became rich because they were smart and worked hard. Women were rewarded because their moral superiority captured the hearts of these successful men.

The men who had money to spend were mainly interested in making more money than they already had. They did not waste time displaying their wealth themselves when their wives could do it for them. At about the time that upper-class men retreated from gaudy colors into the sober "business suit," their women began wearing hoop skirts that rendered them visibly incapable of useful effort.

The new sewing machines of the 1850s made it easier to construct these elaborate costumes, but the intricate trimmings still required untold woman-hours of hand sewing. Hats were alarming structures concocted of ribbons, feathers, and laces. White kid gloves were a luxurious touch; they had to be imported, but rich women threw them away after one or two wearings.

Those who could afford such gear were a small but growing company. On the eve of the Civil War, people were saying that Philadelphia had 25 millionaires, and since New York was the leading commercial city, it may have had more. The few hundred families in each big city who could afford to dress their women out of *Godey's* were important beyond their numbers because they were carefully watched by the thousands of middle-class women who hoped to be rich themselves some day.

Storekeepers had always known that women would pay for a bit of lace that would make their one dress more fashionable, a perfume that scented the handkerchiefs "real ladies" carried, or anything else that made them look or feel like a fashion plate. This woman's market was to grow as prosperity increased the number of women who could afford occasional luxuries. Unusual opportunities opened up for enterprising women who understood their sex.

Fashion officially became an industry separate from tailoring when Worth, the first of the great couturiers to attach his name to his "cuts," opened for business in Paris in 1858. In Williamsburg, Brooklyn, that same year, the wedding of Ellen Curtis and William Jennings Demorest formed the marital/business partnership which established fashion as a separate industry in America, too.

At 33, Ellen Curtis Demorest (1824–1898) was a successful businesswoman in her own right when she married. She knew what rich women wanted because she had grown up in Saratoga, New York, then a fashionable watering place where women came to display their clothes. Her father was a prosperous hat manufacturer who had set her up in business as a milliner to the resort trade, and she had been successful enough to move her business to New York.

Nell, as she was called, gave up her business when she married, but not for long. Watching her maid cut out a dress from pieces of wrapping paper gave her an idea. She thought she could make paper patterns of the latest styles and sell them to women who made their clothes at home. With an accurate pattern, anyone would be able to duplicate the newest Paris fashions.

The idea of cutting the pieces of a dress out of paper first and using the paper pieces as a guide for cutting the cloth did not originate with Nell Demorest's maid. It was as obvious an intermediary step as basting a seam before sewing it. But the everyday operation was especially interesting to Nell because she and her sister Kate had been working for years on a dress chart that would simplify the cumbersome and expensive cut-and-try method of making clothes fit. Cloth was being mass produced. The sewing machine had been invented. If the problem of fitting could be solved, clothing could be mass produced, too.

The paper pattern helped make clothes fit better, but as so often happens, it solved a much more important problem than the one on which the inventor was working. The paper pattern made it possible to sell the *design* of a garment separately from the garment itself. It made fashion not only an industry, but a mass-production industry for a mass market. The paper pattern was as American as the elitist couturiers were French. It brought the aristocratic "cuts" or styles to women rich and poor.

Nell's husband, William Demorest, was quick to see the potential of the paper pattern. A dry-goods merchant, he was an ebullient promoter who was always dreaming up new ways to make a fortune. Some of these were mechanical gadgets. He invented a watch guard, a high-wheeled bicycle, a system for cooking and heating with gas, and accessories for sewing machines which made the fancy stitches popular at the time.

William and Nell made a good business team. He was full of ideas and enthusiasm. She was even-tempered, tactful, and a good organizer. With help from Nell's sister Kate, they attacked the problem of making and selling paper patterns. William devised a mathematical system for cutting the patterns out of tissue paper in a variety of sizes, and packaging them in flat envelopes with colored plates like those in *Godey's Lady's Book.*

The division of labor between the couple remained something of a business secret. Contemporaries suspected that William had all the ideas, and Ellen never contradicted these reports. We know that she quietly supported women in business, employed as many as she could, and publicized women's achievements. We know also that William saw the value of a woman as head of the new business. Since fashions were French, Mrs. William Demorest became, for the rest of her life, Mme. Demorest.

A magazine like *Godey's* was the obvious way to sell the patterns, so in 1860, little more than two years after their marriage, the Demorests brought out the first pattern magazine, *Mme. Demorest's Mirror of Fashions.* It was a picture book of dresses a woman could make for herself with the help of Mme. Demorest's paper patterns. Since the money was to be made on the sale of the patterns, the price of this popular picture book could be lower than *Godey's'* rather steep subscription price. A sample pattern came with each copy, so that a woman could see for herself how the procedure worked.

The patterns were an immediate success. By 1865, William Demorest had over 200 local agents—spinsters and widows preferred—selling the patterns through 300 distribution agencies across the country. The magazine had become a big monthly with a long name, *Demorest's Illustrated Monthly Magazine and Mme. Demorest's Mirror of Fashions,* and a circulation of 60,000.

The pattern designs themselves were Nell's province. She carefully watched the fashion news from Europe, and adapted the extravagant designs to the lives of middle-class women all over the country. The patterns came with instructions for cutting, and were color coded—violet for a bodice, gray for the sleeve. With Demorest patterns to guide them, women in frontier boom towns and in plantation homes of the South could dress like ladies of leisure in New York.

For the genuine carriage trade, Nell opened an elegant dressmaking "Emporium" where she personally attended to the design and fitting of custom-made dresses. She organized the work so well that the Emporium could outfit a woman stopping at a hotel in half a day. She went to Paris for the openings, and in New York presided over fashion openings of her own. Since the Demorests were abolitionists, they made a point of employing black seamstresses to work alongside white ones, and any customer who objected to the mixing of the races was invited to shop elsewhere.

In retrospect, it is hard to separate how much of the Demorest business policy was conviction and how much promotion, and they may not have sorted these motives out themselves. Nell believed in equal employment for women, but she left the talking to others, using her influence to encourage and help. Whatever William's views on the issue, he saw the promotional value of favoring women because they were customers. As employers, the Demorests promoted women and let the world know that they did.

As editors, they consistently reported the achievements of women in every field. For 27 years their magazine carried the column of Jennie June Croly, who wrote the first column of personal advice. Jennie June was more outspokenly feminist than Sarah Hale had ever dared to be. She demanded equality in marriage, education, employment, and the professions, including the right of women to be doctors. She urged girls to train themselves for careers. Nell Demorest and Jennie Croly together helped women start businesses, and they were the leaders in founding the first real women's club, Sorosis.

The Demorests found charming ways to attract attention for themselves and their causes. On Christmas Eve, 1867, Nell gave a masquerade ball for 200 guests who were expected to attend in paper dresses representing famous women of history. Nell came as Queen Elizabeth. Many of the guests were the workroom women who understood the paper patterns, and the *New York Times* reported "the perfect good will with which the fair ones of the company mingled with their associates of color."

Although it is difficult to know which Demorest was the real inventor, Mme. Demorest was credited with a long list of ingenious accessories that were sold by mail through the magazines. These included a spiral-spring bosom pad, a combination suspender and shoulder brace, a small "Quaker" hoop skirt, a comfortable corset, cheap and convenient enough for a working girl, and an "Imperial dress elevator" with weighted strings to raise or lower the skirt so that it could be kept clear of the sidewalk. She also sponsored complexion creams and perfumes.

Selling patterns and gadgets by mail suggested another business: a shopping service for women readers who could not come to New York to buy for themselves. Orders recorded by the "purchasing bureau" during one day called for hats, books, jewelry, hearse plumes, waterfall curls (hair pieces were a big item during the 1860s), boots and shoes, fine leather trunks, parasols, dressing cases, vest patterns, silk cloaks, dress trimmings, two fluting machines, and military hat cords. None of these amenities were easily available in the farming communities where women were struggling to introduce the hallmarks of civilization.

Ironically, William Demorest patented most of the gadgets he invented himself, but failed to patent the paper pattern that was the basis of the Demorest empire. By the time he realized his error, it was too late. Ebenezer Butterick, a Massachusetts tailor, had started selling patterns of men's clothes in 1863 and had patented the idea. The Demorests were first, but they were never able to establish their priority in court, and their business died with them.

While the Demorests were building a mail-order business for women who could not come to New York, retailers in that city were thinking up ways to make shopping an attractive pastime for the near-rich as well as the rich. Before the Civil War, the leading retailer of New York (indeed, of the entire U.S.), was A. T. Stewart, a Scotsman who imported luxury items from Europe and attracted women of the carriage-keeping class by employing handsome young male clerks. Other shops sprang up along Broadway, inviting women to visit.

A Nantucket Quaker by the name of Rowland H. Macy opened a small fancy dry-goods store with a 20-foot frontage on Sixth Avenue, near Fourteenth Street, in the heart of the shopping area. Two years later his business had grown so big that he hired 19-year-old Margaret Getchell, a distant Nantucket cousin, to keep the books. Although she started as a surrogate daughter–helper, she eventually became the first female boss of a sizable retail enterprise and the first woman to demonstrate that women knew how to attract other women into a store.

Margaret Getchell LaForge (1841–1880) had started working as a teacher, but after the removal of one eye she thought that work in a store would be less taxing to her sight. Rowland Macy assured her that no one would ever know that one of her eyes was made of glass.

Macy's was then selling all the bits and pieces a woman needed to complete her costume: ribbons, laces, embroideries, artificial flowers, feathers, handkerchiefs, cambric flouncings, hosiery and gloves. Margaret's job was to take charge of the cash. The post required honesty and intelligence, and Macy was glad to have a relative in the post. It seemed normal to both of them because at home in Nantucket female relatives frequently handled the cash of a store.

Macy's employed so many people, however, that the job of handling cash was really an executive position. Pages and "cash girls" brought the money they took in to Margaret from the counters where the sale had been made, and these clerks had to be trained for the work. As a former teacher, Margaret knew just how to go about training them. She was meticulous, and insisted that every cash slip be made out accurately. "The very act [of erasure] implies dishonesty," she told them.

Everybody liked Margaret. Years later, people remembered the richness and warmth of her voice. She was firm but fair. When a lonely woman was dismissed because it looked as if she had stolen $3, Margaret suspected another employee and took it upon herself to visit the suspect and extract a confession that saved the job of the innocent accused. Margaret lived for the store. At first she took a room across the street from Macy's. She spent extra hours straightening up after the clerks had left.

Stores competed with each other to make their names known. Margaret persuaded her distant cousin Rowland to distinguish his store by putting his trademark, a five-pointed star, on the letterhead and price tags. She spotted current fads and suggested adding products that women needed to pursue them. In order to serve a new interest in country excursions, for instance, she set up a department featuring picnic supplies.

Many of the new products she suggested became the permanent departments that made up the department store: jewelry, housewares, gifts, clocks, silver plate, sterling silver. Especially popular was the house furnishings department, stocking kitchen utensils, wooden ware, bird cages, cleaning supplies, and in 1870 even carriages. Later came books and candy, ice skates, furniture, and fresh flowers. "We shall handle everything except one," she said. "Coffins."

Margaret had many novel ideas to attract women shoppers into the store in the hope that they would see something they wanted to buy. When soda fountains were started in Europe, Margaret installed a marble and nickelplated "fountain" in the very center of Macy's store to draw thirsty shoppers past counters of merchandise offered for sale.

To interest strollers and encourage them to enter, she once dressed kittens in dolls' clothes and displayed them sleeping in the dolls' beds in the store window. While crowds admired the charming display, she hired a photographer to take pictures of the kittens and had the photograph printed for sale. Hundreds were sold.

Rowland Macy was fond of Margaret and treated her like a daughter, and soon she was living in the Macy household. Six years after she arrived, when she was 25, he made her superintendent of the whole establishment, leaving himself free for buying trips abroad. Soon after this promotion, Margaret married Abiel LaForge, a new buyer who was employed because he had befriended Rowland Macy's son when they served together in the Union Army. The LaForges set up housekeeping in rooms over the store, taking their meals at a nearby boarding house.

In 1872, Rowland made Abiel a partner, and the firm became R. H. Macy & Co. Margaret continued to work during her pregnancies and part-time downstairs in the store as soon as one month after her first baby was born. She was two months pregnant with her third child when the partners put her in charge of the store and went on a three-month buying trip to Europe. While they were away, the panic of 1873 struck down sales. One of the measures Margaret took was to institute a grocery department, a feature that has been a money maker for Macy's ever since.

After Abiel became a partner, Rowland expected Margaret to work for nothing, and she continued to do so. Both men trusted Margaret to run the business when they were away, but they differed on how to reward her. "R. H. suggested some present for you," Abiel wrote Margaret while on a business trip with Rowland. "I thought it quite reasonable that, as you had worked there all the spring, some compensation in the way of salary would be the most just way of recognizing your services." Rowland obviously did not agree, because when they returned he gave Margaret a present of furniture instead of money.

Margaret's career was brilliant but short. After her husband's untimely death in 1878, she herself fell seriously ill and died at the age of 38, leaving five children. Dr. Mary Putnam Jacobi, one of the pioneer women physicians, diagnosed her final illness as "chronic ovarity," a term she may have invented to cover her own ignorance.

Nell Demorest and Margaret LaForge contributed something new to enterprise: an understanding of the wishes of women customers. Both were able to make that contribution count because they were fortunate enough to work with men who saw that "the women's angle" was the basis of their business. The woman's market they helped discover was to offer rewarding careers for millions of women in the generations that followed them.

8

MONEY MAKERS
Margaret Haughery, Susan King

A True Woman like Nell Demorest or Margaret LaForge
might help a man make money—or even make it herself if
her family needed it—but she wasn't supposed to make
money merely to prove she could do it. That was for men.

Nevertheless, a few women turned a deaf ear to the message Sarah Hale and Catharine Beecher were beaming at
women in general, and responded instead to the ethic of
enterprise directed at men. Ambitious young women were
not immune to the call of the West and they could be just as
calculating as men, and frequently were more ingenious
when staking out claims to desirable land. In territories
which favored women claimants with children, for instance,
unmarried women were known to borrow a child from a
friend just long enough to qualify as a widow head of
household.

Women participated in the famous Oklahoma land rush of
1889. According to legend, two 18-year-old girls were among
the 20,000 home seekers lined up along the border for the
opening gun. They grabbed the lots that eventually became
the center of a town by jumping off their ponies and setting
up a tent with a sign offering to take in sewing. The sign
"proved" their claim by indicating an intention to do business on the site. Another young woman prevailed on the
engineer of the train carrying settlers to let her ride in the

cab and to stop when she saw land she wanted, just long enough for her to jump out, whip off her skirt, and tie it to a tree as evidence of her claim.

We do not know much about women who responded this way. Their contemporaries dismissed them as jokes or freaks and serious historians mention them, if at all, only in passing. Luckily, however, enough data survive to give us an intriguing glimpse of two who played the forbidden money game and won, when men were making fortunes just after the Civil War.

Margaret Haughery (1813–1882), the "Bread Woman of New Orleans," is an exception to every generalization we've been tempted to make about enterprising women. She had no education at all and never learned to read or write. Her will, leaving a sizable estate, was signed with an X. She had worked as a domestic servant, and nothing we know about her suggests a reason why she did not remain a domestic servant to the end of her days. Her early life was a catastrophe rather than a challenge, and by the time she was 23 she had lost a husband and a child and had no one to support but herself.

Her response to this loneliness was to adopt the poor of New Orleans as her family, and to make money enough to found 11 orphanages, as well as a number of old folks' homes. During the Civil War, she nursed sick soldiers, and developed self-help projects for the families of needy soldiers. She seems to have applied an extraordinary talent for management to organizing her charitable projects as well as to making the money to fund them.

Margaret's parents were tenant farmers in Ireland who brought her to Baltimore, caught yellow fever, and died, leaving her an orphan at the age of nine. She was reared in Louisiana by a foster parent under the guardianship of a Catholic priest. All of the people around her were poor, so she started working as a domestic servant as soon as she was old enough to be worth her keep. When she was 22 she married a sickly Irish immigrant who took her to New Orleans, but a year later both her husband and the child she had borne were dead.

Margaret took a job as a laundress in the St. Charles Hotel, then a showplace for the rich of New Orleans. From her window in the laundry she watched the Sisters of Charity going out to help the poor, and determined to work for them. She was practical enough to realize that their principal need was money. She saved her small wages, bought two cows, and, borrowing a hand truck, sold milk through the streets.

Margaret had business sense and a ready wit that drew people to her. One of the first uses she made of the money she earned from the milk route was to help the Sisters buy a rundown old building that was supposed to be haunted. People passing by were sometimes frightened by the shadows they saw inside at night, but it was merely Margaret and the sisters fixing up their new property after the day's work was done.

The milk business grew. By 1840, Margaret had 30 or 40 cows and was delivering milk in the fashionable new uptown neighborhood of New Orleans. Her charities absorbed as much of her talent as her business. She helped the Sisters of Charity found an orphanage. She designed, built, and raised money for a school for orphan girls that educated them to earn their own livelihood at a skilled trade, so that other orphaned girls would have a better start than she herself had had. In memory of her own lost child, she organized an orphanage for the special care of babies. In memory of her parents, she personally looked after yellow fever victims, and when floods stranded families in the Mississippi, she piloted rescue rafts.

She got into the bakery business by accident. For many years she had supplied milk to a bakery that was failing and could not pay her bill. Finally, she took it over, expanded it, installed new equipment, and made it profitable. Eventually she moved the bakery to a better part of the city and bought steam-operated equipment, a novelty at that time. She stabilized the market by setting up bread routes for delivering bread to regular customers, just as she had delivered milk. Orphanages received bread free, with a delicacy hidden somewhere in the basket to delight the children.

Margaret intuitively used what have since become standard management techniques for getting people to work with each other. In directing flood relief and comforting the troubled, she knew how to divert people from their fears by encouraging them to help someone else, and she often lent money to people to start projects that could make them self-supporting. She contributed to orphanages maintained by all faiths, and aided families of soldiers on both sides of the Civil War. She never turned anyone away, and since so many people came to ask for her advice and help, she had to set up visiting hours for petitioners, many of whom were men in business who respected Margaret because she was successful in making money.

After the Civil War, when foreign trade revived in the port of New Orleans, her packaged crackers became a staple business, one of the city's largest exports. Even at the height of her prosperity, Margaret did not display her wealth. Like other widows of her time, she always dressed in black, and owned only two dresses, one for weekdays and one for Sundays and holidays. If she had been a man, we might have known the extent of her fortune. The best estimate we have is that she donated well over $600,000 to various charities.

During the same years that Margaret Haughery was making a fortune in bread and biscuits, an equally reticent woman was buying and selling real estate in the path of New York City's northward development. Susan King (1818–c1880) was secretive about herself and her business activities. The *New York Times* carried no obituary of her death. But the extent of her charities confirms the impression of associates that she had amassed a fortune of a million dollars.

The career of Susan King has more obvious roots than that of Margaret Haughery. She was born on a farm in Maine. She had little formal schooling, but she had a father who treated her like a son. A government agent who bought supplies for the Army, he took her along on his buying trips and taught her how to bargain for cattle. In the 1840s she came to New York, supporting herself at first by giving guitar lessons.

The city she found when she came was confined to the southern tip of Manhattan Island, but it was rapidly absorbing the farms and woods to the north. Physically rugged, the

young woman from Maine tramped through these un-
developed areas to see which ones would make the most
valuable building sites. At first she brought promising opportunities to investors, but as she prospered, she kept ready
cash on hand to take advantage of opportunities as they
arose. A true speculator, she restlessly moved from deal to
deal. One of her last transactions was the sale, for $250,000,
of the site on upper Broadway on which Union Theological
Seminary was later built.

Susan moved quietly to make her deals, but she came to be
known and respected by speculators interested in the same
properties. One of these was William Demorest, who was
dealing in real estate around Fourteenth Street himself. He
brought Susan home to Nell, who was delighted with her
enterprise and involved her in projects for encouraging
women to become self-supporting. At one point the two set
up a house for "fallen women." But the idea that fascinated
both of them was more ambitious: an international business
importing tea from China that would put hundreds of American women in business selling the tea in their own communities. The Demorests publicized the project, and the newspapers were on hand in 1872 when Susan set forth for the
Orient in a clipper ship appropriately christened *Madam
Demorest*, with a half million dollars of foreign exchange
with which to buy tea.

Susan believed in helping women help themselves, and
she was devoted to the moral as well as the practical value
of money. "The dollar is a language people understand all
over the world," she recalled of her trip. "It chin-chinned
and chow-chowed me all through Japan, China, Chinese Tar-
tary, Borneo, Java, Celebes, the Malacca Islands, among the
cannibals and the heathen Chinese. It has carried me all
around the world. What do I care for the ballot? But now
mark my words, if ever women do get the right of suffrage
it will be through their showing the ability to win the dollar,
and win it just as men do."

In the Woman's Tea Company, Susan brought back the tea
and paid off the investors, but women agents were slow in
appearing, and she eventually withdrew to "let them run the

enterprise themselves." She believed that women should help themselves.

Susan King was a crusty New Englander with a mind of her own, but her success in real estate and in dickering with the "heathen Chinese" was quickly forgotten because nobody knew what to make of her.

She could have been treated like Hetty Green (1834–1916), the notorious "witch of Wall Street" who later made $100 million by speculating in the money market. Hetty has come down in history as a psychopath, but equally paranoid male speculators have been called merely eccentric. Whatever the facts behind these images, they reflect the nineteenth-century stereotype that accepted lapses from morality, and even sanity, in men who made money, while the contemporaneous Cult of True Womanhood made similar behavior inexcusably pathological in a woman.

During the height of the Cult, a woman who made money sounded like a contradiction in terms, hence an impossibility. When such a creature actually appeared on the scene, those who reported her activities tended to mythologize her into a saint or a devil.

By giving her money away, Margaret Haughery achieved the status of a saint. She became a legend while she still lived, and after her death, a statue was erected to her in New Orleans inscribed with the one word MARGARET. Susan King avoided notoriety by shunning publicity except when the public relations–minded Demorests managed it for her.

9

THE CIVIL WAR

Mary Ann Bickerdyke, Annie Wittenmyer, Dorothea Dix, Clara Barton

The Civil War was a national disaster, but it permanently improved the economic options of women. It forced many of them into the mainstream of economic life and created permanent women's jobs for those who wanted to stay there. Women had done men's work in the Revolutionary War, but the Civil War cut deeper into everyday life. Its effect on women was more profound because it came at a time when they were being told what they could *not* do.

According to the Cult of True Womanhood, a woman (or Woman! as she was often addressed) was weak, and could not lift heavy weights. She was sensitive and emotional and could not face harsh realities. She was vacillating and could not make decisions. She had no head for figures and no need to manage money. She was too timid to deal with strangers, too fearful to stand up to opposition, too impulsive to think ahead. For all these essentials of coping she relied, of course, on Man.

But during the Civil War, many a True Woman discovered

to her surprise that she was not really as helpless as she had imagined herself to be. "Our hired man left just as corn planting commenced," Sarah Kenyon, a farm wife in Oneida, Iowa, wrote matter-of-factly in 1861, "so I shouldered my hoe and have worked out ever since, and I guess my services are just as acceptable as his or will be in time to come in my country."

There would be plenty of unexpected work for women to do. Women were the first to realize that a government can't order a million men into the field without organizing their mail, their care in sickness, support and information for their families, and many of the comforts of home that did not require special provision when people lived with their families on farms. The systems that women volunteers improvised to meet these needs laid the foundations for modern military housekeeping arrangements and established new professional careers for women.

The U.S. Army went into the Civil War with hardly any of the human services now provided for soldiers as a matter of course. There was no Red Cross. There was no official organization providing the services of the U.S.O. When President Lincoln called for volunteers to suppress the rebellion in 1861, the 16,000 officers and men of the U.S. Army were healthy young men stationed in the West who needed no medical installation bigger than the 40-bed post hospital at Fort Leavenworth, Kansas.

Within months, this peacetime army's slender facilities were jammed with 250,000 men on trains, in camps, or milling around in search of direction. The army had no plans for a mobilization this size, so all was confusion. Women were appalled at the conditions described in the first letters these men sent home: poor food, no food for 24 hours, shoddy clothing, unhealthy quarters, sudden fevers and illnesses. Almost everywhere they organized local soldiers' relief societies to send "our boys" the comforts of home. They flooded the express offices with parcels addressed to individual units, and sometimes to individual soldiers. Broken glasses of jelly mixed up with books, fermenting sweetmeats, badly preserved canned meats, mounds of clothing, and stationery paralyzed the meager facilities for transporting mail and packages to sometimes rapidly moving troops.

It soon became apparent that informal neighborly help was not going to work. In order to be efficient, volunteer efforts would have to be administered through a formal, national organization with legal responsibility and government sanction.

A group of New York women moved carefully to secure wide acceptance for a plan to create a national civilian soldiers' relief organization. They set up a committee of 92 women whose names carried prestige. Headed by Louisa Schuyler, great-granddaughter of Alexander Hamilton, the committee called a mass meeting at Cooper Union. The big hall was jammed with women and men eager to find better ways to help the troops. A delegation was dispatched to Washington to confer with President Lincoln and the War Department, and the U.S. Sanitary Commission came into being, modeled on the British Sanitary Commission set up to improve British Army medical service in the Crimean War. It was headed by 22 men, but a majority of the actual volunteers and many of the local leaders were women. It had less authority than the British commission, but it was charged with augmenting medical facilities and coordinating volunteer efforts of every kind.

One of the first tasks of the commission was to provide an efficient alternative to the individual contributions which continued to jam the express agencies with broken jelly jars. Branches of the commission set up warehouses in nearly every community to receive contributions and dispatch them where they were most needed.

Two of the most efficient organizers of the commission were Mary A. Livermore and Jane C. Hoge of Chicago. Working as a team, Mary and Jane organized some 4,000 local groups to collect relief supplies which they induced the Illinois Central to ship free to the Union armies in the West. They also persuaded the telegraph companies to send their messages free.

Even when well organized, however, the collection and shipment of supplies was a less efficient way to help troops than raising money that could be spent in the field as needed. In 1863, Mary and Jane organized a Sanitary Fair in Chicago. They hoped to raise $25,000 by selling handwork and unused possessions contributed by women workers. In order to attract a crowd they secured unusual items, such as the original of President Lincoln's Emancipation Proclamation, and persuaded local merchants to close on their opening day. The fair netted $72,000 and was followed by sanitary fairs in other cities.

The fairs offered women a chance to develop working relationships with other women whom they would never have met socially. A regular and generous contributor in Virginia City, Nevada, for instance, was Julia Bulette, the elegant proprietor of "Julia's Parlour," the city's showplace brothel. The fairs were really sizable business enterprises requiring considerable sales and management talent.

During the course of the war, the commission collected well over $25 million in money, supplies, and services. Dr. Henry W. Bellows, president of the commission, found women immeasurably superior to men as collectors of supplies. "No words are adequate to describe the systematic faithfulness of the women who organized and led the branches," he wrote. "They acknowledged and answered, endorsed and filed their letters; they sorted their stores and kept an accurate account of stock; they had their books and reports kept in the most approved forms; they balanced their case accounts with the most painstaking precision. . . . Their volunteer labor had all the regularity of paid service, and a heartiness and earnestness which no paid service can ever have. Hundreds of women evinced talents which, in other spheres and in the other sex, would have made them merchant princes or great administrators of public affairs."

The needs were so various and the franchise of the Sanitary Commission so broad that women could undertake sizable enterprises under its shelter. Patriotism sanctioned activities that would have been regarded as distinctly unfeminine in peacetime. In order to give jobs to wives and mothers of soldiers, Katharine Prescott Wormeley started a clothing factory in Newport, Rhode Island, and delivered 50,000 shirts to the army. When the shirts were delivered, Katharine joined the transport service of the commission, and served on hospital ships evacuating soldiers from the Virginia peninsula, site of one of the bloodiest campaigns of the war. When the operation was so successful that the Army took it over, Katharine became the "lady superintendent" of a general hospital for convalescents at Portsmouth Grove, Rhode Island. As a final contribution, she wrote an unsigned pamphlet, *The United States Sanitary Commission, A Sketch of its Work and Purpose,* which was sold to raise money and enlist workers.

Sanitary Commission workers enjoyed considerable freedom, and some of them used it to cut red tape and compel attention to problems they felt the authorities were ignoring. One of the most forthright was Mary Ann Bickerdyke (1817–1901), a widow with two sons, who worked in hospitals as a $50-a-month field agent of the commission. Known as "Mother Bickerdyke," she was a woman of tremendous energy; her biographer has referred to her as "a cyclone in calico." Leaving her sons with neighbors, she rushed from Galesburg to Cairo, Illinois, with relief supplies in 1861 and served with the armies for the rest of the war. She was a demon for cleanliness, and after a battle gathered up dirty, bloody, and verminous underwear, blankets, and bandages and plunged them into huge cauldrons filled with water, soap, and carbolic acid. She built fires, boiled all the filthy linen, and then hung it on bushes to dry. She induced the Sanitary Commission to provide laundry service on a regular basis, and for a few months, she herself was in charge of a laundry that handled linen for all the Memphis hospitals.

She was popular with generals as well as ordinary soldiers. When a surgeon with whom she tangled appealed to General Sherman, he said: "I can do nothing for you. She outranks me." In a way she did. She carried a pass signed by General Grant authorizing her to go anywhere and to draw on Army quartermasters for any transportation or stores available.

Food for soldiers was always a problem. Even when there were enough rations to go around, the diet was deficient in fruit, vegetables, and dairy products. One of Mother Bickerdyke's exploits was obtaining 100 cows and 1,000 chickens to provide milk and eggs for hospital patients.

When scurvy developed, Jane Hoge and others collected and dispatched tons of vegetables to the Western armies. Local groups staged shows at which admission was by a food donation. There was a slogan, "Send your sweetheart a potato or five onions instead of a loveletter."

Annie Wittenmyer (1827–1900) was one of the free-wheeling commission workers who took single-handed action when she thought the interests of soldiers were at stake. All but one of her five children had died in infancy, and shortly before the outbreak of the war her husband had died as well. When Lincoln called for volunteers, Annie left her one child with her mother and headed for the front lines. In the beginning she went at her own expense, but later she was a representative of the Iowa Sanitary Commission.

She did whatever had to be done. At Helena, Arkansas, she found more than 2,000 sick and wounded men tormented by mosquitoes. Water from the tepid Mississippi River stood in barrels which had held pickled pork, while a barge of ice melted at the river landing because no one had authority to pay for it. Annie paid for the ice herself, and then stayed up one night writing letters for soldiers. The next morning, she took the upbound steamer to Memphis, where she went to the office of the medical director, who was out hunting, and then to the office of the general, whom she insisted on seeing although he was ill.

"I want you, General, to send four steamers immediately, fitted out with cots and supplies, to bring all these suffering men away from that death trap," she ordered. The general said yes, he would do it.

"But General, I want the order issued before I leave the office. Remember, I have no other appeal but the newspapers and the great, generous people of the North who sustain them." The next day she was back at Helena with the good news that four steamers were on their way.

These high-handed tactics won results, but they also won Annie Wittenmyer enemies—a bill was actually introduced in the Iowa legislature to repeal the law that had authorized her appointment to the commission. It was defeated.

One day she visited her brother, Davis C. Turner, in a military hospital in Sedalia, Missouri, just as he was waving away his breakfast in disgust. "On a dingy looking wooden tray," she later recalled, "was a tin cup full of strong black coffee; beside it was a leaden-looking tin platter, on which was a piece of fried fat bacon, swimming in its own grease, and a slice of bread."

At that time, the army had no special provisions for feeding the sick. Regular rations were issued to hospital patients, and anything else that was needed had to be privately supplied. Women who worked in hospitals tried to provide milk, eggs, and fresh vegetables they thought the sick men needed, and many of them set up little stoves to prepare these special dishes for individual patients. Where this improvisation became unwieldy, women had set up regular diet kitchens in the hospital from which all of the patients were served.

Annie undertook to work out a system for running a diet kitchen that could be adopted in every Army hospital as standard practice. In her memoirs she described how the new installations worked:

> 1. The food for those needing special diet was prescribed by the ward surgeons. A bill of fare was provided, with the name of the patient and the number of his bed, for every patient put on special diet; and on this bill the surgeon prescribed his diet by making a mark opposite the articles the patient was allowed. This plan gave the sick or wounded man a chance to express his own wants in regard to food.
>
> 2. These bills of fare were consolidated by the ward-master, and a copy sent to the superintendent of the special-diet kitchen. So the managers of the special-diet kitchen knew just what to cook, and the quantity.
>
> 3. The food thus ordered was prepared in the special-diet kitchen, which, although under separate management, was a part of the hospital.

The kitchens were fitted up with ranges and other suitable conveniences, and were under the management of suitable ladies employed by the surgeons in charge. A storeroom was provided, where the commuted rations of soldiers put on special-diet were stored, also the supplies furnished by the Sanitary and Christian Commissions; and the women in charge carried the keys.

4. These dietary nurses were *not cooks;* they only superintended the work. Many of those who worked in these kitchens were soldiers who were somewhat disabled or convalescent soldiers.

It is the verdict of history that this system of special-diet kitchens saved thousands of lives. During the last eighteen months of the war, over two million rations were issued monthly from this long line of special-diet kitchens, established, many of them, almost under the guns.

Eventually, of course, Annie's diet kitchen became the standard system for feeding patients in every kind of hospital.

Incredible as it seems, military hospitals before the Civil War did not even have regular nurses. Traditionally, sick and wounded soldiers had been cared for by companions, or other soldiers unfit for active duty. With so many men called up, women in both North and South volunteered to nurse the soldiers.

One of the most determined of these was Dorothea Lynde Dix (1802–1881), a New England woman nearly 60 years old, who was nationally known as an advocate of humane treatment for the mentally ill. She had begun this crusade in 1841 when she had discovered, while teaching Sunday school in a jail, that it contained women guilty only of insanity. Her eloquent "memorials" to legislatures resulted directly in 32 state mental hospitals.

Dorothea was not a physician, and she had no hospital administrative experience, but she was well known as a teacher, writer, and lecturer.

She arrived in Washington just a few days after mobilization, and proposed to Colonel Robert C. Wood, acting surgeon general, that she recruit and head a nursing corps of women volunteers. He and others in the War Department objected on the grounds of expense and the possibility that women would add sexual temptations and scandals to the hospital problems. Dorothea Dix reassured them.

"No woman under 30 years need apply to serve in government hospitals," she agreed in her program. "All nurses are required to be very plain-looking women. Their dresses must be brown or black, with no bows, no curls, no jewelry, and no hoopskirts."

The nurses had to be women of unblemished reputation with letters of recommendation from their pastors. Their services had to be requested by hospital surgeons, who could dismiss them at any time. They were to be paid $12 a month, a dollar less than a private soldier, and if they wore uniforms, they would supply their own.

A year after Dorothea Dix went to work in the North, the Confederate Congress legalized women in its hospitals with an act "to better provide for the sick and wounded" that authorized for each hospital two matrons, two assistant matrons, two matrons for each ward, other cooks and nurses as needed, and a ward master for each ward, "giving preference in all cases to females. . . ."

The small Robertson Hospital in Richmond, Virginia, had such a low mortality rate that President Jefferson Davis commissioned its manager, Sally L. Tompkins (1833–1916), a captain so she could continue in charge when the military took over the hospital. She was the only female commissioned officer in the Confederate Army, and during the war, when her hospital treated more than 1,300 soldier patients, only 73 died, an incredible figure for the state of medical knowledge at the time, and considering the fact that the worst cases were sent to that hospital because it provided the best care.

Fears that female nurses would provoke scandals proved illusory. A few of Dorothea Dix's recruits were transferred or dismissed because of "impertinence" to surgeons, but there were no scandals. And though most surgeons were reluctant to work with them at first, they welcomed them as casualties increased.

Louisa May Alcott, the famous New England writer, wrote this vivid account of her nursing chores on January 4, 1863, in the Union Hotel Hospital, in Georgetown, District of Columbia:

> Up at six, dress by gaslight, run through my ward and throw up the windows. . . . Poke up the fire, add blankets, joke, coax, and command; but continue to open doors and windows . . . for a more perfect pestilence-box than this house I never saw,—cold, damp, dirty, full of vile odors from wounds, kitchens, wash-rooms, and stables. . . . I go to breakfast . . . find fried beef, salt butter, husky bread and washy coffee. . . .
>
> Till noon I trot, trot, giving out rations, cutting up food for helpless "boys," washing faces, teaching my attendants how beds are made or floors are swept, dressing wounds . . . dusting tables, sewing bandages, keeping my tray tidy, rushing up and down after pillows, bed-linens, sponges, books and directions. . . . At twelve the big bell rings and up comes dinner for the boys. . . . when dinner is over, some sleep, many read, and others want letters written. The answering of letters after some one has died is the saddest and hardest duty a nurse has to do.
>
> Supper at five sets every one to running that can run; and when the flurry is over, all settle down for the evening amusements, which consist of newspapers, gossip, the doctor's last round, and, for such as need them, the final doses for the night. At nine the bell rings, gas is turned down, and day nurses go to bed. Night nurses go on duty, and sleep and death have the house to themselves.

The Union Hotel Hospital was a crowded, unhealthy place, and after six weeks Louisa Alcott herself became ill with a serious fever and her nursing career came to an end. "I was never ill before this time," she said, "and never well afterward."

For those who could stand it, Civil War work provided invaluable experience that enabled many of the women to move easily into public affairs. In an 1888 Memorial Day address, a quarter-century after Gettysburg, Clara Barton recalled women's work in the Civil War and declared that because of the conflict "woman was at least fifty years in advance of the normal position which continued peace . . . would have assigned her." She herself was the best example.

Clara Barton (1821–1912) began her wartime relief work as a one-woman operation. A former Massachusetts school teacher, then 39, she was copying documents for the U.S. Patent Office in Washington at $1 per 1,000 words when the war began. Except for the summer of 1862, when she was busy on the battlefield, she continued during the war to do enough copying for the Patent Office to earn monthly checks which she spent on relief.

She met the first Massachusetts volunteers to arrive in Washington and reported their needs to New England newspapers. Organizations and individuals there began to send her food and medical supplies. She set up a freelance relief agency in one of her two rooms and then proceeded to distribute, usually personally, what she had collected to soldiers in camps and sometimes on battlefields.

Indomitable and independent, she declined to join the organizations of the Sanitary Commission, Christian Commission, or any of the other war groups doing similar work. "Clara," a biographer later wrote, "at times made herself answerable only to God." But she was not bashful in asking all sorts of people for help. She early won the support of Senator Henry Wilson of Massachusetts, chairman of the Senate Committee on Military Affairs. He gave her letters of introduction, and even intervened on her behalf at the White House.

After the battle of Cedar Mountain in Virginia on August 9, 1862, Brigade Surgeon James L. Dunn was using his last surgical dressings at midnight when Clara Barton arrived, in his words, like "a holy angel," driving a four-mule team pulling a wagon loaded with bandages. It was the beginning of a legend, and the tiny woman, five feet tall and never weighing more than 100 pounds, became "the angel of the battlefield" to her admirers.

Clara sometimes applied the bandages and cooked the food that she and her helpers delivered to the soldiers. She was at both Fredericksburg and Antietam during the fighting. At the latter, she noted in her diary, a bullet passed through the sleeve of her dress to kill a wounded man as she stopped to give him a drink of water.

As the war ended she undertook to learn the fate of thousands of Union soldiers still listed as missing after the emptying of Confederate prisons. When she could not get to see President Lincoln about the project, her friend, Senator Henry Wilson, obtained from him this letter:

> To the Friends of Missing Persons: Miss Clara Barton has kindly offered to search for the missing prisoners of war. Please address her at Annapolis, giving her name, regiment, and company of any missing prisoner.
> A. Lincoln.

It was one of President Lincoln's last letters. Every newspaper in the country published it, and the project won Clara her first national notice.

With several assistants in Annapolis, she set up the office of the General Correspondent for the Friends of Paroled Prisoners with her own funds, though eventually she received some government help. Information began to pour in from many sources: soldiers who had seen their comrades die in battle, families who had sheltered and/or buried soldiers, hospital workers, and even a prisoner-of-war who had been detailed to keep the records of his Union comrades in a Confederate camp. All helped her to identify numbers of dead and missing. She was responsible for tracking down more than 20,000 soldiers whose fate might never have been known otherwise.

Physically exhausted, she went to Switzerland for a rest in 1869 and there learned for the first time about the International Red Cross. At the invitation of Grand Duchess Louise of Baden, Clara helped distribute Red Cross supplies during the Franco-Prussian War of 1870–1871.

She returned to America and organized the American Red Cross in 1881, and using her war-won knowledge of Washington, in 1882 she induced Congress to ratify the international treaty protecting the Red Cross emblem and those who wear it. She headed the American organization for 33 years, and beginning with a Michigan forest fire expanded its activities from war work to disasters of all kinds.

Clara Barton was only one of the women who used the confidence she had gained in Civil War work to influence public affairs afterwards. Jane C. Hoge, the Sanitary Commission worker, raised money to establish the Evanston College for Ladies, which was to become part of Northwestern University. Her friend Mary Livermore became a successful lecturer and woman suffrage leader. Annie Wittenmyer became the first president of the Women's Christian Temperance Union.

The Civil War greatly increased the proportion of women whose circumstances were typical of enterprising women. The war itself was encouragement for women to engage in nontraditional activities. It also deprived many women of husbands and families. In addition to the widows, there were the young women whose potential husbands never returned, or who had spent child- and/or husband-free years during the long war. Finally, the war itself dislocated so many industries and so many lives that it confronted an unusually large number of women with the compelling incentive of a family crisis.

10

RECONSTRUCTION
Frances Leigh

The Civil War provided challenges to which some women of the North could rise, but it overwhelmed most of the women of the South. Many of the widows left to cope alone had been reared in the plantation system which brought the Cult of True Womanhood to its finest flower, and the tradition against gainful employment of "nice women" was so strong in the South that Northern women had to be imported to teach in Southern schools. Some women who found themselves alone had been reared on plantations where they had never been allowed, as girls, to lift so much as a finger. All of a sudden, the fortunes of war required these plantation belles to earn a living in a ruined economy.

Slavery is so abhorrent that it is hard to think of emancipation in other than human terms. The fact remains, however, that the ending of slavery was the most important single economic event of the nineteenth century in America. At the stroke of a pen, emancipation parted slaveowners from millions of dollars' worth of human "property" and put 4 million former slaves into a free labor market as ill prepared to receive them as they were to enter it. In addition, emancipation destroyed the basis of Southern agriculture. Crops, methods, even the size of plantation units had all been based on slave labor.

Women had a special sympathy for their former slaves.

Many had been abolitionists, some even openly, and because they were suddenly required to take responsibility for themselves, they could sympathize with the difficulties confronting newly freed blacks. Almost all of the plantation women felt a dual responsibility: to the plantation itself, as the family business, and to their former slaves. Some dreamed of continuing the old plantation by hiring the blacks they had once owned, but almost all of them failed at the attempt.

One of the few exceptions was an extraordinary woman who succeeded in putting her father's rice plantation on a paying basis using personnel techniques that would provide a rewarding case study for twentieth-century students of management.

In 1866, Frances Butler Leigh (1838–1910) and her father returned from the North, where they had spent the war, to their rice and cotton fields on the sea islands of Georgia. They found that their half-starved former slaves, including some who had been sold to other masters, were willing to work for the old master but no one else. Pierce Butler managed to get a small seed crop of rice planted by offering those willing to work half the crop, but he died the following year, and the freed slaves who had worked for him complained to Frances Leigh that the overseer was cheating them.

"Night after night, when the day's work was over, I sat up 'til two and three o'clock in the morning, going over and over the long line of figures," she wrote. "Not one Negro understood it a bit, but all were quite convinced they had been cheated, most of them thinking that each man was entitled to half the crop. I was so anxious they should understand and see they had been fairly dealt with, that I went over and over again each man's account." Most didn't think she wanted to cheat them, but as one man told her, during the interminable conversations she had with each one, "You see, missus, a woman ain't much 'count."

Planters believed that white men could not withstand the malarial rice fields well enough to harvest the crops, so survival depended on getting the blacks to work. "From the first, the fixed notion in their minds has been that liberty meant idleness," Frances wrote. Those who refused to work, she added, were no worse off than those who worked at plantation wages of $12 a month and rations. "They all raise a little corn and sweet potatoes, and with their facilities for catching fish and oysters, and shooting wild game, they have as much to eat as they want." Blacks were not alone. Dispossessed white planters who used to hunt for sport were now hunting deer for meat, sharing it with other planter families living in shacks they had thrown up near each other in the pine wood. They talked about importing Chinese labor or threshing machines, but they didn't have the money.

"It is very sad to see such widespread ruin and to hear of girls well-educated, and brought up with every luxury, turned adrift as dressmakers, schoolteachers, and even shop girls, in order to keep themselves and their families from starvation," she wrote. "One of Mrs. F——'s nieces paddles her old father over the plantation every morning herself, and while he is giving his orders in the fields, sits on a heap of straw, making underclothing to sell in Charleston."

Frances Butler Leigh was made of sterner stuff. She was named for her mother, the famous British actress Frances ("Fanny") Kemble, who had impetuously married Pierce Butler, whom she met on her triumphant tour of America in 1834. Frances, their second daughter, was born four years later. The aristocratic Butlers looked down on Fanny Kemble because she was an actress: she reciprocated by attacking slavery in print. And while Pierce Butler was as charming as the fictional Rhett Butler of *Gone with the Wind*, freewheeling Fanny Kemble was not prepared to give up strenuous horseback riding and an independent schedule to fit Butler's image of a proper Southern lady. When Frances was eleven years old, her mother and father were divorced. Frances adored her father and became his devoted companion and helper.

She did not have husband or child to distract her from the work of saving her father's beloved plantations until she married the Rev. James Wentworth Leigh at the age of 33. Only after she put the property on a business basis did she move to England, a country her husband preferred. "I have worked so hard and cared so much about it, that it is more to me than I can express to know that I have succeeded," she wrote in 1871. Yet in 1873, after still another overseer had let the work slip, she was back again, rebuilding a building he had not been able to prevent the blacks from burning following a dispute with them.

Succeeding took more stamina and courage than any of the white overseers she employed had been able to demonstrate. She used the histrionic talent of her mother to get "her people" to work. She was convinced that it was her father's "strong personal influence over them" that enabled him to bring in the best crop in the neighborhood during the last year of his life. After he died, "the people" refused to sign contracts for the overseer, so she took over the touchy business of negotiating with them herself.

"The next morning at ten [she wrote], I had the big mill bell rung to summon the people here to sign the contract, and then my work began in earnest. For six mortal hours I sat in the office without once leaving my chair, while the people poured in and poured out, each one with long explanations, objections, and demonstrations. . . . I was immovable. 'No, they must sign the contract as it stood.' 'No, I could not have anyone work without signing.' 'No, they must work six days and rest on Sunday.'" It took two days and a few dramatic confrontations, but in the end, only two made good their threat to leave—"one from imagined ill-health, and one I dismissed for insubordination. The gentlemen [her white staff] seemed to think I had done wonders."

In 1868, when an insurrection was expected, she slept with a loaded pistol under her pillow. The people took to testing her by calling her "Miss Fanny" instead of "Mistress" and they tried speaking to her with their hats on. "This last rudeness I never permitted for a moment, and always said sharply, 'Take your hat off instantly,'" she wrote. "One or two, who seemed rather more inclined to be insolent than the rest, I dismissed, always saying, 'You are free to leave the place, but not to stay here and behave as you please, for I am free too, and moreover own the place, and have a right to give my orders on it, and have them obeyed.'"

The air of command worked. Instead of bribing a black

bully as her agent advised, she had him arrested, and after he escaped, she had him put back in jail. "My agent unfortunately was not much assistance to me, being nervous, timid, and irresolute," she commented. Overseers were often neighbors who had failed on their own plantations, ostensibly for lack of nerve.

Frances Butler Leigh was a worthy daughter of her father. She eventually dispensed with the unsatisfactory white overseers available and directed the work of the plantation herself through black captains. She maintained a school and a church for the free blacks who worked for her at her own expense, and worried about their welfare like a true daughter of Fanny Kemble, the idealist and abolitionist.

Frances Leigh's achievement was a triumph of sheer determination over conditions that did not make economic sense. She succeeded by lavishing prodigious management talent and personal charm on an essentially unworkable system. After she proved that she could make the plantation pay, she went to England to live with her husband. Most of the plantations of the South degenerated after the war into sharecropping operations as unrewarding for owners as tenants. The heroic widows who tried to keep them going drifted into the cities, some to teach school, including schools set up for their former slaves. But never again could Southern women regard themselves as helpless.

11

THE PROFESSIONALS
Myra Bradwell, Lucy Taylor,
Elizabeth Blackwell

The Civil War volunteers had demonstrated that a True Woman could do work of the highest responsibility as long as she wasn't paid for it. But if a woman wanted to enter one of the established professions, she found it jealously guarded male territory.

The sex barrier in the professions was relatively new. In the eighteenth century, women had been "doctoresses," curing ills if they could; women had practised law and preached sermons at a time when these "mysteries" were commonly passed down in families. Eliza Pinckney had picked up enough law in the course of managing the affairs of the plantation to write wills for her poor neighbors. But at about that same time, professional schools were being founded from which women were excluded as a matter of course. When doctors, lawyers, preachers, and eventually the practitioners of lesser "mysteries" organized professional societies, they secured licensing laws which limited entry to those who could prove their qualification by special education or examination. Licensing laws came later to the frontier, but by 1880, all the professions were trying to raise standards and their own incomes by keeping out "undesirables." Women were regarded as undesirable by nature.

In the profession of law, there was a loophole that allowed a woman to learn, even when she could not be licensed or admitted to the bar. There was nothing to stop her from "reading" or studying law in the office of a man admitted to practice; the majority of practising lawyers continued to qualify in this way even after law schools existed for the elite.

The most likely man from whom a woman could learn law was a relative. Before and long after the Union College of Chicago granted the first law degree to a woman named Ada Kepley in 1870, a growing company of wives, daughters, and sisters learned the law by helping the man in the family who was entitled to practice it. Virtually all of these pioneer women lawyers used their knowledge to do the paper work of the office so that practicing males could handle more business, but one of the most creative lawyers of her time used the training she had acquired from her husband to build a separate legal career that did not require licensing or admission to the bar.

Myra Bradwell (1831–1894) was a child of the moving frontier. She was born in Vermont, spent her early years in western New York State, and was twelve when her family moved to Illinois. There she married James Bradwell, a struggling law student of whom her parents disapproved. Myra had acquired enough schooling to teach. In Memphis, Tennessee, she and James ran a private school together, sharing the work as partners. When the Bradwells moved to Chicago, James went into law partnership with Myra's brother there. The firm prospered, and James Bradwell became a judge and a member of the Illinois state legislature.

During the Civil War, Myra was active in the Northwestern Sanitary Commission, and later, in the Soldiers' Aid Society set up to care for veterans after the fighting was over. She had always taken a special interest in the work which engaged her husband and brother, and she devoted more of her time to the study of law after two of her four children died.

Most wives who learned law from their husbands could help make more money by doing the research and writing chores. But Myra's husband was a judge and a legislator, which took him away from his practice. A male law partner could have held the practice for him, but Myra could not appear in court or practice in her own right. Instead, she created a separate career that enabled her both to make money on her own and to improve the practice of law.

In 1868 she founded the *Chicago Legal News* the first weekly law periodical published in the West. Men bent on getting rich quick in the mobile new towns were equally quick to take their quarrels to the law, and lawyers had multiplied to supply the demand. Advertising for the periodical poured in so fast that the first issue was double the four-page size promised in the prospectus.

Although we have no evidence about the Bradwell family finances, it is quite likely that Myra's *News* made her the principal breadwinner of the family. The division of labor in the Bradwell partnership created a powerhouse of both influence and profits. When they set up the Chicago Legal News Company, James used his influence to get a special charter under which Myra could head the business without the legal handicaps that limited married women. James, the legislator and politician, lobbied special acts through the legislature making publication in the *News* legal evidence of laws, notices, and court opinions. Myra, the forthright editor, used the captive audience of lawyers so acquired to push through a long list of reforms essential to transforming the rough and ready frontier courts into a comprehensive system capable of dealing with the greatly expanded legal business generated by progress and prosperity.

With evident encouragement from her lawyer husband, Myra first set out to challenge the prevailing exclusion of women from legal practice. She took the bar examination and passed with distinction, and when she was denied admission first on the ground of being a married woman, and then on the ground of sex itself, she carried the appeal to the Supreme Court of the United States.

The Supreme Court sidestepped a decision by declaring that the states controlled the qualifications for their own bars. This move put the issue in territory friendly to the Bradwells, who succeeded in getting the 1872 session of the Illinois state legislature to pass a law abolishing discrimination in employment. Other women claimed the right which Myra's strategy had won, but Myra did not ask for admission, and never practised as a lawyer herself.

Myra developed all the business possibilities of the paper. She became Chicago's leader in the highly profitable industry of printing cases on appeal. She printed and sold the blanks which lawyers use to draw up legal instruments, and designed at least 75 of the forms herself.

Her response to the devastating Chicago fire of 1871 was a lesson in the possibilities of making money while doing good. The Chicago fire of 1871 was one of the most destructive on record. It burned over three and a half square miles, destroying more than 17,000 buildings and killing 250 people. Like many other Chicagoans, the Bradwells lost their home and furniture, including their private law library and the records of the business, and for the first night, they thought they had lost their 13-year-old daughter, Bessie. When Bessie turned up the next day, hugging the subscription book she had rescued from the fire, Myra took the train to Milwaukee with a copy of the upcoming issue of the *News* for printing. Three days later it appeared, on schedule, with an appeal for law books, a suggestion for a law that would secure real estate titles destroyed by fire, and a suggestion to legal book publishers that they advertise in the *News* because "in no place else in the world will there be such a demand for law books as in Chicago during the next few months." Everybody took the good advice, including a special session of the Illinois state legislature, which passed the Burnt Records Act she suggested.

In part, perhaps, because as a woman she was an outsider, Myra was able to perceive many ways in which the operation of the courts could be improved, and thanks to the influence she and her husband created by their unique partnership, an impressive number of her practical suggestions were enacted into law. She campaigned for clean courthouses and suggested a joint state and county courthouse which was later built. She suggested that real estate deeds be indexed, a simple housekeeping detail which warded off chaos. She encouraged bar associations to codify professional standards. She called for simplified pleadings, better treatment of witnesses in trials, pensioning and retirement of superannuated judges, and a law school education for all lawyers.

Quiet and ladylike, she knew just how to fight sex discrimination. She publicized the plight of a scrubwoman whose wages had been garnisheed to pay for her husband's liquor, and thus won passage of an Illinois statute which secured the right of married women to their own wages. She promoted a law specifically naming women eligible to hold school office in Illinois. When denied the office of notary public on the ground of sex, she had a special bill passed in the legislature which opened this service to women.

Although she did not hesitate to criticize public officials and policies she opposed, she won ungrudging respect from the bar and the bench. In 1890, four years before her death, the Illinois State Supreme Court undertook, on its own motion, to admit her to the bar, thus acknowledging the error they had made in denying her application in 1869.

Equally gratifying was the respect she won from her own family. Both her children became lawyers, and her daughter Bessie followed almost exactly in her mother's footsteps. She married a lawyer and succeeded her mother as editor and publisher of the *Chicago Legal News*.

Myra Bradwell's most interesting innovation was the career she created for herself. If she had been a man, she would undoubtedly have built a profitable practice, but since as a woman she could not serve private individuals for a fee, she took the profession itself for her client and improved the practice of the law for clients and lawyers alike. Her impressive public-service career was in part at least a response to the limitations imposed on women by the conditions under which they managed to acquire their professional knowledge.

A woman could learn law from a man in the family, but unless she was an exception, like Myra Bradwell, licensing laws constrained her to remain his unofficial helper. Women who tried to enter a profession without learning it in the family had a much harder time.

Lucy Hobbs Taylor (1833–1910) wanted to be a doctor, but she had no one to help her. She was born in a log cabin and

managed to acquire enough schooling to become a teacher
in the backwoods town of Brooklyn, Michigan. There was,
however, a physician in that town, and Lucy persuaded him
to give her private lessons in anatomy and physiology. He
suggested that she try entering the Eclectic College of Medicine in Cincinnati, one of the proprietary medical schools
that amounted to diploma mills, but when she went to Cincinnati in 1859, Eclectic refused her because she was a
woman.

One of the Eclectic professors agreed to teach her privately, but the knowledge he imparted brought her no
nearer to the medical degree required for practice. He suggested that dentistry would be an easier profession for her to
enter. Dentists didn't have to make house calls, he pointed
out, and in Ohio at that time, they didn't even have to have
a license.

What he really meant was that dentistry was easier for a
woman to enter because it actually wasn't considered a
profession. Except in the cities, no one cared very much
about the appearance of teeth, and if they rotted, almost
anyone could pull them out. Like preachers and photogra-
phers, who sometimes pulled teeth on the side, early dentists
served sparsely populated rural areas by traveling from town
to town, carrying their tools with them. In the case of dentists, these were usually confined to a file, a few excavators,
a vial of mercury, and silver coin to make fillings. Many
people regarded dentists as little better than the patent
medicine men who traveled the same routes.

Even so, it was not easy for Lucy to find a dentist willing
to teach her. One agreed to teach her secretly if she would
clean his office, but she refused.

In 1859, dentists were trying to organize themselves as a
profession, as doctors had already done. The dental college
in Cincinnati turned Lucy down, but the dean agreed to
teach her privately for three months only, and when she
proved herself in this trial, a graduate of the school took her
on as an apprentice.

Good dentists were hard to find during the Civil War, and
after a few years, Lucy had become a good one. She set up

practice in Cincinnati and later in McGregor, Iowa, where she won a statewide reputation for competence. In 1865, the Iowa State Dental Society admitted her to membership, and helped her to gain admission to the Ohio College of Dental Surgery—which had once rejected her application, along with that of a black man. In 1866 she became the first woman to receive the degree of Doctor of Dental Surgery.

Armed with a diploma, she went to Chicago and set up an office. Only after she was established in business did she consider marriage. At 34 she married James Myrtle Taylor. After his marriage, James quit his job as a painter in a railroad car shop to become his wife's apprentice. Late in 1867, they left Chicago and moved to Lawrence, Kansas, where they set up a practice together. Lucy specialized in false teeth and work with women and children. James worked on the men.

The role reversal of the Taylors makes it easier to see the economic value of learning a restricted profession from a spouse. It made sense for James to become a dentist after his marriage to a wife who was already qualified. He was able to learn at small cost a skilled trade that paid better than the trade he had been following. This, of course, was exactly the situation in which a wife who was an apprentice found herself. By the time James entered dentistry, it was becoming a licensed profession, and as a man he would have had no trouble getting a license so that he could become an equal partner with the wife who had taught him. But if he had been denied a license for any reason, he could probably have added more to the family income by remaining her unpaid assistant than by returning to his job as a blue-collar worker.

Like Myra Bradwell, Lucy Taylor evolved a satisfying marital/business partnership which would be attractive to liberated professional women of the 1970s, but she went into dentistry only because she could not become a doctor. Medicine has always been the most forbidding profession for women. By 1830, a license to practice medicine was required in all but three states, and the license required schooling from which women were excluded. The first woman to achieve Lucy's ambition to obtain a recognized medical edu-

cation was an Englishwoman who brought formidable resources of family connections and personal strength to the
task of breaking the barrier.

Elizabeth Blackwell (1821–1910) was the favorite daughter
of Samuel Blackwell, a British sugar refiner who brought his
large family to America when Elizabeth was 11 years old.
Because he was a religious Dissenter and an intellectual with
liberal ideas, Elizabeth and her four sisters were tutored at
home and studied the same rigorous subjects taught her five
brothers. Books, music, outdoor exercise, and high standards
of personal conduct supervised by four maiden aunts prepared the Blackwell children to pioneer in social reforms.

The Blackwells grew up to practise the sex equality that
they had been taught in their home schoolroom. Elizabeth's
sister Emily was to follow her into medicine, while her sister
Ellen became an author and artist, and her sister Anna a
newspaper correspondent. Her brother Samuel was to become the husband of Antoinette L. Brown, America's first
ordained woman preacher, and her brother Henry was to
marry Lucy Stone, the pioneer feminist who refused to take
her husband's name.

Elizabeth's father presented his children with a model of
self-sacrifice for the sake of principle. He lost his money trying to refine sugar from beets rather than support slavery by
buying cane sugar. When Elizabeth was 17, he died, leaving
his large family penniless in Cincinnati, Ohio, where they
had moved to make a new start. Elizabeth taught school in
the West to make money, but she was restless. She was looking for a large project to fight off what she described in her
autobiography as "the disturbing influence of the other sex."
A friend dying of cancer suggested that she become a doctor,
and the challenge sounded big enough to "place a strong
barrier between me and all ordinary marriage."

Elizabeth was a True Woman who assumed that she could
not be both a doctor and a wife, and she rejected the physical
side of life so thoroughly that no small part of the challenge
of medicine was overcoming her disgust at "the very thought
of dwelling on the physical structure of the body and its
various ailments." But there was a streak of masochism in

her, and after deciding that the course was right, she never wavered.

The obstacles were overwhelming. Influential friends of the Blackwells sympathized, warning her at the same time that no respectable medical school would permit a woman to study physiology in the company of men. Nevertheless, armed with recommendations from all the influential sponsors she could muster, Elizabeth doggedly applied to every good medical school in New York, and when she was rejected, to the less well known, and finally to small country schools.

Geneva College in upstate New York finally accepted her, although they regarded her application as something of a joke. The dean did not want to offend the Philadelphia physician who had urged him to accept this earnest "lady medical student," so he put the application up to the student body. The students were local farm boys so rowdy that neighbors had tried to have the college declared a public nuisance. Amid shouting and catcalls they voted to accept Elizabeth. But while she was there, she won their respect by her quiet determination. She even tried starving herself on the mistaken theory that it would prevent her from blushing during lectures on the organs of reproduction. In 1849, when she was graduated at the top of her class, people came from miles around to view the first woman to complete a medical education in America.

Elizabeth's classmates were content to practice locally on the basis of the 12 months they had spent at Geneva College, but Elizabeth determined to get the best medical education available, and that meant studying in Paris and London. In order to learn obstetrical practice, she had to enroll as a student midwife and follow the course designed for French peasant women at the famous Paris hospital, La Maternité. London was more hospitable. Attracted by her spirit, English doctors let her round out her medical education in the best hospitals.

Back in New York, the actual practice of medicine proved even more difficult than studying it. In that city, "female physician" meant abortionist. No hospital would accept

Elizabeth on its staff, and landlords were so unwilling to have her as a tenant that she eventually had to raise funds to buy a house in which to set up practice. While waiting for patients, she lectured to women on their health needs and set up a clinic for the poor. She was so lonely that she adopted an Irish orphan girl, Kitty Barry, who stayed with her as friend and housekeeper to the end of her life. When the Civil War broke out, she drafted the call for the meeting at Cooper Union that resulted in setting up the Sanitary Commission, but she did not sign her name to it for fear that the "stigma of women doctors" would endanger acceptance of the plan.

Other women followed Elizabeth into medicine. One was Emily, her younger sister. After being turned down by many medical schools, including Geneva College, Emily was accepted at Rush Medical College in Chicago and later at Western Reserve. She joined Elizabeth in New York, and soon there were others who had managed to get into the small, offbeat schools of "eclectic" or "homeopathic" medicine, devoted to theories of disease later repudiated by orthodox physicians. Meanwhile, during the 1850s, medical schools especially for women were set up in Philadelphia, Boston, and other cities. In 1859 Elizabeth estimated that 300 women had managed to get a medical education somewhere in the United States.

Before the Civil War, Elizabeth raised enough money to set up the New York Infirmary for Women and Children, where women doctors could get the clinical experience denied them by hospitals. In 1869, when she returned to England permanently to practice medicine in London, she left behind a small but determined sorority of women physicians dedicated to proving that a woman doctor could be twice as good as a man—if she worked twice as hard.

12

CONFIDENCE BUILDERS
Mary Baker Eddy,
Lydia Pinkham,
Harriet Hubbard Ayer,
C. J. Walker

In the nineteenth century, True Women were expected to be "delicate." Everybody worried about their health. In 1850, a Boston physician estimated that half the women of America suffered from the "real disease" of nervousness, and another talked of importing the future mothers and wives of America from Europe—where, he apparently thought, women were made of sturdier stuff. Sarah Hale scolded her readers to eat simple food, avoid tight corsets, and take exercise. Ailing herself, Catharine Beecher sounded a general alarm over the health crisis of American womanhood.

In general, doctors of the time were neither sympathetic nor helpful. Nineteenth-century medicine was not only bad, but sexist as well. In 1870, a professor of medicine advised his colleagues to diagnose the ailments of women "as if the Almighty, in creating the female sex, had taken the uterus and built up a woman around it." This view related every complaint of a woman to her reproductive system. If a woman complained, as many did, of being "tired," "dull," "uninterested in the family," "subject to fits of weeping, sleeplessness, or loss of appetite," the up-to-date physician might put leeches in her vulva, inject strong chemical solutions into the uterus, or even stick hot iron pokers into it.

Only a determined masochist would risk a repeat of some of the drastic medical remedies prescribed for females. A woman of iron will, Catharine Beecher sought relief from her nervous symptoms in at least 13 different medical establishments, after which her verdict was that "owing chiefly to my own knowledge and caution, I was not injured . . . by any."

Injury, however, wasn't the only concern. A True Woman considered it an insult to feminine delicacy to submit to medical treatment of any kind at the hands of a male physician. Many women of sensibility said they preferred death to physical examination by a strange male, and some may even have paid the ultimate price because of this modesty.

Women doctors were the obvious answer. But not many women followed Elizabeth Blackwell into male medical schools, and there were never enough graduates from the few women's medical colleges to relieve the embarrassment of all the American women in need of medical attention. In retrospect, it is doubtful whether the medical practices of the times could have done much for them.

Much of their illness was undoubtedly organic. Margaret LaForge never fully recovered from the birth of her twins, and she may have suffered damage that modern medicine could have prevented. But the vague and romantic terms in which women described ailments peculiar to their sex suggest that many of these "female ailments" were "in the mind." Since ill health was the only acceptable excuse for rejecting sex with husbands, it is hard to determine whether headaches or strange pains in the lower abdomen were a deliberate defense against pregnancy, an unconscious psychosomatic response to the limitations imposed on women, or straightforward organic disease.

Whatever the nature of their ailments, women found as

little help from orthodox religion as from orthodox male physicians. Male preachers could only enjoin women to submit to the will of God who had created them female, and subject to female disabilities. Insofar as these troubles were psychic, women might find comfort and relief through any one of the mental therapies that were fashionable at the time. Religious revival meetings, spiritualism, mesmerism, health fads, and systems of faith healing all attracted ailing women.

Out of this setting, an enigmatic woman evolved a religion that differed from all others in asserting "the unreality of disease, sin, and death." Mary Baker Eddy (1821–1910) is a controversial figure. Luckily, however, it isn't necessary to judge Christian Science either as science or as religion, or to understand Mary Baker Eddy's personal background and motivation, in order to recognize that the religion she founded met the health needs of nineteenth-century women in a remarkably modern, nonsexist way. Mary did not set out to help her own sex, but women recognized that she spoke to their condition. The Mother Church in Boston publishes no statistics, but according to some estimates, three-fourths of the members and 90 percent of the "practitioners" or paid healers are women, and women frequently serve as presidents of the Mother Church.

Mary's early life reads like a melodrama constructed to illustrate just how awful a woman's lot could be. Sickly as a child, she was the youngest of six children born on a New Hampshire farm. A mysterious spinal defect and a tendency to fits and tantrums kept her out of school much of the time, but she was an avid reader on her own. Her father was strict, but her mother favored her and may have indulged her because of her physical frailties. After attending Sanbornton Academy, she married her sister-in-law's brother. It was the first of three marriages, each a disaster in its own way.

Her first husband, George Washington Glover, died six months after the wedding, leaving her pregnant and in such ill health that she had to go back to her parents for nursing and give up her baby son to be reared by foster parents. For nine years she was so nervous and hysterical that her family had to care for her as if she were an infant, rocking her to quiet her agitation, and trying all sorts of cures.

In 1853, she married Daniel Patterson, an itinerant dentist. She later termed this marriage "a very unfortunate mistake." It began ominously. She suffered an attack of "neuralgia in the spine and stomach" just before the marriage was to take place, so the bridegroom had to carry her downstairs for the wedding ceremony. Later, her health always seemed better when he was away on business or in the Civil War. They were finally divorced in 1873. Her third husband was Asa Gilbert Eddy, an unimaginative sewing-machine salesman who died five years after their wedding.

Mary's career did not begin until she was 45 years old, and it began, characteristically, with disaster. She slipped on the ice in Lynn, Massachusetts, and hurt her back badly. According to her own account, "on the third day," February 4, 1866, she rose from her bed, having healed herself by reading the Bible. It was on that day of the "Great Revelation," she wrote, that "I discovered the Science of divine metaphysical healing which I afterward named Christian Science."

During the next three years she sought the secret of "mind healing" and perfected her ability to remove from the mind the wrong thinking that she believed caused physical ills. Mary's personal magnetism attracted followers. According to Sydney Ahlstrom, professor of modern church history at Yale, she carried all through her life "a certain aura of excitement, so that not even those who parted from her in anger seemed to regret the association." "Demonstrations" or testimonials of those who said they had been cured of various illnesses brought students to her. She was able to earn her living, though sometimes precariously, by healing individuals, lecturing on her system, and teaching others to heal by her methods.

Mary referred to money as "supply," and taught that a "sufficiency of supply" was the natural outcome of spiritual understanding. As she attracted followers, she put the new religion on a sound financial basis. Over a period of eight years, she single-handedly taught a seven-lesson course in mind healing to 4,000 students, each of whom paid her $300.

The fee was high, but the course was vocational. After completing it, students could become practitioners who could collect fees for their services in healing. Because they prescribed no physical treatment, practitioners did not have to be licensed as doctors, and the new calling attracted women.

All during Mary's early years she had been busy writing a book on her theories. In 1875, the Christian Science Publishing Company, formed by two of Mary's students with $2200 capital, brought out the first edition of *Science and Health*. Before her death in 1910, each of its subsequent editions, 382 in all, became, in its turn, the authorized text for Christian Science. Sales of *Science and Health* have since returned sizable, though unreported, royalties to the Church.

As the faith spread, so did Mary's problem in controlling it. In 1889, Mary took heroic action to maintain her leadership over a movement with 20 churches and 33 teaching centers scattered across the country. She disbanded the Metaphysical College she had established to train healers in Boston, dissolved the Boston Church, and a few years later "disorganized" the National Christian Science Association, which had been an earlier attempt to band the adherents together. There were recurring factional disputes among the followers, and leaving them to quarrel among themselves, she retired to her native New Hampshire. There, as "Pastor Emeritus," she reorganized the church into an iron-clad bureaucracy that insured not only her personal control during her life, but the continuation of her policies after her death.

Under the reorganization, all religious authority was vested in a hand-picked, self-perpetuating board of directors, which prescribed the same order of service for every Christian Science Church in the world. The directors scheduled specific readings from the Bible and *Science and Health*, executed by "Readers" who were not to be permitted to interpret the texts they read. The National Association was replaced by the "Mother Church" in Boston, to which all practitioners, leaders, and believers belonged wherever they lived. Branch churches were no more than buildings. New members of the Church had to pass inspection by a group called "First Members." Although the plan was elaborate, its intent was to create an impregnable fortress from which Mary Baker Eddy could control Christian Science. The Mother Church directed all activities, and Mary Baker Eddy directed the Mother Church.

At the age of 87, she struck back at a flood of adverse newspaper and magazine articles with a public relations stratagem of stunning simplicity. In 1908, she directed her trustees to start a daily newspaper, the *Christian Science Monitor,* with two aims. One was the reporting of Christian Science; the second was the creation of a good, national, public-service newspaper that would, in the words of an editorial written by Mrs. Eddy in the first issue, "injure no man, but [would] bless all mankind." While it often lost money, and had to be reduced to tabloid size in 1975, the *Monitor* has become one of the most respected newspapers in the country.

Mary "passed on" at the ripe old age of 89. In addition to a personal fortune of more than $2,500,000, she left behind that rare phenomenon, a well-organized and well-financed church. The Mother Church in Boston is now the center of a complex of glass and concrete office buildings that cost $75 million. Scientist church buildings around the country are often the newest and finest in town. Every member pays a minimum head tax of $1 a year, and most are affluent enough to give much more. There are Sunday offerings, profits on the publications of the Christian Science Publishing Society, and profits on Mary's writings. The publisher maintains that with the exception of the Bible, Mary Baker Eddy's *Science and Health, With Key to the Scriptures* holds every printing and publishing record.

Christian Scientists can collect Medicare benefits for stays in Christian Science sanitariums, and the Mother Church has been able to obtain copyright protection for *Science and Health* beyond the usual 56 years.

Excluded from medicine, religion, and big business management by virtue of her sex, Mary Baker Eddy created a centralized bureaucracy as efficient as any large corporation. Without specially favoring or segregating women, Christian

Science helped women to cope with the psychosomatic ailments that male-dominated medicine could not cure, and they in return became its principal supporters.

The prevailing culture created medical problems for women. Victorian prudery inhibited women from consulting physicians, and doctors were so ignorant that they often made matters worse. Beyond that, the belief that the vocation of women was to be wife and mother made them worry unduly about anything that affected their sexual organs or their capacity to bear and raise children. Traditionally, women had always looked to each other for help on these problems, but the demand for advice and reassurance was always greater than a woman could satisfy through the grapevine. While Mary Baker Eddy was evolving her philosophy of Christian Science, another woman, of Lynn, Massachusetts, was inventing a way to commercialize the neighborly reassurance women sought from each other.

The maternal visage of Lydia Pinkham (1819–1883) has gazed upon countless American women from bottles of her Vegetable Compound for nearly a century. Although her name and photograph became the trademarks of a multimillion dollar business, and she herself was an instinctive promoter, she turned to enterprise late in life when her husband went bankrupt, and she did not live long enough to enjoy the great profits of her success.

Like so many other enterprising women, she came from a family of activists. She was the tenth of twelve children born to a shoemaker and farmer, William Estes, and his second wife, Rebecca, strong-minded people who left the Quaker sect because they thought it was too soft on slavery. Both of the Estes were reformers who took pleasure in debate and controversy, and their friends included William Lloyd Garrison, the abolitionist, and Frederick Douglass, the great black orator.

Lydia attended Lynn Academy, became a teacher, and immersed herself in the fight for the abolition of slavery. After becoming an active member of the local branch of the Female Anti-Slavery Society, she helped organize and became secretary of the Freeman's Institute, a debating society which was then unique in admitting both women and men.

It was at an Institute meeting that Lydia met Isaac Pinkham, a widower with a daughter. They were married in 1843, and had five children. Isaac, who had been both a trader and shoe manufacturer before his marriage to Lydia, now turned to real estate and dragged his growing family through one disastrous venture after another.

For 30 years Lydia bore the mounting debts and constant removals to shabbier quarters like a True Woman, revealing her disappointment and bitterness only in entries in her journal. She noted her sadness at the death of Nathaniel P. Rogers, a minister friend to whom she may have been romantically attached as well, and named her second son after him. She kept a careful account of expenditures, at one point charging her grown sons for room and board. The "Rules for Success in Business" she wrote in her notebook the day after her fortieth birthday, sound like a reproach to her husband, Isaac:

> 1st—Make all your purchases as far as possible of those who stand the highest in uprightness and integrity. Men of character.
>
> 2nd—Enter into no business arrangement with any one unless you are well satisfied that such person is governed by a strict sense of honor and justice.
>
> 3rd—Engage in nothing of business at arms length, and be sure you are well acquainted with whatever business you may engage in.
>
> 4th—Be satisfied with doing well and continue in well doing. A sure sixpence is better than a doubtful shilling, which motto, be governed by.
>
> 5th—If you own land, do not neglect to set out fruit trees and bushes a single year after owning it, till enough is set out.

Lydia's notebooks also contain recipes for home remedies which she passed around to neighboring women in the same way that women exchange recipes for food. We know what was in her famous Vegetable Compound because she adapted a formula for a "uterine tonic and sedative" from the 1870 edition of the *American Dispensary* by Dr. John King of Cincinnati and wrote it down in her journal. Lydia's recipe called for unicorn root, fenugreek seed, life root, black co-hosh, and pleurisy root, all botanical drugs available from American sources, especially the Caribbean area. Black co-hosh was a plant first used as a medicine by Massachusetts Indians. Pleurisy root was a milkweed believed to be a remedy for pleurisy. Lydia mixed everything in an 18-per-cent solution of alcohol, and offered her tonic free to ailing women friends, who praised it.

The panic of 1873 forced Isaac Pinkham into bankruptcy shortly after his thirtieth wedding anniversary. He could no longer initiate any business ventures. While Lydia and her sons were talking about what they could do to support the family, legend has it that a party of women from Salem ar-rived to buy some of the medicine of which they had heard. Lydia was a bit flustered, but sold them six bottles for five dollars. The Pinkhams soon decided to go into business with the compound, and a new kitchen was installed in the cellar of their home, where the compound was mixed.

"Success was immediate," Lydia wrote in a later advertise-ment. At the start the business was a partnership of Lydia and her favorite sons Daniel and William. Isaac had to lie low to avoid his creditors, and the bankruptcy seems to have crushed his spirit. Although the family tried to make him feel useful and sought his advice, his contribution seems to have been limited to reading aloud to the rest of the family as they bottled the compound together in the evening.

Lydia was general manager and treasurer. Long experi-ence with penury had trained her in careful budgeting, and in order to keep up appearances, she allocated funds for luxuries as well as necessities. Everything else went into handbills advertising the compound, which her sons dis-tributed whenever they were not employed at paying jobs.

Lydia wrote the copy herself. "Only a woman can under-stand a woman's ills," she declared in hundreds of newspaper advertisements. "Lydia E. Pinkham's Vegetable Compound is a Positive Cure for all those Painful Complaints and Weaknesses so common to our best female population." In a company-encouraged biography published in 1931, Robert Collyer Washburn writes that Lydia convinced herself that the compound was the salvation, and she the savior, of the human race. Her promotions listed dozens of symptoms, embellished with painful-sounding adjectives describing the woes of women of all ages and circumstances, and offered hope for a quick cure for every ailment, even sterility. "A Baby in Every Bottle," one slogan promised. Because "many a dutiful daughter pays in pain for her mother's ignorance," Lydia implored mothers to inform girls of bodily functions once thought too delicate to discuss. She invited schoolgirls afraid to ask their mothers to write to her directly, and they did.

Lydia's distrust of doctors and surgery was evident in the testimonial letters she published in her advertisements. "I underwent the horrors of local treatment but obtained no benefit," one thank-you note read. Lydia wrote that working girls were "often held back by an illness they do not understand."

She revived her early interest in politics and wove her political populist beliefs into the advertising copy, especially when her son Dan ran for the state legislature in 1878. "People who pay for government mismanagement," she wrote, "are today suffering from kidney complaints, dyspepsia, indigestion, and could surely, speedily and permanently be cured by . . ." the compound. There was no aura of quackery about Lydia's sincere attempts to heal and advise, and the compound was at least safe and free from contamination.

No one really knows who thought of putting Lydia Pinkham's likeness on the bottle, though many people tried to take credit for suggesting the successful trademark. Lydia had a special photograph taken for it: a True Woman could risk even public exposure for her family. The sons registered the label, with Lydia Pinkham's face as a trademark in the Patent Office, but did not attempt to patent the formula or process.

In 1881, both Dan and William died of tuberculosis, which they may have contracted by their exertions in plugging the business. Lydia herself died in 1883, five months after she suffered a paralytic stroke. Ironically, her husband Isaac lived on until 1889. And the big rewards went to Charles and Aroline, the two children who had been least active in building the business.

According to Sarah Stage, an assistant professor of history at Williams College who is studying the cultural influence of Lydia Pinkham's Compound, the Pinkham Medicine Company violated all Lydia's rules of good business. The advertising agent employed by the company did not qualify as a man of character, nor was he governed by any strict sense of justice or honor. Shortly after Lydia's death, Charles discovered that the agent had been grossly and systematically overcharging them on commissions for placing advertising. The family knew little or nothing of the drug business when they began to market the Vegetable Compound, and in their financial desperation surely risked a sure sixpence for a doubtful shilling by mortgaging the house to pay for advertising.

But this was the real breakthrough. Newspaper advertising proved a more effective way of reaching customers than handbills, and at one time the Pinkhams were plowing 85 percent of their receipts back into advertising. The "Department of Advice" which enlivened the ads continued long after Lydia's death. Correspondents simply consulted a coded copybook to compose letters in her style and name, as if she were alive.

Sales of the Compound, which had been $300,000 a year when Lydia died in 1883, reached $1,300,000 in 1898. The anti–proprietary medicine crusades of the American Medical Association and several magazines in the next two decades reduced them only temporarily. Publication of a photograph of Lydia's tombstone in the *Ladies Home Journal* in 1904 was regarded by the company as a help: it proved that she had actually lived and was not a mythical character as some suspected. Sales peaked at $3,800,000 in 1925, but food and drug laws began to restrict the claims that could be made for the product. In 1968, Lydia's descendants sold the business to Cooper Laboratories, Inc. In 1973, Cooper closed the Lynn plant and moved production to one in San German, Puerto Rico, closer to the source of the ingredients. Sales were $750,000 in 1974.

Newspaper advertising and modern promotion made the Vegetable Compound a big success, but the secret of this success was Lydia Pinkham herself. The product she sold was not only her tonic. Her maternal visage and her reassuring words about female functions, such as menstrual periods, alleviated excessive worries fostered by a culture that valued women above all for their sex. When those worries made women sick, the harmless Compound and Lydia's advice could make them really feel better.

Lydia Pinkham was the first of many women who made themselves nationally known trademarks. A few years after Lydia's likeness appeared on her bottled Compound, another woman, Harriet Hubbard Ayer, lent her name to a product which promised to enhance a woman's attractiveness to men.

When women weren't worrying about how they felt, they were worrying about how they looked to the opposite sex. A woman's face was her fortune, but in the 1870s she wasn't supposed to do anything to improve it beyond dusting her nose with a dab of powder on a hot day. However, nothing prevented women from talking with each other about how to improve their complexions, and gossiping about what other women were reported to be doing as beauty measures. Lily Langtry, for instance, the actress known to be the mistress of the Prince of Wales, was supposed to have rubbed her face with minced raw meat and to have acquired her alabaster complexion by rolling naked in the morning dew.

Harriet Hubbard Ayer (1849–1903) was not the most successful of the cosmetic queens who have successively reigned over dressing tables since her day, but she developed the promotional technique that all of them have since used. She had the initial advantage of being herself the glamorous woman other women want to look like. During 17 years of marriage to a leading Chicago business executive, she spent her time reading, writing, entertaining, and dressing regally at home and abroad, But her husband did not share her cultural interests, and in 1882 she took her two small daughters and went to New York to live. The next year, Herbert Ayer lost his money and Harriet had to make her own living.

Her good fairy did not desert her immediately. A fashionable furniture store in New York hired her as a saleswoman, expecting to draw curious crowds to view the great lady fallen on evil days, but Harriet turned out to be a shrewd saleswoman who did not mind being pitied if she made her commission. Soon she was traveling in Europe to find pieces of furniture for her special customers, visiting on business the people and places she had known when she herself was a lady of leisure.

One of her stops was the shop of M. Mirault, the chemist on Boulevard Malesherbes in Paris who in her palmy days had concocted for her a special violet Parma perfume which she had made her personal trademark. Always on the lookout for interesting new products and services, Harriet recalled the story Mirault had told her about a cream his grandfather had made for Mme. Recamier, the beauty who had plotted against Napoleon. According to Mirault, it had kept her face as young as a girl's for 40 years. Acting on impulse, Harriet bought the formula from Mirault so that she could manufacture it herself.

American women were beginning to use special soaps and creams to protect their complexions against the sun, and Harriet felt they were willing to do more. In 1886, James Seymour, a rich Chicago customer who admired her taste, backed her with $50,000—provided she would put her own name on the cream.

Harriet agreed. By day, she continued to sell furniture, but at night she fiddled with the formula, tried it on herself and her mother, and let her imagination run wild writing pamphlets about Mme. Recamier, her beauty secret, and how Harriet Hubbard had discovered it. Mme. Julie Recamier's faultless complexion was the most striking feature of David's famous portrait of her reclining on a sofa. Medical ointments were considered socially acceptable, so Harriet at first pretended that she had been given the cream by a Frenchwoman as a remedy for sunburn.

Harriet's social position and literary ability made the Recamier ointment a sensational success in its first six months on the market. Harriet either knew all the great ladies or knew how to get to them, and she induced many of them to endorse Mme. Recamier's formula as prepared by Harriet Hubbard Ayer. And to prove she was willing to go for broke she put the Hubbard coat of arms, as well as her name, on the jars. Such personal publicity was not yet acceptable and it cooled the ardor of a suitor named General Grubb who had been offering her the chance to marry her way back into society.

Harriet enjoyed what the French called a *succès de scandale*. People like Mrs. Stuyvesant Fish, the society leader, made a special visit to her shop to view the daring woman who put her name and her family coat of arms on a jar—and when they came to stare, they bought the product. Abroad, Lily Langtry endorsed the cream. Harriet turned out more long testimonials about the cream's virtues, including obviously fictional stories about unnamed society women who were rescued from blemishes and freckles.

The success lasted only a few years. Harriet, who had been divorced from Herbert Ayer and was no longer courted by General Grubb, was finally sued by James Seymour, according to one story, because she refused his advances. To complicate her private life, her daughter Hattie had married Seymour's son, Lewis, a move which did not prevent Seymour from allegedly plotting to break her mind or her health. Eventually he persuaded Hattie to commit her mother Harriet to an insane asylum. When Harriet was released, she lectured about the treatment of the insane, and helped organize legal help for similar victims. But the cosmetic company languished, and the right to the line of products she had established, and the use of her name—Harriet Hubbard Ayer —were eventually sold by her heirs.

There is a postscript to her story. In 1896 she applied for a job as a reporter on the *New York World*, just when that paper was creating a woman's page for its Sunday edition. Always facile with words, she dashed off a health and beauty column on the spot for editor Arthur Brisbane and was hired.

She was an ideal columnist, and adapted easily to her new audience. Instead of Parma violet perfume, the trademark of her great-lady days, she now became known for a working-woman's costume of jacket, shirtwaist, and skirt cut off four whole inches from the floor. She experimented on her own with cold creams, antiperspirants, and an anti-kink preparation for straightening the hair of blacks, but gave them away instead of selling them.

Harriet succeeded in the cosmetic business because she was a talented writer and promoter. In her later columns and pamphlets, she gave women sensible advice on diet and health that could really improve their appearance. She assured them that it was their moral duty as women to take any means to make themselves attractive.

It was a message women wanted to hear. When Harriet Hubbard Ayer started her business, American women used cosmetics with discretion. In 1941, at the outbreak of World War II, cosmetics and beauty was among the nation's twenty largest industries, three-fourths of the women of the country were users of cosmetics, and more than a half billion dollars was spent on preparations intended to improve the appeal of the female face.

Men quickly moved in on the new bonanza, but the enterprising women who managed to make themselves trademarks have been among the biggest female fortune builders of the twentieth century. Both Helena Rubenstein and Elizabeth Arden left estates valued at more than $20 million.

Even more unusual was the fortune, estimated at $1 million, left by C. J. Walker (1867–1919), inventor of the "Walker Method" of straightening black African hair. At a time when most blacks were segregated in poor neighborhoods, her "colored woman's palace" at Irvington-on-Hudson, designed by black architect Vertner Tandy at a cost of $250,000, attracted incredulous attention.

Madame Walker, as she called herself, loved the shock she created. The Walker method (vigorous shampooing, brushing, and straightening with hot iron combs) came to her allegedly in a dream. Like the other cosmetic queens who followed in Harriet Hubbard Ayer's footsteps, she dramatized herself to promote her products. Her wealth was an important sales argument for the millions of black women whose notions of female beauty, as well as of the good life, were otherwise based on the appearance and lifestyle of whites.

Unlike white women enterprisers, Madame Walker made more money than any black man of her time, and she made it without the help of outside encouragement or an unusually good education for a woman. Born on a Louisiana farm, orphaned in childhood, married at 14 "to get a home," she supported herself and her daughter for 18 years as a washerwoman in St. Louis. In order to remedy the defects in her own education, she hired a tutor to teach her to speak properly.

Madame Walker was a genuine system builder. Starting with herself, and then neighbors, she demonstrated the method from door to door, training converts to convert others. Soon she had a nationwide corps of "Walker agents" in white shirtwaists and black skirts, making "house calls" all over the United States and the Caribbean.

Many blacks no longer care to straighten their hair, but the Walker method boosted the self-confidence of earlier generations of black women by making it possible for them to follow prevailing fashions in hair styles designed for whites. Like Madame Walker, some of the most successful women have been the enterprisers who have found new ways to help other women solve the problems American culture has created for them.

13

INSTITUTION BUILDERS
Henrietta King, Eliza Nicholson

After the Civil War, the American economy hit a new stride. Technical progress increased productivity at record rates. Business firms grew larger. Small firms tended to expire with their founders, but a few acquired what appeared to be a life of their own that enabled them to survive into the 1970s. This seldom happened by accident. Almost always, somebody planned the firm's future, and in a number of cases, that person was a woman.

One was the King Ranch in Texas, a multinational corporation which in the 1970s was raising cattle on 11,500,000 acres of land in Australia, Argentina, Venezuela, and Brazil, as well as on the home place in Texas. The King Ranch drew income from oil, racehorse breeding, game preserves, and many other ventures, but its greatest achievement was the production of beef by scientific, assembly-line methods.

This impressive spread can be credited to the business ability of a remarkable woman who began with 500,000 acres of Texas land she inherited in 1885 along with a debt of $500,000.

Henrietta Chamberlain King (1832–1925) was the self-reliant only daughter of a preacher in Brownsville, Texas. After teaching briefly, Henrietta married Richard King, a steamboat master who had just become a rancher. Captain King took his 22-year-old bride to the ranch he had bought on Santa Gertrudis Creek, 40 miles inland from Corpus Christi.

Richard King was a romantic who envisioned a vast empire. One of his ambitions was to buy all the land along the Gulf of Mexico between the Nueces River and the Rio Grande 150 miles to the south, and he almost succeeded in doing so. Another was to induce the government to buy and fence a strip of land a mile wide extending from Brownsville to Kansas over which he could drive cattle to market. Though railroads were beginning to crisscross the Southwest, he was still working on the grandiose idea of this trail when he died of cancer, leaving all of his estate "to my beloved wife, Henrietta King, to be used by her and disposed of precisely the same as I might do if I were living."

Henrietta had managed the ranch frequently while the captain was away on business trips. And during the Civil War, when his beef fed the Confederate armies of the West and he sold Confederate cotton in Mexico, he had been forced to flee to escape Yankee raiders; Henrietta, seven months pregnant, remained to defy them. She had been so resolute in defending the ranch against the outlaws and renegades who infested the neighborhood in the early years that they were said to have stayed away when they knew she was there alone.

In 1885, when Henrietta took over permanently, the ranch was in debt; Richard King had been buying land and spending heavily for fencing at a time when drought was forcing the slaughter of cattle and depressing hide and beef prices. Soon after the funeral, Henrietta named her prospective son-in-law Robert Kleberg as her manager, and she accompanied the young people on their wedding trip the following year.

Henrietta and Robert attacked the financial problems of the ranch together. In spite of Richard King's dying injunction "not to let a foot of dear old Santa Gertrudis get away," they sold several thousand acres to pay the most pressing debts.

Henrietta gave young Robert increasing responsibilities, but it was not until ten years after he became manager that she gave him her power of attorney. They conferred on ranch business every day, and he made no important move without consulting her. They dropped the cattle drives Richard had loved, and shipped their animals by rail. The railroad was less romantic, but it was quicker, surer, and often cheaper in terms of the beef it saved. Henrietta and Robert encouraged a rail line through their ranch by contributing land for the right of way and for a new town called Kingsville, three miles east of ranch headquarters.

Although she was more than 60 years old at this time, Henrietta planned much of Kingsville herself and donated the land for its churches. She owned and ran its lumber company, weekly newspaper, and cotton gin, as well as nearly all the cotton gins between Corpus Christi and Brownsville. An ardent advocate of temperance, she saw to it that Kingsville had no saloons by inserting a clause forbidding the sale of liquor in every deed she gave.

Henrietta and Robert were constantly on the watch for new scientific developments that could solve the problems of the ranch. One of these problems was water. In the drought year of 1891, 12,000 cattle had to be shipped to the Indian Territory to save their lives. That fall Henrietta helped finance a Department of Agriculture experiment in rainmaking. Bombs, dynamite, and gas-filled balloons were exploded on the ranch, but little rain resulted.

A few years later, Robert showed Henrietta a newspaper article about a new heavy well-drilling machine being made in Nebraska. They bought one for a local driller. In 1899 he struck water. The gushing flow of artesian water from a depth of 532 feet protected much of the ranch from the hazard of drought.

Captain King, the romantic, had bred cavalry, police, and work horses. When the automobile replaced these animals, Henrietta King and Robert Kleberg began developing racehorses and bought or bred three Kentucky Derby winners, Bold Venture, Assault, and Middleground.

The most profitable application of science to ranching was to be an improvement in the breeding and care of cattle. Information on animal diseases was collected at the ranch. When a rabid coyote bit Willie Chamberlain, Henrietta's younger half brother, a local doctor rushed him to Paris where Louis Pasteur had just discovered a rabies vaccine. Willie's life was one of the first that was saved by the vaccine. In gratitude Henrietta built and named a hospital in Corpus

Christi for Dr. Arthur E. Spohn, the local physician who accompanied Willie to Paris.

The Kings were among the first to dip their cattle to protect them against tick fever. They gradually replaced the picturesque but scrawny longhorns of earlier times with fatter and more tractable animals. Over years of experimental breeding during which they cross-bred Brahmas and shorthorns, the King Ranch produced the only authentic new breed of cattle to be developed in North America, the Santa Gertrudis breed. It yields a high proportion of usable meat, is resistant to disease, and thrives in unfavorable environments. King Ranch, Inc., has introduced it to many other countries.

Henrietta thought in terms of dollars as well as land. She paid off all the captain's debts within ten years after he died and began buying more land. When her holdings reached a million acres, the publicity made her a national figure. In 1907 she was offered $10 million for the ranch, but she turned it down.

The ranch had become a huge enterprise which required leadership as well as administrative skill. Henrietta provided both on a queenly scale. She ceremoniously visited all parts of her domain at least twice a year. In between these visits, managers of outlying properties reported at headquarters and were entertained at her ranch house. Though her hospitality was open handed, she had a few inflexible rules. One required that women wear dresses and men coats at dinner. Another decreed that at breakfast everybody had to eat a cereal. She kept 80 varieties on hand and nobody refused when she asked, "Will you have hot or cold cereal?"

She was nearly 86 when she made her will, in which she tried to protect the estate from being dissipated. She had cause for concern, for palsy had crippled Robert Kleberg in 1916. His sons, Robert, Jr., and Richard, were running the ranch under his direction. The will set up trustees who were required to keep the holdings intact for a decade. In 1925, Henrietta King died at the age of 92. All 200 of the King Ranch cowboys, dressed in range clothing and riding range horses, accompanied her on her last journey to the Kingsville cemetery.

Henrietta had inherited a half million acres of land and a half million dollars of debt. She left an estate of $5.4 million and more than a million acres, but this was just the beginning. Oil was eventually discovered on the land, adding $12 to $18 million dollars a year in income to the corporation that was formed by Robert's sons to operate their share of the ranch.

The growing economy of the late nineteenth century that created agribusinesses like the King Ranch required the dissemination of information on a wide scale. To supply this demand of the expanding nation, newspapers had to grow too.

At the end of the Civil War, most daily newspapers were short-lived journals created to express the political opinions of their owners. After rugged competition, a few of these sheets managed to survive by transforming themselves into big, stable, common carriers of local, national, and international news of culture, society, business, fashion, food, books, entertainment, and sports, interpreted by columnists of varying opinions, and enlivened with illustrations and cartoons.

One of the few who succeeded in making this transformation was Eliza Poitevent Holbrook Nicholson (1849–1896), who was such a True Woman that she refused to cover divorces lest they shock the sensibilities of her readers.

Eliza always regarded herself as a poet. She grew up on a lonely farm in Mississippi, went to boarding school, and managed to get some of her poetry published under the pseudonym Pearl Rivers. On a visit to New Orleans, she caught the eye of Ava Morris Holbrook, owner of the New Orleans *Picayune,* and he offered her the position of literary editor of the newspaper. Although her family did not want her to work in a newspaper office, she moved to her grandfather's home in New Orleans and took the job. In 1872, when she was 23, she married the 64-year-old Holbrook. Three years later he died, leaving her the *Picayune* and a debt of $80,000.

Friends urged her to declare bankruptcy and take the $1000 the law allowed a widow, but Eliza decided to fight it out instead. She called the staff together and made a little speech. "I am a woman. Some of you may not wish to work for a woman. If so, you are free to go, and no hard feelings. But you who stay—will you give me your undivided loyalty, and will you advise me truly and honestly?" Most stayed. As a boss, she made diffident suggestions, inspiring rather than directing the able staff she assembled.

Two years later, she married the paper's business manager, George Nicholson, and then they ran the *Picayune* together. They divided responsibility the way Sarah Hale and Louis Godey had done: he managed the business side, she the editorial work.

She set up "departments" to appeal to special interests, and chose able men and women to run them regardless of their political affiliation. In her search for good people, she even hired former officers of the Union Army.

Her most controversial innovation was a society column, then regarded as a shocking invasion of privacy. She gave other women a chance, among them Elizabeth Gilmer, better known to two generations of readers as Dorothy Dix, the syndicated columnist of advice to the lovelorn.

Eliza's editorial policies were designed to win a wider appeal for the paper and emphasized human interest and public affairs rather than politics. The *Picayune* campaigned for temperance, for protection against cruelty to animals, and for an end to organized crime. She saw to it there was something for everybody in the paper: "Lilliput Land" for the kiddies, a family health column, comic drawings, an expanded literary section, articles on notable women, and suggestions and encouragement for women who worked.

She successfully developed the Sunday edition of the paper into "the library of the masses," as one of her biographers put it. In her 20 years as head of the paper, the Sunday section circulation grew from 6,000 in 1878 to 30,000 in 1891.

Eliza moved with the times. In 1886 she installed the new electric lights in the *Picayune* office. During the next five years, she doubled the amount of telegraph news she bought so that she could cover national and international events of importance to the growing overseas trade of New Orleans. She opened bureaus in other cities. When advertisers crowded her news pages, she was able to raise her rates.

By appealing to all political persuasions as well as many

different interests, she converted the *Picayune* into a solid common carrier of news that attracted readers of all political persuasions.

Eliza's childhood does not seem to have marked her for enterprise. She enjoyed neither an exceptional education nor exceptional encouragement from the childless uncle and aunt who reared her on a backwoods plantation on the border of Louisiana and Mississippi. Moral support, as well as the family crises which stimulated her to achieve, came from her husbands, both of whom were old enough to have fathered her. She was between husbands when she made the critical decision to run the *Picayune* herself, and the first of her two sons was not born until she was 32 years old.

Eliza's marriages may seem to have been strategic, but they were not unhappy, and no one could say that she did not live up to the highest standards of True Womanhood and True Motherhood. After Nicholson died, she kept the paper going for her two sons, and when dying from influenza, she appealed to the staff from her deathbed and made them promise to "support her sons until they were old enough to run the paper themselves." They did. The *Picayune* remained in the Nicholson family for the next generation, and eventually merged into the *Times-Picayune,* which became the leading newspaper of Louisiana.

Henrietta King and Eliza Nicholson made stable permanent institutions of parochial enterprises because they happened to be married to the men who founded them. The failing enterprises Henrietta and Eliza rescued grew and prospered because these women brought new management talent to their development. Their histories suggest that management talent is not exclusively male, but that women seldom head large-scale enterprises only because they have seldom been given the chance to do so.

But the scarcity of women at the top does not mean that large-scale enterprise was hostile to women. In fact, the opposite was true: as business firms grew bigger towards the end of the nineteenth century, they came to depend heavily on the clerical work of women at the bottom.

14

WOMEN IN THE OFFICE

Mary Seymour, Katharine Gibbs

In 1879, a 33-year-old school teacher opened a school to teach women how to use the new typewriting machines which were being demonstrated in stores and hotel lobbies with attractive young women at the keyboard as a sales come-on. Mary Seymour's Union School of Stenography and Typewriting at 38 Park Row in New York City was not the first business "college" to offer instruction in typewriting, but it was the first to confine its student body to women.

Before this, some of the schools which taught penmanship, bookkeeping, and business practice may have admitted women on occasion, but they seldom sought out women students. As a self-supporting single woman herself, Mary Seymour knew that thousands of women would be willing to pay tuition in order to get a foothold in office work.

They were needed. Big organizations required an unexpected volume of paperwork. The bigger the organization in which a given task was done, the more paperwork the task seemed to generate. The federal government had discovered this during the Civil War, when the mountains of paperwork required to keep a million men in the field sometimes seemed a bigger threat to the Union than the Confederate armies. Until that time, men had kept whatever records the small federal government had needed. When the war broke out, however, competent males were hard to find, and in 1861, women were recruited to clip Treasury notes by hand.

By 1865, 447 women were working for the federal government as clerks, all getting $600 a year, a salary that was set high to compensate for the high cost of living in Washington.

The women stayed on afterwards, and in 1870, Congress ruled that women employees were to be graded and paid like men. As Civil Service regulations became more complicated, government bureaucrats found ways to classify women so that they could be required to do the same work men did at lower pay.

Equal opportunity was hard to enforce in government jobs because competition among women for clerical jobs was keener than competition among men. Budget-minded bureaucrats could always find a superior woman willing to do the work of the next job up on the ladder, but a superior man had to be paid what he was worth because he could make money more easily than a woman in other lines of work. When employers in business as well as in government quickly discovered that women clerks were talent bargains, they concluded, not unnaturally, that women were better suited to the tasks by virtue of their sex.

S. S. Packard, founder of the proprietary business school that still bears his name, claimed to have been the first to see that stenography was "especially adapted to the clear brain, quick fingers and methodical habits of a resourceful girl."

Directors of business schools, feminists, employers, and the women themselves soon agreed that women were better for all except the most skilled jobs in stenography or those which required travel, then regarded as unsuitable for "ladies." "I wouldn't take men in place of these girls in any circumstances," an employer is supposed to have testified in a magazine article of 1893 which reported a sizable increase in the number of women clerks. "Men are troublesome. They complain about trifles that a woman wouldn't notice. The office boys don't suit, or the temperature of the building is too hot or too cold, or the light is not properly adjusted. Then, if they have a slight headache, they stay at home. Most of them are married, and their wives fall ill, or their mother-in-law comes on a visit, and all these things are made an excuse for absence. The women come whether they have headaches or not. They never want a day off to attend a baseball match. They undertake the work with a full understanding of what is required of them, and they are steadfast in the performance of their duties. . . ."

Other employers may not have agreed with these sentiments, but the conclusion of this interview states a point of view that was standard policy in many New York offices of the time. "There is only one thing we exact over and above their business qualifications," the employer being interviewed said. "We do not employ a woman unless she lives at home with her family." More important than the supposed virtue of home-living women, of course, was the fact that they could thus afford to work for less pay. At a time when some women typists were earning $15 a week (which was more than most women could earn elsewhere), a male typist with less competence could command $20.

Since female "typewriters" generally left work when they married, requiring a trained replacement, Mary Seymour's new school found a rapidly growing market. At that time, females were filling only 5 percent of what we would now call white-collar office jobs—clerks, copyists, bookkeepers, accountants, as well as stenographers and the new "typewriters." Two decades later, her competitor, S. S. Packard, complained that women had taken over the field so thoroughly that it was hard to find candidates for the "many stenographic positions which can be filled only by young men."

Mary Foot Seymour (1846–1893) opened her school just at the right time, and with a born promoter's enthusiasm for exploring new opportunities that she inherited from her father. A lawyer, land agent, and writer, Ephraim Seymour pioneered a succession of new ventures until he died in the gold mining town of Nevada City, California, when Mary was five years old. Ephraim Seymour's widow took the four children back East to live with relatives, and eventually settled in Jersey City.

While attending private schools, Mary Seymour developed her talent for writing. Some of her stories for children were published, and in 1874, the first year Remington shipped typewriters on a commercial basis, she was teaching second grade in Jersey City. But like so many other nineteenth-century women, Mary Seymour was in ill health much of the time, and while laid up she taught herself the art of shorthand with the idea of becoming a court stenographer.

Shorthand reporters were usually men. It would have been considered unseemly for a woman to appear in public to take down the longwinded speeches of congressmen, or to appear in court to record proceedings. However, the tedious work of transcribing the notes into longhand could be done by women in private. No one quite knows how Mary Seymour managed to become accepted as a court reporter who would herself take notes as well as transcribe them, but she did, and very quickly became successful enough to hire other women to help her. As her business grew, she realized that the women could work faster if they were trained to transcribe the notes that they took directly on the new typewriting machines. Furthermore, if businessmen were being persuaded to invest in those new machines to cope with the increased flow of paperwork, they might be persuaded to hire trained women to do the work.

Mary Seymour's new business college would make it all possible. She used all the tactics of a contemporary marketer to sell her product—training, demonstration, placement, and education—and she set up four separate firms. The Union School of Stenography and Typewriting trained new women students. The Union Stenographic Company employed women stenographers who could be temporarily lent to businessmen to demonstrate the virtues of stenography in the private office. Other women were placed in permanent positions—without an agency charge to employers—by a separate employment bureau, Union Stenographic and Typewriting Association. Mary Seymour also founded a publication, the *Business Woman's Journal,* which she used to recruit new students and to maintain standards for the new occupation.

When she spoke to a newspaper reporter about her enterprises, Mary Seymour deftly combined an appeal to potential women students with reassurance to potential employer clients of the placement bureau. "By far the greatest difficulty I have to contend with, is to keep my best operators with me," she said. "Although I pay them liberal salaries and do everything I can to secure their services permanently, they are in constant receipt of offers that men would be glad to receive. Many pupils of the school receive offers of positions at salaries varying from $8.00 to $12.00 a week before they have finished the six months' course of instruction. I mention this for the purpose of showing how popular the employment of women clerks has become, that is, if they are properly trained for the work."

Then she closed in on the doubts of reluctant employers. "Business men tell me that they prefer women as shorthand amanuenses for one particular reason. It is because, contrary to accepted tradition, women are less likely than men to disclose the business secrets of their employers. Then, too, they are more faithful and more apt to remain for a long period in the service of one employer."

Her statement on equal pay was straightforward and re-markably militant. "Of course, a number of employers engage women under the prevailing impression that they will work for lower wages; but while this is true in the majority of cases, it is equally true that efficient women can command as high salaries as men, particularly if they refuse to work for less, which is usually the case." As she succeeded in business, Mary Seymour became a more active feminist, directing her energies into open advocacy of woman suffrage and of the broadening of employment opportunities for women.

The *Business Woman's Journal*, which she launched in 1889, carried advertising for typewriters, safes, pencils, and textbooks, and offered recipes, fashions, articles about successful women, and service articles, such as "Hints to Women Who are Ignorant of Business: How to Keep a Bank Account" and "How Poor Girls May Learn A Profession." Occasionally, Mary Seymour could not resist throwing in one of the children's stories she liked to write under a pseudonym. After the magazine had appeared, she took the unusual step of incorporating the small publication as the Mary F. Seymour Publishing Company and selling out her interest to women investors in all parts of the country on terms as low as $2.50 a month. All the officers were women.

In 1892, the magazine became the *American Woman's*

Journal, which announced that it aimed to help and inspire women in every sphere of life. The few issues that appeared before Mary Seymour's untimely death, after an illness of four days, suggest that had she lived she would have moved from business education into the business of publishing. One of her purposes in incorporating the *Journal* had been "that not being dependent on the life of one individual, its chances of perpetuity may be increased," but the *Journal,* with its startlingly modern outlook, did not survive its founder more than a few years.

Meanwhile, back at the office, women who had been hired to take letters were taking over the business housekeeping of bureaucracy, cleaning out the cuspidors, dusting the tops of the desks, and making the office boys behave. Some of them easily fell into the role of office wife to the men for whom they worked and were rewarded with the coveted title of secretary.

The first secretaries had been male—young men apprenticed to government officials to learn the art of politics or government by helping with the paperwork. The term persists as the title of cabinet members in Britain and the United States. The first big business leaders had male secretaries, too, young men who were being trained for managerial roles. But by the time of World War I, enough women had become the assistant closest to the boss to create a market for stenographers with a new kind of training.

Katharine Gibbs (1865–1934) was 46 when she became a widow in 1911, with two sons to support and no business experience whatsoever. Educated in finishing schools, she was well aware that she had never learned what it took to make a living. But she was sure she could devise a course of study for women which would really prepare them for the kind of intelligent assistance to executives that a liberally educated woman could offer if trained in the nuts and bolts of the commercial world.

Against the advice of friends, she sold her jewelry to set up a school that would be different from existing business schools. She directed it exclusively to women who wanted to be secretaries. She taught them business law, liberal arts,

English, and other broadening disciplines useful in assisting a man of large affairs who would expect from a secretary the same grace a proper wife was expected to display in managing his elaborate home.

The first Katharine Gibbs School in Providence, Rhode Island, profited from the World War I demand for women to replace men in business organizations. Women poured into the school so fast that she had to restrict enrollment. New schools were founded, and Katharine Gibbs became a large business herself.

The private secretary became a female unless otherwise noted. According to a *Fortune* analysis of September, 1935, a businessman wanted "something as much like the vanished wife of his father's generation as could be arranged—someone to balance his checkbook, buy his railroad tickets, check his baggage, get him seats in the fourth row, take his daughter to the dentist, listen to his side of the story, give him a courageous look when things were blackest. . . ."

It was not finger dexterity or low wages alone that accounted for the preponderance of women secretaries, *Fortune* continued. It was sex. "The modern office necessitates a daily, intimate and continuing relation which is much more possible between a man and a number of women than between a man and a number of men." Men can't be good secretaries, the analysis concluded, because they are too ambitious to be devoted to the humble work. When secretaries became preponderantly female, the title, of course, no longer meant apprentice manager.

As organizations grew bigger and more complex, the distinctions between "men's jobs" and "women's jobs" became more arbitrary, and more oppressive to women. One reason is obvious from the shape of any bureaucratic table of organization. The table of organization is not a ladder, on which the lowest paid may hope to rise, rung by rung, as early nineteenth-century journeymen wage workers expected to do, but a pyramid. In a technical and specialized organization, all workers at the bottom of the pyramid have to be highly skilled, but there isn't enough room for all of them to rise to the top no matter what their competence.

Some way has to be found to keep the workers on the bottom productive and happy. The way it has usually been done, of course, is to recruit these workers from a class or caste carefully taught not to expect to rise. When women were needed in these jobs, it was easy to persuade them to accept their place at the bottom by telling them that this bottom placement was only temporary until they married and embarked on their true career as wives and mothers.

To entice women to the low-paying jobs at the bottom, employers went to special pains to portray the work as especially "feminine."

The telephone company kept women at the physically confining switchboards by assuring them that "hello girls" were more tactful and attentive to subscribers. The typewriting companies solved the problem of providing operators for their new machines by declaring that the nimble fingers of women made them better at the work than men who, in any case, would have demanded higher wages.

Similar arguments rationalized the use of women in scientific and technical drudgery. According to a book published by the *New York Tribune* in 1898 entitled *Occupations of Women and Their Compensation,* Thomas A. Edison employed 200 women in the "more delicate details of his electrical invention," and there was room for women astronomers as human "computers" of star positions in the days when these calculations had to be made by hand. In photography, the *Tribune* went on, women could work at mounting, spotting, finishing, and retouching the negatives as well as in "getting the confidence of subjects, particularly children."

Employers did not hesitate to invoke the sanctity of dependence on men to keep their young women workers content with low wages. According to a Department of Labor inquiry of 1910 into working conditions for women, supervisers in department stores implied that women who complained of low wages were unattractive. "Haven't you a man friend to help support you?" they would ask.

15

SEX WOMEN
Miriam Leslie, the Everleighs

In Victorian America, women were so often told that their sexual attraction was their most valuable asset that it was natural for some of them to look for a way to use it to make money. The potential of being exploited by women was so unnerving to men that the worst thing they could say about a woman was that she "used sex" to get ahead. Yet even at the height of the Cult of True Womanhood, some women brilliantly capitalized on their "natural" assets.

The most dramatic of these was Miriam Leslie, who "used sex" in and out of marriage to build a journalistic career for herself and to expand the publishing empire she inherited.

Miriam Follin Squier Leslie (1836–1914) was the daughter of a New Orleans commission merchant with international cultural and business interests. He tutored Miriam at home and taught her to make herself understood in five different languages, but learning did not make her entirely high minded. As a girl, she was sexy and seductive. She craved excitement, and from the very beginning she knew how to make it. After a shotgun marriage, later annulled, she went on the stage as a protégé of Lola Montez, an internationally famous actress who was having a love affair with Miriam's brother.

Miriam herself attracted many men, but in 1857 she gave up the stage to marry Ephraim George Squier, an amateur archeologist with interests in Central America. He had published a newspaper for Spanish-speaking residents of New York and written about Latin America for *Frank Leslie's Illustrated Newspaper*. Frank Leslie was a promoter with a stable of publications, and during the Civil War, he invited Ephraim to become one of his editors. Miriam helped her husband translate books and learned both the editorial and the business side of publishing from him. Soon she was editing Leslie's *Lady's Magazine* and delivering a handsome profit on it.

Frank Leslie and Miriam Squier were very much alike— quick, flamboyant, changeable, insatiably ambitious. They always had business to discuss, and since Frank was estranged from his wife, he moved in with the Squiers, whose household was managed by Miriam's mother. It soon became obvious to everyone but Ephraim that Miriam and Frank were lovers. Ephraim's eyesight was failing and he was frequently away. Sometimes the three traveled abroad together, and on one occasion, when they were in England, Ephraim was arrested for an old debt incurred in that country. It certainly looked as if the jailing had been arranged for the convenience of the lovers, but Ephraim remained cheerful.

"Don't bother about me in the least," he wrote his wife from jail. "have a good time and in that way best please your E.G.S." Miriam cheerfully complied. She visited London theaters and art galleries with Frank, who sent the prisoner a box of sausages, steaks, chops, and herring, and bailed him out after he had collected material for an article entitled "Two Weeks in a British Bastille."

The threesome continued this way until 1872, when Frank's wife finally agreed to a divorce. Miriam then confronted Ephraim with trumped-up evidence for divorce and freed herself to marry Frank Leslie. Ephraim went insane, but the Leslies managed a glittering social life on several continents, which they exploited for its business advantages. Miriam wrote articles about their travels, with an instinctive awareness that publicity for the Leslies was good for the circulation of their publications. Miriam had always been strikingly beautiful, and as Mrs. Frank Leslie, clothes and jewels became the tools of her trade.

When they appeared at the inauguration of Samuel J. Tilden as governor of New York in 1875, Miriam was bedecked with $70,000 worth of diamonds. At their palatial country estate in Saratoga, New York, they entertained notables such as the emperor of Brazil, and they traveled around in their own $35,000 Palace Pullman car made for exhibit at the Centennial Exposition.

Inevitably the bubble burst. The panic of 1877 toppled the Leslie empire. The enterprising editor of a Western newspaper dug up all the scandal surrounding Miriam, from a two-year marriage that had to be annulled when she was nineteen, to the titillating details of the Squier-Leslie menage. By 1880, Frank was not only broke and fighting for his property, but suffering from cancer of the throat. At the office Miriam held off the creditors and kept the publications going. When word came that Frank was near death, she rushed to his bedside. According to her, his last words were, "Go to my office. Sit in my place, and do my work until my debtors are paid."

Unlikely as the injunction sounds, it's just what she did. She had her name legally changed to Frank Leslie, a move that later generations might label "penis envy." Meanwhile, she dealt with 17 lawsuits, including a contest of Frank's will by his sons. She pruned out unprofitable publications and built the circulation of the two remaining ones by beating the competition to the news. When President Garfield was assassinated, *Frank Leslie's Illustrated Newspaper* was on the street in record time with sketches and a full account. She understood every aspect of production as well as of reporting and finance. Soon she was flashing around at the opera, touring America and Europe, and creating gossip on three continents with her love affairs. At 55, she married a 39-year-old brother of Oscar Wilde, whose conversation charmed her, but when he turned out to be no help at the office and a drunk as well, she divorced him.

Two years later, she once again rescued her publications from bankruptcy brought on by the panic of 1893 and the ineptness of the managers to whom she had leased them. When she was 62, she had to return from retirement to take over the Frank Leslie publications once again, restoring them to such financial health that she was able to sell them for a half million dollars a few years later. In her seventies she was planning to marry a former gentleman-in-waiting to the King of Spain, but 70-year-old Don Teodoro Martel y Fernandez de Cordoba died before the wedding. In 1914, at the age of 78, Miriam died, leaving nearly half of her $2 million estate to Carrie Chapman Catt for "the furtherance of the cause of Woman's Suffrage."

Miriam Leslie was much more than a matrimonial adventuress, but that's what she seemed to those who subscribed to the mores of her time.

While men resented women who used a sexual tease to win material advantages for themselves, they had nothing but respect and even affection for the honesty of two women who made a million dollars delivering sex as a straightforward commodity.

Prostitution had flourished more or less openly in the womanless mining towns of the West. But glamorous as legend made them out to be, the madams of "parlor houses" in Nevada and Colorado disappeared or died broke after the boom subsided. It remained for two sisters from Virginia to make money out of prostitution by using the tried and true methods of big business.

The Everleigh sisters were born Aida (1864–1960) and Minna Simms (1866–1948) in Stanardsville, a small town in Greene County, Virginia. They concealed their origins to avoid possible embarrassment for relatives, and friendly biographers joined in the deception by describing them as products of Kentucky.

Their father, George Montgomery Simms, was a lawyer successful enough to send them to private schools and to provide lessons in dancing and elocution. They grew up to be trim, alert women who most of their lives were regarded as being ten years younger than their ages.

In her early twenties, Minna married an older man named Lester, and a little later Aida married his brother. Both marriages ended in less than a year, with Minna complaining that her husband was "a brute, suspicious and jealous" who had attempted to strangle her. The sisters moved to Washington, D.C., and there joined a traveling theatrical troupe as actresses.

Playing dramas, mostly of the *East Lynne* type, they toured the country. They were in Omaha, Nebraska, early in 1898 when a $35,000 inheritance enabled them to quit and become entrepreneurs. After careful consideration, the sisters decided to start a bordello for visitors to the Trans-Mississippi Exposition opening in Omaha that year. They had no firsthand knowledge of such places, but they remodeled a small building and lined up attractive women, some of them actresses from the road show.

When the exposition closed two years later, they had increased their capital from $35,000 to $70,000. But with no exposition to lure travelers, their business vanished. The local sports of Omaha refused to pay $10 for a woman or $12 for a bottle of wine, and the young madams had to look for a more promising location.

Chicago was most appealing. Thousands of men attended conventions there, sold cattle at the stockyards, and transacted business of all kinds. Other bordellos flourished in the city but the sisters planned to outdo them all. They became the Everleigh sisters, concocting the name from the "Everly yours" with which their grandmother signed her letters.

They bought a going establishment on South Dearborn Street—lease, fixtures, women, and good will cost them $55,000. They discarded the fixtures, discharged the women, and had an army of workers redecorate and refurnish the buildings. With a new staff of young women, many of them new to Chicago, they opened on February 1, 1900, as the Everleigh Club. Within a short time it became known as the most luxurious and most profitable bordello in the country.

"No house of courtesans in the world," noted the *Chicago Tribune,* "was so richly furnished, so well advertised, and so continuously patronized by men of wealth and slight morals." Even the critical Vice Commission of Chicago reported that the Everleigh Club was "probably the most famous and luxurious home of prostitution in the country."

Over the next decade, the sisters plowed much of their profits back into the club, spending $200,000 on paintings, statuary, and draperies. They had an art gallery, a ballroom, a library, and a music room. There were twelve soundproof parlors known as the Gold, Moorish, Silver, Copper, Red, Rose, Green, Blue, Oriental, Chinese, Egyptian, and Japanese Rooms. The music, the food, and the 30 women usually in residence were as magnificent as the decor.

"I talk with each applicant myself," Aida once explained. "She must have worked somewhere else before coming here. We do not like amateurs. Inexperienced girls and young widows are too prone to accept offers of marriage and leave.

"To get in a girl must have a pretty face and figure, must be in perfect health, must understand what it is to act like a lady. If she is addicted to drugs, or to drink, we do not want her. There is no problem in keeping the club filled. We always have a waiting list." The girls received half their earnings without the inflated deductions which were customary elsewhere.

Most Midwest prostitutes seem to have been farm girls of native Anglo-Saxon stock who wanted to better themselves in the city. Nineteenth-century investigators assumed that poverty drove them into a "life of vice," but feminist historians are resurrecting the disregarded evidence that a substantial minority chose prostitution as a means of earning a living because of "personal inclination."

At a time when women were available for as little as $2 in other establishments only a few yards away, a man had to pay $10 just to get inside the Everleigh Club. He was greeted with "How's my boy?" by Minna, who customarily wore a diamond dog collar, diamond bracelets, and a stomacher of diamonds, emeralds, and rubies. He was then allowed to buy wine at $12 a bottle, spend perhaps $50 for dinner, enjoy a resident siren briefly for $25 or in a more leisurely manner for $50 or more.

There were discounts for politicians in exchange for protection, and for newspapermen who frequently publicized the club. When big news broke after midnight, the city desk men of the *Chicago Tribune* knew that they had to call Calumet 412—the phone number of the club—to assemble reporters and editors.

When Prince Henry of Prussia arrived in New York in 1902 to pick up a yacht built for his brother, Kaiser Wilhelm II of Germany, the ship news reporters routinely asked what he wanted to see in America.

"I would like to visit the Everleigh Club in Chicago," replied Prince Henry—and he did.

The businesslike sisters, who were never personally involved with any of their visitors, ran charge accounts for important patrons and early began to cultivate corporate and expense-account business. Chicago held its first automobile show the year the Everleigh Club opened, and the motor men made it their second headquarters during show week for the next decade. On some nights an auto show exhibitor's badge was required for admission.

When a reform mayor closed the club in 1911, the sisters auctioned most of its furnishings and left Chicago with about $1,000,000 in cash, jewelry worth $200,000, furniture valued at $150,000, and $25,000 in bills owed by club clients.

Though some of their fortune was wiped out in the Great Depression, neither ever needed to work again, and they lived out the rest of their lives in quiet retirement. They lived in a brownstone house in New York filled with furniture from the Everleigh Club until Minna died in 1948. Aida gave up the brownstone and its furnishings were auctioned. The elder sister then returned to Virginia, where she died at the age of 95.

The Everleigh sisters made the logical retort to a business economy that discriminated against them on the basis of their sex; they found a way to capitalize on the very fact that excluded them from the business world.

16

PROFESSIONALIZING HOUSEWORK

Ellen Richards, Fannie Farmer, Alice Lakey

No matter what else they do for a living, women have been expected to shop, keep house, feed their families, and get the laundry done. They've been brought up to believe that this work of consumption is more important than anything else they do because some high-minded women of the nineteenth century established homemaking as a profession that all women should be proud to practice.

Housewives needed this boost. By the end of the nineteenth century, their economic role had become anomalous: money had become so important a measure of value that an unpaid worker did not command the respect accorded those whom the Census called "gainfully employed," and while it made sense to reorganize and mechanize the work of production in factories on which a profit could be made, there was no such urgency to improve the efficiency of the work women were expected to do at home. Housewives were less productive than factory workers and they knew it.

The enterprising women who codified homemaking into a

formal discipline wanted to apply science to housework to make it as productive as the work done in factories. But the successful establishment of this new profession for women affected the course of the economy much more directly. It assigned to women the responsibility for deciding what the family should buy and how these products and services should be used. It made women professional consumers, and this, in turn, helped to direct the thrust of the American economy towards goods consumed by families in homes. With a woman as a manager, each household would buy and use many more products. Every family had to have its own washing machine, even if it was used only a few times a week. Every home had to have its own modern kitchen in which food could be scientifically prepared.

Professionalizing the work of women was not a new idea. Catharine Beecher had tried to do it earlier in the century. When not campaigning for normal schools, she was writing and speaking on behalf of establishing a discipline she called "domestic economy." But the time was not ripe. The woman who finally achieved her dream, Ellen Richards, called the discipline "home economics."

Like so many other enterprising women of the nineteenth century, Ellen Swallow Richards (1842–1911) escaped the heavy sex-role conditioning of her time by skipping the early years of school. Both her parents had been schoolteachers, and they taught her at home. But to the despair of her mother, described by Ellen's husband later as "a small-minded woman with no conception of what her daughter was," Ellen was a tomboy. As a girl, she helped her father plow and pitch hay, and also helped him keep two stores.

Ellen wanted more than anything else to go to college. She taught school to get together enough money, but when her mother's health failed, she left to keep house for her father. After accumulating $300, earned and borrowed, she entered Vassar at the advanced age of 25.

Ellen's health had been delicate, but Vassar unleashed such boundless energy in her that she used to knit while climbing the stairs all the way up to her fifth-floor room to avoid losing a single minute. "The only trouble here is that they won't let us study enough," she complained to her diary.

"They are so afraid we shall break down."

One of Ellen's favorite professors was Charles A. Farrar, who stimulated her interest in chemistry. Professor Farrar told his students that analytical chemistry "means very nice and delicate work, fitted for ladies' hands," and he urged them to be "very thorough in the laboratory." Ellen was overjoyed when he allowed her to help him with his work.

In 1870, when Ellen was graduated from Vassar, chemistry was emerging as a new science that could be applied to improve everyday life in many ways. One way was health. Pioneer chemists were coming to suspect a relationship between dirt and illness, but the germ theory of disease had not yet been discovered, and cleanliness in water supplies, homes, and hospitals was still motivated by common sense, esthetics, and the old adage that cleanliness is next to godliness, rather than by scientific proof.

Ellen wanted to learn more about chemistry, but no advanced schools were open to women. Two commercial chemists to whom she applied regretted that they had no need, at the moment, of an apprentice. One suggested that she try to get into the new Massachusetts Institute of Technology in Boston.

M.I.T. was then only five years old and wary of taking on a female, in spite of enthusiastic recommendations from her Vassar professors. But the school admitted Ellen Swallow as a special student without tuition; in this way they could say she really wasn't enrolled in the event that her presence turned out to be embarrassing. Characteristically, Ellen didn't realize that she was being snubbed, but gratefully accepted what she interpreted as a scholarship.

"I am winning a way which others will keep open," she wrote in 1871. "Perhaps the fact that I am not a Radical or a believer in the all powerful ballot for women to right her wrongs, and that I do not scorn womanly duties, but claim it as a privilege to clean up and sort of supervise the room and sew things, etc., is winning me stronger allies than anything else. Even Professor A. accords me his sanction when I sew his papers or tie up a sore finger or dust the table, etc. Last night, Prof. B. found me useful to mend *his suspenders*, which had come to grief, much to the amusement of young

Mr. C. I try to keep all sorts of such things as needles, thread, pins, scissors, etc., round and they are getting to come to me for everything they want and they almost always find it. . . . They leave messages with me and come to expect me to know where everything and everybody is."

Like many other pioneers, Ellen Swallow accepted self-exploitation as a privilege. "They say I am going ahead because Professor Ordway trusts me to do his work for him, which he never did anybody else," she concluded her letter. "I am only too happy to do anything for him."

"She was a quiet little thing," Professor Robert Hallowell Richards recalled of her first year at M.I.T., during which he taught her mineralogy. He asked her to marry him, and during their engagement, she helped him translate German technical books which contained information needed for his lectures.

They were married in 1875, and Ellen used her new security as a faculty wife to help other women get as much schooling in chemistry as she had been able to get for herself. She persuaded M.I.T. to accept funds from the Woman's Education Association of Boston to convert a small gymnasium into a "Woman's Laboratory" where women, many of them already teachers, could learn chemistry. Ellen contributed $1000 a year for upkeep out of her own pocket, and on one occasion came up with an extra $50 to get the laboratory swept to her own exacting standards of cleanliness. By 1878, separate education for females had been abolished at M.I.T. and women were admitted directly on the same footing as men.

Success put her out of this unpaid job, but Ellen was never entirely happy unless she was serving as the faithful, behind-the-scenes assistant to some man. "Professor Richards' work this summer is on an electrical process, and I cannot help him much," she wrote in 1883, the year that the Woman's Laboratory was torn down to make way for a coed chemistry building. "Everything seems to fall flat. I feel like a woman whose children are all about to be married and leave her alone."

Other men relied on her help. In 1869, Massachusetts established the first state Board of Health and asked Professor William R. Nichols to investigate water pollution. Nichols was opposed to education for women, but accepted Ellen's assistance on this pioneer public health project. Samples of drinking water arrived at M.I.T. from all over the state. As his assistant, Ellen made almost all of the official tests of the purity of water for the State of Massachusetts until this routine was taken over by a state laboratory in 1897. Ellen also tested foods for the presence of poisons and adulterants, and eventually tested sewage and even air for the presence of disease agents.

In 1884, when she helped Professor Nichols set up the first laboratory in the new discipline of "sanitary chemistry," she was appointed to the faculty of M.I.T. as a full-fledged paid instructor of sanitary chemistry. In that capacity, and at an instructor's rank and pay, she taught the analysis of food, water, sewage, and air to the pioneer sanitary engineers who set up similar laboratories all over the world.

Ellen was increasingly involved in the contemporary movement to apply science to the improvement of every aspect of everyday life. Her knowledge was sought by the philanthropically minded Boston women who thought that the health of the working classes—and perhaps even their debilitating taste for hard liquor—could be altered by teaching poor girls to prepare "scientifically" nutritious meals at low cost. Ellen taught experimental classes, and in 1890 set up the first American public kitchen which demonstrated the preparation of wholesome foods it also sold, a technique for nutrition education later adopted by Jane Addams at Hull House in Chicago.

"Scientific eating" developed rapidly. Ellen taught experimental courses, designed public exhibits, wrote some of the first U.S. Department of Agriculture pamphlets on nutrition, and helped Boston set up one of the first school lunch programs in the United States.

Ellen's energy was prodigious, and her interests so omnivorous that her sister-in-law called her "Ellen-cyclopedia." She tested groceries for adulteration and fabrics and wallpaper for arsenic. She set up the science section of a correspondence school for women.

At home, she practised what she preached. Meals in her sunny, sensibly furnished home were simple, without rich

gravies or sauces. Plants and short washable curtains replaced heavy draperies set at the windows, and rugs replaced
heavy carpets. Ellen was one of the first to adopt the vacuum
cleaner, gas for cooking, shower baths, the gas hot water
heater, and the telephone. Ellen's servants were sent to
cooking school and given typewritten lists of what to do,
"with just enough information to keep the household running smoothly . . . but not enough . . . to be confusing."

Although her efforts were expended in many different enterprises, the goal was always the same: the application of
science to the improvement of homemaking. In the last years
of her life, she gathered all of her interests together. She
invited friends interested in raising the status of housekeeping to discuss standards, practices, and programs for a new
profession, intended, in the words of her summary, "to teach
the American people, chiefly through the medium of the
schools, the management of their homes on economic lines as
to time and energy." In 1908, this group formed the American
Home Economics Association with Ellen as first president.

The practitioners of this new profession decisively influenced agriculture and food industries. Their findings on
the nutritional value of orange juice made it a breakfast staple and built the huge citrus industries of California and
Florida. Their teaching has cut the consumption of bread,
potatoes, and fatty meats such as pork, and increased demand for fruits, vegetables, eggs, and milk.

Changing food habits was uphill, missionary work. Science
was all very well, but many rebelled against applying it to
what they ate. Some reacted to the appeal for a balanced diet
like the woman who said, "I don't want to eat what's good for
me. I'd ruther eat what I'd ruther."

The early home economists realized that the only way to
get people to eat what was good for them was to make those
good foods palatable. There was ample room for improvement. Sentiment has vastly overrated the quality of the home
cooking experienced by most turn-of-the-century Americans. The credit for greatly improving the taste as well as the
nutritional value of the American diet goes to a contemporary of Ellen Richards and fellow Bostonian, Fannie Merritt
Farmer (1857–1915), who did more than any other person to

bring the standards and practices of the scientific laboratory into the kitchens of America. She popularized explicit definitions ("to bake is to cook in an oven"), clear, exact directions, and exact measurements, down to an eighth of a teaspoon, instead of the "pinches" and "walnuts" of traditional recipes. Since its first appearance in 1896, her *Boston Cooking School Cook Book* has become the "kitchen Bible." It has sold four million copies in eleven revisions—one of the most profitable ventures ever published by Little, Brown & Company.

Fannie was not an especially good cook herself. The daughter of a poor printer, she was stricken with paralysis at 16, and was hardly able to struggle about on her own for ten years. A family friend hired her as a mother's helper and encouraged her to enroll in the Boston Cooking School in 1887. The Boston Cooking School was founded in 1879 by the same Woman's Education Association which gave Ellen Richards money for the Woman's Laboratory at M.I.T. The school provided the handicapped woman with a congenial career as a teacher, and she eventually headed the school from 1894 until 1902 when she started her own Miss Farmer's School for Cookery.

Fannie's greatest contribution to scientific cookery was to show her pupils how to make traditional dishes turn out the same every time. In 1896, she called on Little, Brown with a batch of her tested recipes, and suggestions for meal planning and nutrition. The editors were so dubious that they insisted that Fannie pay for the publishing of the first edition.

The book was an instant success. In subsequent editions, Fannie added traditional recipes from well-known restaurants, cleverly reconstructing dishes whose recipes were supposed to be secret and testing them herself until they met her exacting standards. She guided the inexperienced cook through the steps of making sauces such as Hollandaise so explicitly that they could be made by anyone who could read plain English. Fannie Farmer thought of herself as a leader in the movement for improving health through diet. "The time is not far distant," she wrote, "when a knowledge of the principles of diet will be an essential part of one's education. Then mankind will eat to live, will be able to do better mental and physical work, and disease will be less frequent." She took her greatest satisfaction from teaching the principles of nutrition for the sick to nurses, hospital dietitians, and students at the Harvard Medical School, and in encouraging Dr. Elliott P. Joslin to pursue the origin of diabetes in the failure of the body to digest sugar. Like the pioneer home economists who were her inspiration and associates, she was not only a professional homemaker, but a social reformer.

As women learned to do a better job of homemaking, they realized how little control they had over the goods and services they no longer provided for themselves. Big business determined the price and the quality of the many products every woman had to buy. The schools her children attended, the medical services available at hospitals, the very safety of the streets on which her children played, were controlled by bureaucracies notoriously unresponsive to individuals. Women isolated at home could not get these bureaucracies to listen to their complaints, but when they were organized in women's clubs, they were able to secure important reforms.

The women's club movement began as a protest against segregation. In 1868, a group of newspaperwomen were excluded, on the basis of their sex, from a reception given by the Press Club of New York City for Charles Dickens. Because women weren't supposed to lunch unescorted in public, the fourteen eventually met regularly in a room over Delmonico's fashionable restaurant on Fifth Avenue.

The rebels decided that women would never get anywhere until they had a club of their own, like the resplendent Union, Manhattan, and Union League clubs of New York, all of them off limits to women except by special invitation. They pledged themselves to the "advancement of women through unity and cooperation" and adopted the name Sorosis. One of their first projects was to invite the all-male Press Club which had excluded them from the Dickens reception to a breakfast at which males were forbidden to speak or "do anything but sit still and eat and be talked and sung to." The males came and survived the ordeal.

This was the beginning. Almost simultaneously, women's clubs sprang up in other American cities. Not all of them were as feminist as Sorosis, but the clubs undertook to improve their members' minds by reading and discussing books, and to improve their communities by supporting local charities and advancing projects ranging from clean streets, kindergartens, and help for the poor to such causes as the protection of American Indians, temperance, and even the eradication of the "social evil," a euphemism for prostitution. And since women were generally excluded from higher education, most of the clubs promoted the education of women, including the education of poor women in the science and art of homemaking.

In 1889, Sorosis invited 97 women's clubs to a sisterly celebration of its twenty-first birthday. Those accepting formed a permanent central body, the General Federation of Women's Clubs. The consolidation strengthened the power of women to exert political influence on public issues, and its formation coincided with a shift of interest from personal development to reform. "Dante is dead," the president of the GFWC declared in 1904, "and I think it is time that we dropped the study of his *Inferno* and turned our attention to our own social order." Membership in the clubs affiliated with the General Federation grew from 500,000 in 1890, the year it was founded, to over 2 million in 1910.

Local clubs that had sprung up in response to special problems federated into national bodies which could undertake long-range programs of research, publicity, and lobbying on the basis of funds supplied by local member clubs. Just as local enterprises were being merged into national firms, so the local women's clubs federated into national organizations such as the National Council of Jewish Women (1893), the National Association of Colored Women (1895), the National Consumers League (1890), and the Congress of Mothers (1894), which later became the National Parent-Teacher Association (PTA).

By 1906, women's clubs had become so powerful that they were a decisive influence in passing the Pure Food and Drug Act. Through their own organizations, women all over the country wrote a million letters to Washington demanding federal standards for the labeling and purity of food and drug products. The individual most responsible for the million letters was Alice Lakey (1857–1935).

Until she was 46 years old, Alice Lakey lived a sheltered and unusually private life even for gently bred women of her time. Ill health shaped her childhood and early adult life. An only child, she lost her mother at the age of six, and her father retired from the ministry because of ill health. As a young woman, she herself was so frail that in 1888 she had to give up a concert career as a singer which had taken her to Europe. She returned to the United States, where her father had gone into the insurance business, and the whole family retired to Cranford, a little town in New Jersey which promised the peace and quiet Alice and her father both needed.

The campaign for pure food attracted Alice not only because of family health problems, but also because her father was finicky about his food. In 1903, she invited Dr. Harvey W. Wiley, chief of the Bureau of Chemistry of the U.S. Department of Agriculture, to speak at the local improvement association.

The Cranford Village Improvement Association was hardly an important platform, but Harvey Wiley was a crusader who never turned down an opportunity to speak. In the public mind, practitioners of the new science of chemistry were divided into two parties: the villains, who were using it to preserve the color, flavor, and texture of foods shipped long distances from farm to store, and the heroes, who were trying to protect the ultimate consumers from the potentially harmful effects of the "additives" they did not know they were buying.

Harvey Wiley was the leader of the heroes. His Bureau of Chemistry had analyzed dairy products, lard, and maple sugar, tea, coffee, and canned vegetables. All were found to contain foreign substances, some of which, such as the coal-tar dyes used to color butter and cheese, were obviously dangers, while others, such as pieces of rope in prepared meats, were not exactly what the customers thought they were buying. Other investigations showed that drugs were far from pure. Some drugs worried temperance workers because of their high alcoholic content, or because they contained harmful narcotics, while others were useless concoctions which kept sick people from going to doctors who could really have helped them.

Harvey Wiley's answer was to lobby for legislation that would protect the consumers. A persuasive speaker, he enlisted Alice Lakey in the cause the first night she heard him, and much later, after years of working closely with him, she could liken him, without a smile, to Moses and Lincoln.

Alice mobilized the women's clubs into an army of well-organized, well-heeled supporters willing to work at the drudgery of letter writing and doorbell ringing without pay. Branching out from her local Cranford Village Improvement Association, she took a traveling display of adulterated foodstuffs to women's clubs. Everywhere she went she urged women to write their congressmen and their president in support of Wiley's bill.

At the 1904 convention of the General Federation of Women's Clubs in St. Louis, she distributed 1000 pamphlets about adulterated foods and drugs and secured the appointment of a pure-food committee. In the following year, she was one of the six citizens who persuaded President Theodore Roosevelt to support Wiley's Pure Food and Drug Act.

Alice continued to lobby for social reforms as adroitly as the special interests lobbied against them. In 1919, when her father died, she continued the insurance publication he had founded and enlisted the network of women's clubs in promoting life insurance to protect income and accumulate funds for the college education of children.

Meanwhile the mobilization for World War I made important use of the national women's organizations and stimulated the formation of many more. Women's groups were enlisted to run bond drives, do relief work in Europe, knit huge quantities of socks and sweaters, and stage meatless, butterless, and wheatless days to insure adequate supplies to the men at the front.

During the Civil War, women had been organized on a geographical basis. This made sense when almost all women were homemakers. By World War I, enough women worked outside the home to make it worthwhile to organize them on the basis of occupation as well.

In May, 1918, the Young Women's Christian Association, itself a national organization since 1881, called a meeting of career women in business and the professions and chose a

Kentucky lawyer, Lena Madesin Phillips (1881–1955), to head the group. Madesin, as this early feminist liked to be called, was the daughter of a judge who encouraged her to study law. At the age of 36 she was the first woman to graduate from the University of Kentucky Law School with honors. She set up practice in Nicholasville, Kentucky, to be near her 80-year-old father—"the center of my life"—but in order to relieve her from any sense of obligation to stay with him in Nicholasville, he told her he had sold the house and would be living with an older daughter. There was nothing to keep her at home when the YWCA War Work Council offered her the paid position in New York City.

The first Business Women's Conference of 100 nationally known women knew that they had more than a wartime job, and that, in Madesin's words, they had established "an alliance of business women of the United States which will be a tremendous power for the betterment of women." Of the many resolutions proposed, one which failed called for "suitable dress in business," which was an attempt to bar the peek-a-boo blouses and French heels which were then fashionable. Disapproving silence likewise greeted a resolution asking for a "standardization of morals." The women meant business.

After the armistice they did not disband. Madesin, by now a full-fledged organization professional, toured the country enlisting local clubs of business and professional women to attend a convention at St. Louis in July, 1919, which formed the National Federation of Business and Professional Women's Clubs. It adopted the slogan "equal pay for equal work," and pledged itself to support vocational training for women. Since then, the BPW has sponsored research about working women and has worked for a long list of public policies for women, including the child labor amendment, establishment of a Federal Women's Bureau and a Children's Bureau, Federal aid to education, the Equal Rights Amendment, and the State Status of Women Commissions. The idealism of women which had formerly been expended on campaigns for the abolition of slavery, temperance, and moral uplift was turned to the consumer concerns of women themselves.

17

THE INNOVATORS
Maggie Walker, Kate Gleason

The social reformers and consumer advocates made women aware that the big business monopolies of the 1880s and 1890s controlled the prices of everything women bought. Women were also hurt as enterprisers when those same big business-men bought or squeezed out small firms. When a family business was swallowed up by a national company, the female relatives were likely to be eased out by the new management. In a small business, it has always been good for morale, and good for women, to have family members take an active role. But in a large company the employment of relatives becomes an evil called nepotism, and it is a threat to the formal rules that a large-scale enterprise must enforce.

Small business did not entirely disappear under the vicious competition of the monopolies, as the political rhetoric of the day asserted: their owners often continued to succeed because they pursued opportunities which the big companies either ignored, or created opportunities in allied fields. An example of a market ignored was life insurance for blacks.

Life insurance became a big business following the Civil War. It made sense for the increasing population that had left the security of the farm for wage work in cities, and it made special sense for the former slaves who had few friends or relatives nearby to help them in sickness or death. During Reconstruction, the insurance companies had accepted blacks as insurance risks, but following an actuarial study made by the Prudential Life Insurance Company in 1881, indicating that blacks were shorter-lived than whites, most companies reduced the benefits or raised the premiums of black policyholders—or simply refused to insure them at all. In addition to this unpromising actuarial information, insurance companies were handicapped because their sales methods were not well adapted to the black community.

Into this void stepped a black institution, the mutual benefit fraternal society, which a friendless black man or woman could join, for modest monthly dues, and be sure of a visitor if he were sick, a decent burial with mourners if he died, and some help for the surviving family. In order to attract and hold members, the societies had to offer social and religious reassurance. One of the most successful organizers of this service was a remarkable black woman, Maggie Lena Walker (1867–1934), who was literally born in a mansion. Her mother, Elizabeth Draper, was an assistant cook in the Van Lew household, and she had married William Mitchell, its handsome young mulatto butler.

Elizabeth Van Lew was a rich and eccentric spinster who set her cook's daughter an example of independence extraordinary for any woman. Known as "Crazy Bet" because she sometimes feigned madness as a cover, she was an abolitionist who spied for the North without leaving Richmond. From her elegant home, she helped Northern prisoners escape and passed information to the Union forces. When Richmond fell, she raised a huge American flag over her home. General Grant personally visited her to thank her and gave her an armed guard to protect her against reprisals. Elizabeth Van Lew had freed many of her servants before the Civil War, and took a special interest in their personal development.

The household afforded its servants not only an exceptionally good education, but unusual encouragement to enterprise as well. Little Maggie was a special favorite who browsed in the library and was spoiled by everyone except her own mother.

After the Civil War, Maggie's father became head waiter at the St. Charles Hotel, a job which enabled the Mitchells to set up housekeeping for themselves. They sent their daughter to Armstrong High School for blacks, which was run by impoverished white women who took special pains with their pupils and encouraged Maggie to prepare for a teaching career. The outlook changed abruptly through exactly the kind of personal catastrophe against which life insurance protects. Maggie's father was found dead, apparently robbed and murdered, in the James River. Maggie's mother had to take in washing to support her two children. Maggie helped by picking up and delivering the laundry, but she stayed in school, and cemented her ties with the future leaders of the black community.

The Armstrong class of 1883, with which Maggie graduated, protested against the current practice that scheduled their commencement exercises in a Negro church, for which there was no fee, while students from the white high school were graduated in a theater for which the school paid rent. Wendell P. Dabney, the class spokesman who became a nationally known publisher, contended that since black parents paid taxes like white parents, black students had as much right as the whites to a theater which cost the school system money. The white principal told her Armstrong class that she could get a theater for them if they would agree to separate seat locations for the white and black members of the audience, but the class refused. Rather than go to the church, the Armstrong class of 1883 graduated in its own auditorium.

After graduation Maggie went to work in her old school as a teacher. Three years later she married Armstead Walker, son of a prosperous black building contractor, and retired to bear three children. While at home, she became active in the Independent Order of St. Luke's, a black fraternal organization she had joined as a girl of 14.

The black secret societies were modeled on their white counterparts, such as the Masons and Odd Fellows, which had always supplied mutual help to their members in sickness and in death. But unlike their white models, the black "fraternities" admitted women, and since black women frequently found themselves in need of help, they were often the leaders in forming them. St. Luke's, one of a dozen or so benefit societies in Richmond, had been founded in 1867 by Mary Prout, an ex-slave, to minister to the sick and bury the dead.

Even a small benefit scheme required an inordinate amount of paperwork and detail for its volunteer members. Volunteers visited the sick, administering small payments earmarked for them. They had to collect and record weekly fees from a thousand or more individuals. It was easy to make errors, and squabbles could blow up into major feuds in the atmosphere of secrecy characteristic of fraternal organizations. In 1899, the secretary-treasurer of St. Luke's resigned on the ground that members weren't cooperating, the order was not growing, the treasury was empty, and the work was too heavy for the $300 a year he was paid. Maggie Walker, who had been an active volunteer, agreed to take over at $100 a year and was unanimously elected.

Maggie found only $31.60 in the treasury against the potential claims of a thousand members. She faced an impossible task. She had to collect dues, verify cases of illness and death, keep the books, and pay the claims. She not only taught herself, but sharpened her skills by taking business courses in a commercial school, including a course in salesmanship.

A benefit society is stronger if it is bigger, and Maggie's predecessor was right in complaining that the order could not survive if it could not sell itself to a larger number of people. She doubled the membership during her first year in office, and kept the books meticulously.

The religious flavor of St. Luke's helped it to grow. Though it offered a hundred-dollar policy without doctor's examination, it refused to insure anyone who did not confess his or her faith in the Supreme Being. A devout church worker, Maggie had a flair for public speaking that served her well in the organizational battles a fraternal officer had to win to survive. She was an eloquent persuader in the same evangelical tradition that would eventually produce Martin Luther King.

One of Maggie's first projects was a juvenile division which encouraged children to study the Bible, save, keep clean, and work. Dozens of youth clubs were formed all over the South.

When a child had saved a whole dollar, he or she was encouraged to deposit it in a savings bank. In 1902, Maggie convinced St. Luke's to sponsor the St. Luke's Penny Savings Bank. In 1910, the failure of the True Reformers' Bank, founded by a rival secret society, led to a state law which required the separation of secret orders and their banks.

With Maggie as president—supposedly the first woman bank president in the country—St. Luke's Bank and Trust Company became a depository for the city of Richmond's tax, gas, and water departments, and once, when Richmond's white banks could not lend more money to the city, St. Luke's financed a $100,000 loan which enabled the public schools to continue.

During these years of growth, Maggie built new quarters for the order and the bank, and a comfortable home for her family with a spacious, awning-covered veranda.

When Maggie Walker died in 1934, she left a personal estate of $40,000 and an organization strong enough to survive the Depression. The insurance organization she had built from scratch, and with very little guidance from its white predecessors, had collected more than $3 million in premiums. The Independent Order of St. Luke's owned a four-story brick building with lodge rooms, an auditorium, and a press for publishing the *St. Luke's Herald*, its own paper. It employed black women as clerks at a time when black women were barred from white-collar work. They wore white uniforms and started every morning with prayer.

In 1976, extensive private and government health, unemployment, and life insurance plans were available to black and white alike, but the Independent Order of St. Luke's still existed. The St. Luke's Bank and Trust Company founded by Maggie Walker weathered the Depression of the thirties and survived in downtown Richmond as the Consolidated Bank & Trust Company. The Maggie L. Walker High School of Richmond was teaching both races and sexes.

Insurance for blacks is an example of the kind of special market which big business was willing to leave to smaller firms. But there was another class of opportunities for small and medium-sized firms. Small companies with a special skill could supply a service or product that big companies could not have made as cheaply or as well. The automobile industry has created a network of such small suppliers.

As the pioneer car manufacturers dwindled down to the few big survivors, they found that it paid them to let small machine shops make special parts for them. The shops which could find a place for themselves as suppliers to the assembly lines were protected by the umbrella of the big companies who financed, advised, and helped them with business services they could not otherwise have afforded.

Only a few of the thousands of small machine shops all over the country were able to join the automobile industry network. Most machinists did not have the business sense or the sales ability required. One of those who succeeded was not the machinist himself, but an articulate daughter who did the selling for him.

Kate Gleason (1865–1933) was the daughter of William Gleason, who had emigrated from Ireland and become a machinist in Rochester, New York. Her mother was a suffragist and family friend of Susan B. Anthony, and her father encouraged her to be active and independent. She wore her hair short and straight in a day when girls wore long curls or braids, and she played with boys when other girls were busy with their dolls. "They didn't want me," she recalled. "But I earned my right. If we were jumping from the shed roof, I chose the highest spot; if we vaulted fences, I picked the tallest." When her eldest brother, her father's chosen assistant, died, Kate resolved to take his place. "I walked down to the shop, mounted a stool and demanded work," she told a reporter after she became successful. "At the close of the day he handed me one dollar, my first pay. I had no pocket, so I tucked it in my dress, and lost it on the way home. My mother and grandmother made a terrible fuss."

Her father liked to have her around the shop to keep the books and help with the business paperwork. Kate enrolled as a special student at Cornell University, but had to leave before the end of the year because business at the machine shop was slow. Kate's father could no longer pay the salary of the man he had hired to replace her in the shop office.

Kate's recollection of how she received the news was a story she later told on herself to charm her customers. As she told it, she took her father's letter out on the campus and sat under a tree where she thought no one would see her, but a fellow student discovered her crying. "He choked up and said brokenly that he was awfully sorry, but that just at present he couldn't be more than a brother to me. I tried to convince him that I was crying at leaving *college*, but he attributed that statement to my maidenly modesty, and in the end I walked off furious, if broken-hearted." She returned to the shop.

William Gleason and his younger sons were more interested in designing and making machine tools than in marketing them. Influenced, at least in part, by feminist principles, they allowed Kate to become the traveling salesperson of the Gleason Works, and she was superb at it.

The early automobile industry was aggressively male. Suppliers selling big companies entertained them lavishly and sometimes in questionable places. Kate could not, of course, take her prospects to the Everleigh Club. Instead, she developed the art of telling amusing stories, and at one point in her selling career affected elaborate hairdos and carried violet-garnished muffs to dramatize the advantage she enjoyed on the basis of her sex.

The demand for machine tools is extremely sensitive to changes in the economy, and in the recession of 1893 the market was poor. Kate encouraged her father to work on an invention with which he had been tinkering. It was a machine that made bevel gears much faster, cheaper, and more reliably than could be done by filing the rough castings of the part by hand.

Bevel gears transmit power around a corner. In an automobile, the bevel gears in the rear axle carry power from the engine, transmission, and propeller drive shaft to the rear wheels. In the 1890s, they were used principally in bicycles, but the device had a bright future.

Kate saw that there was a much bigger market for the gears themselves than for the planer her father had invented to make them, and she set out to sell both to the shops making bicycles and early automobiles. A persuasive saleswoman, she made such good presentations that most people in the automobile industry thought she had invented them herself. Henry Ford called the Gleason bevel gear planer "the most remarkable machine work ever done by a woman." Kate was never able to persuade her purchasing agents that her father was the inventor and machinist, and that she herself had not developed the gears. She traveled all over the country and eventually all over the world, introducing bevel gears and planers to the international automobile industry and other industries as well.

In 1913, when the Gleason Works was prospering, Kate had a falling out with her father and brothers for business reasons that the family have never made public. The parting was friendly, however, and Kate decided that she should be the one to leave. "It seemed to me that my experience would make it easier for me to go into a totally different line of business than it would be for my brothers, who, up to that time had specialized on the shop end of the work," she explained. "It was heartbreaking, because it meant leaving father and all the friends I loved."

Kate left the Gleason Works with enough money to experiment in new ventures. The outbreak of World War I created a demand for her services in the Rochester business community. When the male president of the First National Bank of East Rochester was called to service in France, she took his place.

Another assignment that challenged her ingenuity was her appointment as receiver of a bankrupt machine-tool shop that was $140,000 in debt. The creditors hoped only that she could retrieve 10 percent on their investment, but three years later she was able to announce a profit of $1 million.

The opportunity that interested Kate most as she surveyed the local scene from her desk in the bank was the need for low-cost housing. She was sure that costs could be cut if builders adopted the mass-production methods of the car makers she had learned when she was selling the bevel gear planer.

The most imaginative of the eight new businesses she

financed was Concrest, a community of 100 six-room houses in East Rochester. Instead of concentrating on luxury housing, Kate aimed to serve working-class families which were paying inflated wartime rentals of $65 a month for four rooms.

Concrest houses were small, but Kate loaded them with extras that she knew would delight women. Each kitchen came equipped with porcelain-lined gas range, sink with mixing faucet, laundry tray with aluminum cover, refrigerator, kitchen cabinet, ironing board, and even a cookbook, a mirror, and a powder puff. She included extras that moved prospects to sign: built-in bookcases, window shades, stair rods, screens, and a brass-trimmed woodbox on wheels. In 1921, she was able to offer all this for $4,000.

Kate's financing plans anticipated low-cost housing projects built after World War II. She knew that working-class families could not afford conventional mortgages, so she sold her houses on the basis of a small down payment and payments of $40 a month which could be budgeted like rent.

She brought construction costs down by using concrete and adapting mass-production methods. "My particular inspiration for method came from a visit I made to the Cadillac factory a few years ago, when Mr. Leland showed me the assembly of the eight-cylinder engine. All this work was done by one man, but he was furnished with a cabinet on wheels, which contained every part he needed and only as many parts as he needed," she wrote in an article on Concrest in a building trade magazine. Mr. Leland was Henry Leland, the engineer who founded the Cadillac Company and put the first electric self-starters in its cars. "It is not at all likely Mr. Leland knew this one assembler out of the 8,000 men in the factory," she recalled, "but in showing me the work, he put his hand on the man's shoulder as though he were his friend and said, as I remember, 'This man assembles our engine complete in eight hours, so that it complies with all tests, and it used to take two men four days.'

"We try here to follow Mr. Leland's methods as closely as possible, by having the stock on the job ahead of time, as needed. On very hot days, or to show our appreciation for necessary overtime, we serve occasional cool drinks or ice cream, and on dismal, cold days, we occasionally serve hot coffee and doughnuts. This is done without any idea of being benevolent."

Kate used mass-production methods to cut costs. She settled on a standard house plan, orienting the units in different ways on the site to avoid a monotonous appearance. She developed a special system to mix and pour the concrete from a telescoping tower with mixer, hopper, and chute mounted on wide-tired wheels for easy mobility. She bought materials in quantity when she could get a low price, and used hardware and electric fittings from the five-and-ten-cent store. But cheap did not mean shoddy. Concrest houses were built, she said, to last a hundred years. She took the same methods to Ladies' Island, Beaufort, South Carolina, where she set up an economically viable, low-cost recreation colony for artists and writers, and in 1927, after studying adobe buildings she demonstrated that it was practical to build similar modern houses of poured concrete in Sausalito, California. She demonstrated that housing could be mass produced and sold to working-class families on an easy payment plan, and anticipated later home-financing systems.

Both Kate Gleason and Maggie Walker were gifted saleswomen who identified a market that big business was not yet reaching. And both were good enough businesswomen to keep small risky enterprises solvent.

18

HELPERS
Mary Follett, Josephine Roche,
Mary Richmond

Women have traditionally taken the initiative in helping those unable to help themselves: children, minorities, soldiers, prisoners, the sick, ignorant consumers, even other women. Even True Women like Catharine Beecher and the Civil War workers were willing to defy male authority on behalf of those they felt were being victimized.

In the 1890s, enterprising women rallied to the support of a new class of victims: employees working for big organizations which viewed them as "labor" if they worked for hourly wages, or "personnel" if they wore white collars and were paid by the week or month. By the end of the nineteenth century, more Americans were working for wages or salaries paid them by employers than were working "for themselves," and the frontier was considered closed. This meant that there was no "free" land in the West to provide an alternative livelihood for workers unwilling to accept unfavorable conditions of employment, or for those whom employers could not or would not hire.

Many jobholders worked in small firms where the boss knew all his workers by name and directed them as if they were his family, but this system broke down in the companies that were so large that workers had to be known by a number. The problem had been foreseen by philosophers who had speculated that machines would strip workers of their personal identities, a danger as frightening as physical mutilation. Karl Marx had warned that "wage slaves" would revolt against the impersonal system that alienated worker from work.

The problem was no longer theoretical when thousands of workers were recruited to build ships and make munitions for World War I. In spite of the incentives of patriotism and high pay, doubling the number of workers did not build a ship in half the time. Instead, exasperating "human problems" delayed urgent military schedules. Wildcat strikes and seemingly petty disputes slowed production. It became obvious that large workforces could not be managed like small ones.

When employers turned to the emerging social sciences for advice, the theorist who proved most helpful was a soft-spoken, unassuming, but intense intellectual who never met or appeared on a payroll in her entire life.

Socially and culturally, Mary Parker Follett (1868–1933) was a proper Bostonian, whose family ran a granite quarry in Quincy, Massachusetts. She adored her father, and had to interrupt her studies to care for her invalid mother and a younger brother, but she never married, and never had any other family obligations. An inheritance from her grandfather and her father enabled her to devote her entire life to studying how people treated each other.

At first she looked for the answer in books, studying economics, government, and history at the Society for the Collegiate Instruction of Women by Professors and other Instructors of Harvard College, which was later to become Radcliffe College. There she made friends with eminent Harvard intellectuals like the historian Albert Bushnell Hart. She also studied at Newnham College, Cambridge, England, and in Paris. She took time out to write her first book, an analysis of the office of the Speaker of the House of Representatives, before receiving her bachelor's degree from Radcliffe at the age of 29.

She then turned her attention to observing human interaction in real life. In 1900 she set up a debating society as one of a group of activities for poor boys and girls in Roxbury, Massachusetts. She was so impressed by the success of informal neighborhood groups that she eventually persuaded the city of Boston to open school buildings to community groups in the evening as a matter of civic policy. As she watched people work together in these groups, she began to develop two sets of ideas that were to have important consequences. The first was that democracy could never be realized through big, impersonal political parties, but only through small, autonomous groups of neighbors. In 1918, her book setting forth this theory, *The New State*, attracted favorable attention from intellectuals disillusioned by the failure of representative democracy to bring about social reforms.

Her second theory applied the Hegelian notion of thesis, antithesis, and synthesis to the resolution of conflicts between people. She believed that people grew and changed each other by talking out differences of view to find out what each party really wanted. Once real interests were identified, a new solution could emerge that would not require either side to back down or compromise.

Mary's favorite example was a window that one person wanted open and the other wanted shut. The conflict was insoluble so long as the issue was defined as the position of the window, but if the two talked to each other about it long enough, it might appear that what one really wanted was more air, while what the other really wanted was protection from a direct draft. Once these real interests were identified, the conflict could be resolved by opening a window in an adjoining room.

This concept, set forth in her 1924 book *Creative Experience*, offered harassed business managers an exciting new handle on the personality clashes and intractable human problems that so often frustrated their best-laid plans. Mary would be able to show them how this rather abstract notion could be applied to "labor" problems.

Mary liked to talk to business people because they spoke out of their own concrete experience instead of in generalities and were more willing, she found, than scholars and politicians to try experiments. She felt that business could do something about the reforms intellectuals merely discussed. "Industry is the most important field of human activity and management is the fundamental element in industry," she told an audience of Oxford scholars in 1926.

If Mary loved business people because they were practical, the repressed philosophers among them loved Mary because she provided a rationale and a vocabulary for their most puzzling experiences, and they found her surprisingly well informed about what went on in their shops. Vocational guidance work with her Roxbury young people had introduced her to the realities of industrial work. In 1912 she had founded and partly funded the Boston Placement Bureau, which was so successful that in 1917 it became the city's Department of Vocational Guidance. She had also served on some of the wage boards established to set rates under the 1912 Massachusetts minimum wage law for women, an exercise that had carried her into the nuts and bolts of "meeting a payroll."

This work had acquainted her with employers, among them the manufacturer Edward Dennison and the merchant Lincoln Filene, both of whom gathered liberal thinkers around them and experimented with forward-looking programs for making business more humane as well as more efficient. Mary may have had these New England uplifters in mind when she told her Oxford audience that "it is among business men (not all, but a few) that I find the greatest vitality of thinking today." An eager listener, she was just the kind of sympathetic woman to whom a hard-boiled man of large affairs didn't mind expressing his half-formed thoughts and feelings.

Out of these encounters, Mary formulated theories of the decision-making process in organizations, the relationships between formal and informal organizations, and the role and function of the executive, topics taught to students of business administration in the 1970s. As her theories developed, Mary progressed from listening to business leaders to writing and speaking to them.

She was successful because she was able to illustrate her

theories with practical advice. Give orders in terms of the work to be done, rather than the relative status of the chief and subordinate, she suggested. In explaining the importance of semantics, she pointed out that a "Complaint Department" invites complaints, and would really function better if rechristened "Adjustments."

She told business leaders that business created not only profits and products, but opportunities for people to interact with each other and so develop better human relationships. She thought that management was a profession, and that it should be formally organized like law and medicine with a body of principles taught in schools, a code of ethics, and a recognition of responsibility for the public welfare.

Business has taken Mary's advice. Corporation presidents now proclaim their "public responsibilities" and send their rising managers to study management science. The kind of advice she gave to individual business leaders has since become a formal service offered by management consultants, virtually all of whom are males. Interestingly enough, the few women who have established themselves as management consultants have almost all specialized in personnel management—the problems of people that drew Mary Follett into the worlds of business and industry.

When labor became a public issue, women tended to side with the workers. Organizations to help the working classes attracted women college graduates eager to put their education to work reforming society. The New York Consumers League, formed in 1891, attempted to make consumers a countervailing power that could force big business to treat workers as well as consumers. The Womens Trade Union League was more radical; it aimed to educate and organize women in the garment trades, and it actively assisted strikers.

The most innovative of the new helping organizations was the settlement house, best described by its inventor, Jane Addams (1860–1935): "I gradually became convinced," she wrote in retrospect, "that it would be a good thing to rent a house in a part of the city where many primitive and actual needs are found, in which young women who have been given over too exclusively to study, might restore a balance of activity along traditional lines and learn of life from life itself; where they might try out some of the things they had been taught."

With the help of a college classmate, Jane opened Hull House in Chicago in 1889. Hull House served as an informal headquarters for like-minded social reformers who stopped by to work with neighborhood people for months or years. It became a nucleus not only for the kind of group activities that Mary Follett recommended, but for a long list of reforms ranging from stricter labor regulations and better municipal government to the establishment of juvenile courts and the right of labor to organize. Soon settlement houses were established in other cities. Though men were always accepted, the leaders and most of the workers were socially conscious women.

The determined social reformers found new ways to make business listen to them. One of the most dramatic demonstrations was provided by Josephine Roche (1886–), a woman who openly declared herself an enemy of the business practices that had made her family rich. Her father, John J. Roche, an associate of John D. Rockefeller, owned a coal-mining company in Colorado. At 12, she wanted to visit the mine. When her father said no, it's too dangerous, she flashed him a devastating retort: why then, is it safe for the miners?

Like many other rich girls growing up in the West, which was short on suitable potential husbands for one of her station, she was packed off East to school. From the point of view of her family, Vassar was a disastrous choice. Secretly suffragist, bursting to prove that college was not wasted on women, the Vassar class of 1908 was a hotbed of social reform.

Josephine did everything a proper young reformer was expected to do. At college, she worked in a Poughkeepsie settlement house. After college, she went to work as a probation officer for the Denver Juvenile Court, but then went back East to Columbia to study sociology in search of answers to the problems of poverty and deprivation she had encountered in the field. She returned to Denver to become that city's first policewoman, and earned a reputation for being tougher than the males in cleaning up prostitution.

Like other socially awakened young women of her time, she resolved the conflict between marriage and career in favor of career. A brief marriage ended in divorce, leaving her free to work with the Committee on Public Information and the Children's Bureau in Washington.

Then, in 1927, the death of Josephine's father made her the largest single stockholder of the Rocky Mountain Fuel Company, which was guilty of all the labor abuses Josephine was fighting. Miners paid by the weight of the coal they mined were being gypped at the scales. Ventilation was poor, and the men lost time because the company didn't provide good transportation underground. John Roche had employed Pinkerton men to spy on "agitators."

She could, of course, have sold it, but would transferring the moral responsibility to another be right? While she was trying to decide, the dreaded "wobblies" of the anarchist International Workers of the World (I.W.W.), infiltrated the company in spite of the efforts of the Pinkerton men, and fomented a riot in which six miners were killed. The liberal State Industrial Commission investigated the riot and recommended that the workers form a real, rather than a company-dominated, union. Josephine decided to implement this verdict.

"I found myself," she said later, "with a complete laboratory to thresh out all the theories I had evolved in my research work." Once her mind was made up, she was as decisive as John D. Rockefeller himself might have been. She told her stockholders that the miners needed a real union and she was going to see that they got it. She next used her stock interest to appoint an unlikely set of new officers. In due course, a man known for his liberal political views became president of the company. The lawyer who represented the United Mine Workers became the company counsel. When infuriated stockholders unloaded their stock in protest, she bought it and strengthened her own control.

The contract negotiated by the new company officers gave the workers important benefits: $7 for an eight-hour day; arbitration of grievances, and improved working conditions.

In return, the miners undertook to justify the pay rise by increasing productivity.

Josephine didn't stop with improving the ethics of the company's labor relations. She withdrew from the agreements with other mine operators in the state who eliminated competition by splitting up markets among them. Her competitors fought back by slashing prices, cutting wages to do it. Josephine's miners responded by lending her half their wages and peddling Rocky Mountain coal to small users in the state who sympathized with their cause. Unions all over the state joined in a boycott of nonunion Colorado coal.

By 1932, the worst year of the Great Depression, Rocky Mountain Fuel had won its Colorado war. The company had nearly doubled its share of the coal mined in Colorado. Its workers were employed more days per year and at higher pay than those of any other company in the state, and they enjoyed the lowest accident rate per ton of coal produced. In 1935, male-oriented *Fortune* Magazine paid Josephine the ultimate compliment: "She took over her inherited business when it was in grave danger, pulled it out of a crisis which male executives had been unable to handle, challenged and defeated the most powerful competitive interest in her industry, if not the country, and carried her concern through the succeeding depression."

Unlike the magnates usually profiled in *Fortune*, Josephine did not pursue her business triumph. After proving her laboratory experiment, she ran for governor of Colorado in 1934 and lost. President Roosevelt appointed her Assistant Secretary of the Treasury in charge of the U.S. Public Health Service. A close friend of John L. Lewis, the thundering, bushy-browed organizer of the United Mine Workers, she became one of the three trustees of the union's Pension and Retirement Funds, the first of the multi-million-dollar union pension funds. In spite of her capitalist origins, Josephine Roche chooses to identify herself in *Who's Who* as "labor organizer."

Upper-class women seldom were able to use the power of ownership to show big business how a model employer ought to behave, but they could talk to industrial leaders as social equals, and they knew how to go about implementing reforms. Many of them learned the arts of politics to help secure legislation which now guarantees most American working women and men a safe environment, minimum wages, maximum hours, unemployment insurance, reliable labor statistics, and retirement with a Social Security check coming in every month for life.

But what of the many workers who couldn't find jobs? The employers who attracted farm youngsters to work in factories were not responsible for feeding them and their families when they were no longer needed, or when they fell sick and could no longer work. But some provision had to be made for them. As far back as the Civil War, "friendly visitors," most of them women, had doled out their own money to the destitute of their neighborhoods, but this informal system could not take care of the number of human rejects congregating in newly industrialized cities.

As they had in the Civil War, women saw the need for organizing the work of welfare which had formerly been done on a sporadic, personal basis. Local agencies for collecting and disbursing funds began to proliferate.

These small, amateur agencies usually had a hard time accounting for the money because there were no generally accepted rules about how it should be spent. At the same time, there were so many agencies that some needy could get help in more than one place, while those in the greatest need were overlooked, and often left to die, because they had no friends or relatives to make their wants known.

The financial panic of 1873 intensified these problems and called attention to the British charity organization movement. In England, local agencies cleared their cases with a central "charity organization society," which provided no direct relief itself. By the end of the 1870s, American counterparts were in operation in most Eastern seaboard cities.

These struggling new societies encountered all the problems of running a large-scale operation, and in addition had to face some deep-seated social issues raised by the evidence of poverty they brought to light. It became obvious that part-time volunteers couldn't operate the bureaucracy required no matter how warm-hearted they were; that relief merely encouraged some people to "work the system"; and that state governments might have to supplement charity in tiding over the temporarily dislocated as well as in support-ing the "social basket cases" that had been the responsibility of local communities since colonial days. The economic threat to the well-being of cities and the sheer size of the task interested civic-minded males with "business experience," but it was a remarkable woman of working-class origin who sparked the movement to set objective standards for dealing with the poor, a woman whose first encounter with charity was as a $50-a-month fund raiser employed on a trial basis by the Baltimore Charity Organization Society.

Mary Richmond (1861–1928) was the daughter of a carriage blacksmith from Belleville, Illinois. She was the only one of four children to survive infancy, and she had lost both par-ents to tuberculosis, then a disease of poverty, by the time she was seven years old. Eager, intense, and like so many nineteenth-century females frail of health, she was brought up by her grandmother and two maiden aunts who ran an extraordinary boarding house in Baltimore.

Mary's grandmother was interested in spiritualism and took her along to seances, but she didn't send her to the public schools because she didn't like the system under which bright students were kept from asking too many ques-tions by being sent to tutor the dull ones. By any standard, Mary would have been one of those hapless bright ones. As an adult, she could not remember a time when she could not read. School-teacher relatives and the residents of the board-ing house gave her books to read, and one boarder urged her to keep a notebook. Dinner-table conversation, as she remembered later, might be about the resurrection of cats, antivivisection, or the rights of women.

When she was 11 years old, Mary was admitted to school on the basis of an examination, and although she had trouble adjusting to the social life of her contemporaries, she was graduated from Baltimore's Eastern Female High School at the age of 16. She went immediately to New York City to work with her aunt in a publishing house that specialized in radical books.

All during Mary's twenties she lived close to the edge of

the poverty and unemployment which was beginning to disturb thoughtful Americans. When her aunt fell ill, Mary supported her for the rest of the aunt's life. When Mary herself became sick, she was afraid she had tuberculosis because her parents had died of it. She could not stop working, and though she followed the doctor's orders about caring for herself, she did contract malaria. She then returned to Baltimore, where she worked as a bookkeeper.

She wanted to be a teacher, but for that, she lamented, "you have to have an education or political pull"—and she had neither. She was 28 when she answered an ad for a job as assistant treasurer of the Baltimore Charity Organization Society, looking, as her interviewer later recalled, "pathetically young" but talking so earnestly that she sounded "like the Ancient of Days."

Mary was remarkably successful in attracting sponsors, who encouraged her, guided her intellectual growth, and helped her learn the ways of the world from which her timidity and poverty had excluded her. At the outset of her new job, friends financed a week of study at the Associated Charities of Boston with its general secretary, Zilpha D. Smith, who introduced her to books on the subject.

At the Baltimore Society, she quickly acquired another valuable mentor, John Glenn, a Harvard graduate who served as volunteer chairman of the executive committee. Although he was totally blind, he was a scholar and a connoisseur of philanthropical literature, and when he discovered that the new employee was avidly reading up on his favorite subject, he suggested that they join forces. Their discussions of the authors she read to him provided the richest possible training in the philosophy of welfare.

Mary Richmond often said that she had to learn social work and do it at the same time. Her first duties included fund raising and reporting on the allocation of funds, and her rise was meteoric. Two years after she was hired, she was general secretary of the Baltimore Society, a post formerly held by university-educated men.

She was a social theorist at heart, and like Mary Follett she thought a great deal about the human relationships she observed in her daily life. Although she never made many "friendly visits" herself, she analyzed those that other workers were making, and analyzed their encounters with clients to find out why they so often failed in their objectives. Systematic herself, she was convinced that the failures were due to inadequate information, and she urged the paid investigators to report more fully. When blunders still persisted, she looked for better solutions.

While hammering out a code of practice for investigating cases, she was also strengthening the organization of the society itself. To the art of personal persuasion she brought not only enthusiasm and homey erudition, but a talent for observing, listening, and encouraging other people to express their views—talents she insisted could be taught to social caseworkers.

Recognition quickly followed in the burgeoning new discipline. In 1899 Mary was asked to head and reorganize the Philadelphia Society for Organizing Charity. She did not fire anyone, but placed capable people in strategic posts, supplied them with data, and inspired them. In 1909, the new Russell Sage Foundation asked her to create its Charity Organization Department, and she moved from Philadelphia to New York.

From her central position at Russell Sage, Mary Richmond was able to move the new profession toward her goals through writing, editing, sponsoring institutes for case workers, and eventually participating in the founding of schools of social work that taught, in organized form, what she had taught herself through reading, observation, and research. In 1917, she published *Social Diagnosis,* the most widely used textbook for social case investigating of its time.

Mary Richmond was not a psychologist. She believed that people were influenced by their social environment and could be helped when the faults of their situation were remedied. Her view was superceded by that of the Freudians who converted the casework interview into a miniature psychiatric session. However, more than any other single person, she molded the present curriculum of social work training—which at the graduate level combines classwork with apprenticeship, the route she herself took in her own self-education. And although the Freudian cast to casework was to dominate private practice, the technique of investigating she developed was applied to the public assistance programs of the New Deal by her student, Jane Hoey.

Social work was a new profession, an organized way of doing work that women had always done. But it remained an underpaid career on the assumption that like nurses and teachers, women caseworkers were only biding their time until marriage. Like the teaching of children and the tending of the sick, the relief of the poor in America has been subsidized by the willingness of trained women to work for less pay than men of equal competence.

19

FASHIONS
FOR EVERYONE II
Ida Rosenthal, Nell Donnelly

Women continued to make their own dresses at home long after they gave up other home manufacturing. The paper pattern had made fashion available to any woman with time, a minimum of talent, and a sewing machine. By varying a basic pattern, a woman could dress in the current style and express her own individuality with accessories and trimmings. And a nimble-fingered woman could dress as if she were rich.

There is evidence that the rich found this irritating. In 1900, *Vogue* Magazine, then an arbiter of fashion, proclaimed that "the great lesson our women have to learn is to dress according to their position in life."

American women never had to learn this lesson. A new kind of industry was evolving in New York City, one that would eventually meet the contradictory wishes of American women for cheap mass-produced dresses that looked neither cheap nor mass-produced.

The industry began in a small way. Immigrant tailors had begun to mass-produce women's suits the way men's suits had been manufactured as far back as the Civil War. Even as the editors of *Vogue* were writing, other immigrant venturers were gambling on mass-producing the garment that went with suits, the shirtwaists immortalized in the drawings of the "Gibson girls" by illustrator Charles Dana Gibson.

Garment manufacturing was a risky business, undertaken by small family firms willing to gamble their savings on an idea. Fiercely competitive with others in the same line, they were as dependent on neighboring lines as the shirtwaist on the skirt. But because they were small, they could afford to make short production runs of each model, and to vary a basic design so that customers didn't have to worry about "seeing themselves coming and going." They could also move fast enough to "knock off" or copy the successful design of a competitor or a high-fashion import from Europe.

The massive switch to ready-to-wear occurred after World War I. In 1920, when the community of symbiotic competitors moved together into specially designed fireproof buildings on Seventh Avenue in New York, there were only half as many dressmakers in the country as there had been ten years earlier. Only the most adept dressmakers could compete with Seventh Avenue, and one of these founded a profitable new garment industry in the course of her attempts to fit her customers better.

Ida Rosenthal (1889–1973), founder of Maidenform, Inc., the first manufacturer of brassieres, started dressmaking in Hoboken, New Jersey, and later moved her home and business to Washington Heights, New York, where her daughter Beatrice recalls playing on the living-room floor around the feet of seamstresses pumping away at sewing machines. In the early 1920s, Ida prospered and moved her business to a smart shop on Manhattan's Fifty-seventh Street. In those days, she recalled, a woman who paid $125 for a dress expected it to fit, regardless of her own shape, and the short straight flapper dresses popular after World War I were revealing an infinite variety of female shapes.

Ida was inventive enough to work on the shape, rather than the dress. She began to make, for each customer, a simple two-cup container for her breasts, snapped in the back. Customers discovered that their personal "brassieres" made their other dresses look better too. Ida was soon making and giving one away to every customer. Customers liked them and came back for more.

Ida's husband William was one of the early ready-to-wear dress manufacturers. In 1924, he quit this risky line and helped Ida mass-produce brassieres. A gifted designer who later became an amateur sculptor, he addressed himself to the complex puzzle of designing a system for mass-producing brassieres for all sizes and shapes of women.

William had to begin from scratch. There were no standard sizes for women's clothing as good as the standards uniform manufacturers had been able to set up for men's clothing. Each manufacturer worked out his own, and that is what William had to do to design a production system for brassieres. He started by dividing women into figure types, and then designed a different style of brassiere for each, the precursors of the familiar A, B, C, and D cup sizes. But since a small woman could have big breasts, and a big woman small breasts, all of the cup styles had to be made in all of the dress sizes. Production instructions for each size and style required the development of sets of measurement: nipple to nipple; shoulder strap to shoulder strap, and so forth.

The instructions were used to make the first brassieres one at a time, but soon William developed a mass-production system under which brassieres were assembled from parts, as automobiles are assembled. Suppliers were close to each other in the new garment center, so that a small manufacturer could buy hooks and eyes, elastic, and boxes, and hire specialists in garment labeling, selling, advertising, and distribution. As they prospered, they attracted competitors, but the Rosenthals remained the leaders.

They divided the management of the enterprise on the basis of their respective talents. William managed production, the "inside" work that usually goes to the wife of a couple in business together. Ida was the business head, the "front man" who managed promotion, selling and finance. A small but dominant woman, she used to maintain control over clients who towered over her 4-foot 11-inch height by commanding them to sit.

It was a happy marriage both personally and occupationally. Ida and William Rosenthal came from the same East European Jewish culture in which women frequently managed practical affairs so that their husbands could devote themselves to scholarship and religion. Ida's own mother kept a store while her father studied the Talmud.

Maidenform, Inc., remained a family business, and management descended on the distaff side. Ida groomed her daughter Beatrice for management in the same way that business founders groom their sons. "When I graduated from Barnard College in 1938," Beatrice recalls, "I had to start learning all over again, there was no formal training school in those days. I started, as did many of our executives, at the sewing machine, I worked in various other departments in Bayonne, too, and in 1939 I came to New York and worked on advertising." Although probably unaware that executive development specialists advise the practice, Ida often deferred to the judgment of her daughter even when she disagreed in order to cultivate her sense of responsibility. When Ida Rosenthal died in 1973, the company, under Beatrice's management, was offering "new" soft-line brassieres which resembled the original model Ida had designed for the flapper era.

The Rosenthal story is a classic example of the way custom work is industrialized, but Ida did more than found a successful manufacturing business. She founded an industry that speeded the adoption of mass-produced dresses by making it possible for them to fit as if they had been custom made.

In the early days of the garment industry, most manufacturers concentrated on high-priced line copies of Parisian imports, or low-priced line "housedresses," shapeless garments intended simply to cover a woman's body when she was alone at home with her immediate family. The first to see that American women wanted fashionable clothes to wear every day, even—and perhaps especially—when alone with their husbands, was an American woman who lived far from the burgeoning clothing industry. Nell Quinlan was born on a Kansas farm in 1889, the youngest of twelve children, and the first 26 years of her life were a predictable sequel: schooling at a Parsons, Kansas, convent; high school and business school; a job as a stenographer in Kansas City; marriage, at 17, to Paul Donnelly, a man who lived in her rooming house and worked in the city as a stenographer too.

Nell was less conventional than she looked. She wanted to go to college, then a rare privilege largely confined to daughters of well-to-do city professional families. Even more rare, for a pre-World War I Kansan, was Paul Donnelly's willingness to help his wife realize this ambition. Instead of saving for the down payment on a farm or house, as other young couples did, the Donnellys saved enough in one year out of their joint earnings for Nell to enter Lindenwood College, a woman's school in the St. Louis suburb of St. Charles. She was the only married student at the school—a distinction that set her apart and made her feel as odd as the Chinese student in her class. Nell was bright, and both the Quinlans and the Donnellys knew it. With help from both families, Nell was graduated in the class of 1909.

For the next seven years she kept house, but with no children to keep her busy, she took up sewing and became good at making her own clothes. One Christmas she made colorful dresses of her own design for her sisters. They were enthusiastically admired by friends who wanted comfortable everyday dresses that did not look like the bungalow aprons, Mother Hubbards, and other garments offered in the stores for wear at home.

In 1916, Nell checked the market out with Kansas City stores. In one after another she asked the clerk for a "smart little dress" she could wear while doing her housework. Everywhere she got the same answer: highly paid designers couldn't spend their time designing cheap dresses that couldn't be sold at a big profit. Nell did not argue with them. She went home, made up a dozen "dress aprons" that would allow a woman freedom of physical action without making her look like a frump, and persuaded the buyer of the George B. Peck Dry Goods Store in Kansas City to put them on sale as a test. Every one was sold by noon of the first day, and the buyer ordered several dozen more.

At the time her husband was not enthusiastic about the

prospect of setting up a garment factory in the house, but as he told a reporter, "I always felt that Nell was smart," so he backed her with $1270 from his savings. Nell installed two power machines in the attic, hired two girls to help, and was soon turning out two dozen dress aprons a day. When Paul returned from the service after World War I, the dress apron business had outgrown the attic and had to be moved to a location in downtown Kansas City, near the department stores. Paul quit the Barton Shoe Company, where he had been credit manager, and became president of the new Donnelly Garment Company, while his wife took the post of secretary-treasurer. He handled financial strategy. She designed the dresses, hired the workers, and supervised the selling.

The company prospered during the 1920s, sometimes grossing as much as $3.5 million a year, but it flourished alone in Kansas City without following the pattern being set by the growing dress industry on Seventh Avenue.

At a time when American designers enjoyed no credibility, the Donnellys put Nell's signature on their product, shortening the name to Nelly Don. It quickly became a valuable trademark, known everywhere for sensible, wearable, attractive dresses at a price women could afford. Although more than a third of the dress manufacturers on Seventh Avenue went out of business during the four years after the stock market crash of 1929, Nelly Don maintained its sales, and took advantage of the market by adding good wool and silk dresses at low prices.

Nelly paid special, personal attention to the quality of the clothes that went out under her name. As a girl, she recalls her mother warning her against making a dress out of material that she had picked up at five cents a yard. "Don't put work into that," she told her daughter. "It will fade." Nell ignored her mother and carefully assembled a charming dress with tucks and time-consuming detail—only to discover that it *did* fade. At Nelly Don, she insisted on having every fabric tested for fading. To insure good fit, she made every new design up in every size and tried it on an actual woman of the size and age for whom it was intended before going into production on the model. While Seventh Avenue concentrated on selling new styles, Nell aimed at repeat business from women who had to live in and with the clothes they bought.

Nell's Depression prosperity involved her in an unfortunate incident that changed the course of the business and her life. In 1931, she and her black chauffeur were kidnapped and held for $75,000 ransom. Former Senator James A. Reed, the Donnellys' lawyer, secured her release after 34 hours without ransom. Within a year of this incident, at the age of 43, Nell divorced her husband and married her 72-year-old lawyer, and they had a son, Nell's only child. Under the divorce settlement, Nell retained control of the company and became its president. She sold her controlling stock for more than $1 million some ten years before retiring in 1954.

Ida Rosenthal and Nell Donnelly succeeded because they found ways to contribute to the mass-production of women's clothing at the time the industry was developing after World War I. Because they were women, they saw a need that escaped the attention of the men in the business. Men were not dressmakers who struggled to make women's dresses fit, nor did they face the embarrassment of answering the door in a shapeless "housedress."

Like Nell Demorest and Margaret LaForge before them, these two women used their special insights as women to build an economic role for themselves.

20

WORLD WAR II
Olive Ann Beech, Tillie Lewis

Rosie the Riveter was the heroine of World War II. She was an all-American girl who worked in an office and had a boyfriend. When the boyfriend volunteered to go into the service, Rosie went to work in an airplane plant where they taught her how to rivet. It was dirty, it was dangerous, it was patriotic, it was fun, and the pay was great.

Rosie was making more money than she had ever dreamed a woman could make, but most of the things she wanted to buy were rationed or unavailable, so she bought war bonds through the payroll deduction plan.

At the end of the war, Rosie's boyfriend came home. Rosie laid aside her tin hat. She cashed her war bonds, added the proceeds to the money he had saved from his Army pay, and with the GI mortgage he could get, they were soon settled down in a nice little house where they raised four children and bought a refrigerator, a washing machine, a car, and a backyard barbecue.

The story of Rosie is the story of what happened to most women who helped win World War II in the defense plants. After the war, most of them found themselves running homes in the suburbs. But a few women who were in the right places at the right times found themselves running big businesses.

One of them was a secretary who had married her boss.

Olive Ann Beech (1903–) was the business manager who converted a small commercial plane enterprise into a huge defense company that supplied the planes on which 90 percent of all American bombardiers and navigators were trained in World War II.

Olive Ann was the daughter of a Kansas carpenter and building contractor. When she was only seven years old, her mother set her up with a bank account, and by the time she was 11, she was writing checks for all the family bills. After attending business school, she worked as a bookkeeper and office manager for an electrical appliance firm in Augusta, Kansas. In 1924, when her boss died, she went back home to Wichita.

There she found a $20-a-week job as bookkeeper for the Travel Air Manufacturing Co., formed a few months earlier by Walter Beech and two partners to make small commercial airplanes. There were only 12 employees.

Walter Beech was a former Army pilot who had built and raced planes. Born in Pulaski, Tennessee, he had only a grammar and night-school education. Like many aviation pioneers, he was a charming but sometimes difficult character. A swashbuckling bachelor, he opened fire on Olive Ann, his first woman employee, the day she started work. "Leave the married men alone!" he ordered.

"Don't worry," she retorted. "I'm not going to bother you either."

Money was scarce in the early days of Travel Air at Wichita. Walter and his colleagues sometimes took passengers for joyrides from the Kansas wheat fields at one dollar a head, with Olive Ann selling the tickets. She also began to handle the money back at the office, and soon was promoted to office manager and secretary to Walter, who was president and general manager.

One day when he failed to return from a trip on schedule with money to meet the payroll, she called on the Fourth National Bank and Trust Company and asked for a loan of $2000. The surprised bankers were not sure of her authority, but gave her the money.

By 1929, Travel Air had become the leading manufacturer

of small commercial planes, and Walter Beech was able to merge his company on favorable terms with Curtiss-Wright. In his new position as Curtiss-Wright executive, he had to move to New York, so he married Olive Ann and took her along. Neither liked the change, and two years later they were back in Wichita starting a company of their own.

Walter was president of Beech Aircraft Corporation, and Olive Ann was secretary-treasurer and director, but if Walter thought he was saving the salary of his right hand "man" by marrying her, he reckoned without Olive Ann's business sense. No matter how lean the earnings, she insisted on receiving compensation for her services.

The earnings were at first nonexistent. Walter and "O. A. Beech" (as she liked to be called) started operations in a deserted factory with a few former Travel Air workers. Not a plane was sold the first year, and only one was sold in the second year. In order to boost sales, Olive Ann suggested using women pilots in the 1936 transcontinental race. The Beech plane won.

In the late thirties, defense contracts transformed the little private plane company into a huge and critical war industry. The buildup began in 1938, when Beech sold its first million dollars' worth of planes. By 1940, the military backlog of orders climbed to $22 million. But while their business was booming, all was not well with the Beech family. In June of that year Walter was in a coma with encephalitis from which doctors feared he might never recover. Nearby, on the same floor, O. A. Beech was awaiting the birth of their second daughter, Mary Lynn.

From her bed in the maternity section of the hospital, O. A. Beech began to run the company, and she ran it with an increasingly firm hand. There was plenty to do. Orders were mounting and Beech Aircraft needed money beyond the capacity of the local banks to supply. While Walter was still disabled, Olive Ann arranged for a $13 million loan from the Reconstruction Finance Corporation, and later negotiated $50 million in revolving credit from 36 banks to finance the production of aircraft.

Walter came back to work, but he never fully recovered.

Olive Ann had to cope with all the management problems of sudden expansion. In order to keep the assembly lines going night and day, she had to recruit and train people who had never worked in factories before. When production facilities were inadequate at Beech, Olive Ann found subcontractors to make some of the parts.

Sales reached a wartime peak of $122 million in 1945. When Walter died of a heart attack in 1950, Olive Ann became president, chairman of the board, and chief executive of the company—functions she had been exercising for a decade. In 1968, when she was 65 years old, she turned the presidency of the company over to a nephew, Frank E. Hedrick, but continued as chief executive. The secretary who married the boss remained in charge of a business that in 1974 had sales of more than $240 million.

Olive Ann had the reputation of being a tough boss, but she survived in a tough business. She supplied business management and a steel spine to a flamboyant aviation pioneer who was delighted to turn the finances over to her. She did so well that Beech Aircraft has made a profit almost every year, and nearly all of its planes, some of which are priced at more than a million dollars each, are sold before they are made.

Defense contracts enabled new small enterprisers in many industries to survive their growing pains and grow big. One who made good use of this opportunity was one of the first women to get a cannery going in California. Manpower was short on the farms and in the canneries, but the armed forces were begging for more production, and the only way to deliver it was to find and train workers who had never seen the inside of a cannery.

During World War II, this woman stood along the assembly line of her plant personally showing new workers how to peel Italian tomatoes. When they couldn't do the delicate operation fast enough, she tried canning tomatoes in their skins. It worked, and other hard-pressed canners followed her lead.

Tillie Lewis (1901–) introduced the Italian tomato industry to California in the first place. One of a very small group of self-made enterprising women, she had long dreamed of growing, canning, and selling the small, tangy, pear-shaped tomatoes called pomodoros that make Italian spaghetti sauce unique.

She was born Myrtle Ehrlich in Brooklyn. Her father was a Jewish immigrant who ran a music store. Her mother died when she was a baby. She didn't like her stepmother, and nobody objected when Tillie quit school at 12, lied about her age, and went to work folding kimonos at $2.50 a week for a Brooklyn garment manufacturer. When Tillie was 15, she married a grocer twice her age just to get away from home.

The way she likes to tell the story, the idea of growing pomodoros popped into her head the only time she volunteered, on a Sunday, to help take inventory for her husband. Looking over his stock, she wondered why the high-priced tomatoes and tomato pastes were all from Italy. Why couldn't these special tomatoes be grown in the United States?

Nobody seemed to know. She asked experts at the Brooklyn Botanical Gardens. "Wrong soil and climate," they explained, but they didn't say what soil and climate were right. She did learn that people had said the same thing about French grapes but that wine makers had transplanted the vines successfully to California and made fortunes. She had never been to California but figured that what worked for grapes and wine might work for tomatoes.

She read about tomatoes in the public libraries and wrote to experts asking why pomodoros couldn't be grown in the United States. Those who replied were not encouraging and some suggested she forget the whole idea. She didn't forget it, but it was years before she could do anything about it.

After she divorced her husband, she worked as a "customer's woman" for a stockbroker for a time and went to business school at night. Soon she was selling securities on commission, and she was good at it. In 1932, one of the gloomiest years of the Depression on Wall Street, she earned $12,000.

One day in 1934 she read on the office news ticker that Congress had imposed a 40 percent tariff on pomodoro imports. If she was to do anything about her long-cherished dream, she realized this was the time. She bought a new hat and a Berlitz book of lessons in Italian, and invested her savings in a second-class passage to Naples aboard the S.S. *Vulcania.*

On the way over she had the luck to meet Florindo del Gaizo, a Naples canner who was the leading exporter of pomodoros. He was interested in the tariff too, and feared that it would cut down on the 700,000 cases a year he sold in America. He was also fascinated by the little red-haired woman in the big hat who had never been in a cannery but talked confidently of growing and canning pomodoros in the United States. The courtly Italian toured her through his cannery, showed her pomodoros growing around Naples, and entertained her in his home.

She left happily two weeks later with a cashier's check for $10,000 and four bags of pomodoro seedlings. Under her arrangement with Florindo del Gaizo, he would send her canning equipment and an expert to install it. She would undertake to grow, can, and market Italian-style tomatoes in the United States, and for this she was to be paid a salary of $50 a week.

Florindo was the closest thing to a male sponsor Tillie ever had. "I will never forget him," she says. "He was the first person to believe in me."

She named their enterprise Flotill Products, Inc., a combination of his first name and her nickname, and, in commemoration of its casual launching, designed a trademark picturing a champagne glass and a sprig of pomodoros. She had never been to California, but she had the names of business people who might be able to help, and they suggested various sites for her to visit. The San Joaquin Valley looked like the best place because it had soil and climate much like that of Naples. She found a canner who agreed to pack on a cost-plus basis.

The first real snag was the reluctance of farmers to plant the seedlings she farmed out to them. They were used to growing round tomatoes, onions, and potatoes, and they didn't think pomodoros would grow in the San Joaquin Valley.

Tillie induced them to promise to plant enough to can

100,000 cases of whole tomatoes and 100,000 cases of tomato paste. Then she set out on a one-woman tour of the East to get wholesalers to buy the crop she expected. Before the tomatoes were even grown, the whole crop had been sold.

The pomodoros grew beautifully, but there weren't enough of them. The farmers had been so doubtful that the pomodoros would grow that they had not been willing to risk all their acreage on the new crop. Tillie had to answer to the angry wholesalers. The second year she had her own cannery in Stockton, the crop was bigger and there was a profit, but there were always problems. Tillie had to learn all about commercial canning. In the beginning, she used secondhand equipment that was always breaking down. Once, just when tons of tomatoes were waiting to be processed, a steam boiler stopped working. At the very moment Tillie was wondering what to do, the wail of a railroad whistle reminded her that locomotives produced steam.

"I called up the Santa Fe and asked how much they would charge to lend me a locomotive," she recalls. "The man who answered was sympathetic and said they would charge only the switching fee of $7.50. 'Good,' I said 'I'll take two.' The tomatoes were saved."

Florindo del Gaizo died in 1937, and to keep control of the enterprise Tillie had to borrow $100,000 to buy his stock. A vice president of the Banco di Napoli in New York loaned her the money, and she gratefully said: "If I can ever do anything for you, please don't hesitate to call me." Pearl Harbor ended operations of the Banco di Napoli in New York, and in a letter the banker reminded Tillie of her promise. She sent him tickets to California for himself and his family and created the job of vice president and treasurer for him in the company. He held the post for 27 years.

In 1940, AFL cannery workers struck her plant, though she was paying more than the union asked and providing additional benefits. The strike was settled with the help of Meyer Lewis, western director of the AFL, and a year later he became her general manager. Seven years later, they were married.

As an independent canner, Tillie had to find some way to

establish consumer recognition of her brand name. One of her assets was the attention she attracted as the only woman canner in the business. Her own attempts to reduce led, in 1952, to the first artificially sweetened canned fruit. The diet pack turned out to be popular and profitable. When she sold her controlling shares in Tillie Lewis Foods, Inc., to the Ogden Corporation in 1966 for $9 million, she became that billion-dollar company's first woman director.

World War II made large-scale enterprises out of small firms producing something that was needed for the war, and a few of these were headed by women like Tillie Lewis and Olive Beech who made the most of the opportunity. But most women went to work because extra hands were needed, and industry became accustomed to the convenience of being able to call on them.

Each major American war has permanently liberated women from some restriction on their freedom. The Civil War had made it respectable for them to leave their homes to work in public. Their contribution to World War I secured them the vote. World War II offered married women the option of working for money when they needed it, and at the same time gave to industry a badly needed flexible labor reserve.

21

THE VOCATION OF WOMANHOOD II

Beatrice Gould

It's now an open secret that Rosie didn't really want to go back home after the defense plants closed. A survey conducted by the Women's Bureau reported that 80 percent of the women who had worked during World War II would have liked to continue in their jobs. Most of them quit because the jobs that remained were given to returning veterans, and a subtle campaign in the press portrayed women as eager to start the families they had deferred so long.

Rosie went home and the women's magazines did their best to make her like it. In the 1940's, women's magazines had come a long way from *Godey's Lady's Book*. They were no longer reasonably innocent entertainment and edification for women, but "media" for carrying advertising messages. Sarah Hale's spheres were resurrected to sell soap, cosmetics, floor wax, refrigerators, and many other consumer products which newly affluent millions could afford for the first time.

Women were the targets for all these products, and in her book, *What Makes Women Buy*, advertising copywriter Janet Wolff describes the creatures who would buy them:

> Women feel a strong desire for security—though emotional and social much more than economic or

physical. When these appeals are used in selling, they should show an awareness of . . . women's need of approval in both home life and outside activities . . . and women's dependence on others for economic security.

The emphasis on romance and youth, plus the acceptance of "sex" today, makes selling appeals based on enhancing beauty and attracting the opposite sex rate high.

Women feel a great desire for enjoyment and convenience . . . [But] These desires cannot always be used directly as appeals, for many women feel guilty about having too many pleasures and comforts.

Contemporary living has heightened women's strong need for self-esteem and personal pride. . . . Almost every product and service has the potential ability of fulfilling this need through building women's dignity or adding prestige to family and household jobs.

Women who worked as copywriters based their advertising appeals on the sexist notions Betty Friedan has labeled the feminine mystique. The mystique was of great importance to women advertising copywriters because it was their ticket of admission to the advertising "game." They constantly reminded their bosses that as women, they knew best what other women wanted.

The most enduring of the successful women in advertising has been Bernice Fitz-Gibbons, the daughter of an Irish immigrant dairy farmer whose career in store advertising spanned 40 years. She coined both the Macy's slogan, "It's Smart to Be Thrifty," and the Gimbels retort, "Nobody, But Nobody Undersells Gimbel's." Gimbels had to pay her $90,000 a year to get her.

"I've never claimed that women should take over the advertising business," she wrote in her lively autobiography, *Macy's, Gimbels, and Me,* nor did she believe that only women could write copy addressed to other women. In her office, men often wrote fashion copy, but she reports that there are some consumer reactions men simply don't see.

Male toy buyers, for instance, failed to predict the success of a doll that gets sick with the help of accessory Bandaids, crutches, casts, and removable chicken-pox marks. They were revolted and thought little girls would be revolted too.

"And women not only know what little girls like," Fitz continued, "they also know what is good for breakfast. Eastern Air Lines, eager to improve its reputation for good food, [had] announced that it would serve a 9:00 A.M. breakfast of eggs benedict. Apparently the agency [did] not have a woman on the account. Any woman would know that nothing could be more repulsive to a queasy stomach or a hangover from the night before. . . ." Advertising agencies, she concluded, are "overmanned and undergirled." Famous for her slogans, she gave them one for nothing: *If you want more legal tender, hire more of the female gender.*

In order to deliver the largest possible number of customers to advertisers, the women's service magazines concentrated on the one thing all the customers had in common: homes and families. "Marriage is a woman's business," Beatrice Gould, editor of the *Ladies Home Journal*, told me once. "We are a trade journal for wives."

The advertising and the women's magazines in which it appeared were too essential to be left to women. Both on the magazines, and in the advertising agencies, control was firmly in the hands of men. For many years, Beatrice Gould was the only woman at the top of the masthead of a major woman's magazine, and she was there as coeditor with her husband Bruce. In October 1946, when the *Journal* sold more than two million dollars' worth of advertising, a peak never before attained by any magazine, Beatrice Gould looked like a woman who was exercising real economic power. Let us take a look at this woman and the nature of the power that she exercised.

Beatrice Blackmar Gould, who refused to divulge her birthdate to *Who's Who in America*, had an exceptional education. Her father was a small-town Iowa school superintendent who worked his way through college a year at a time, and her mother was the librarian of the normal school he attended. Beatrice herself remembered an idyllic, apple-pie childhood built around family dinners during which "everyone talked" and the children were permitted to argue "providing it was about books, or the Civil War."

Beatrice had models of achievement at home. "My parents seemed to have an unbounded confidence in their own abilities," she recalled, and her mother was especially competent. A good cook, she was also an expert seamstress. When she was in her fifties, Mrs. Blackmar earned an M.A. degree at Columbia, and after thirteen tries, received a driver's license at the age of seventy-three.

At the University of Iowa, Beatrice met and subsequently married Bruce Gould, an English major who dreamed of becoming a playwright. Like so many ambitious young people of their time, they went to New York to seek their fortune. They both worked on newspapers, wrote for magazines, and even wrote plays together, one of which, *Man's Estate*, was produced on Broadway in 1929.

Beatrice was well established as a writer and kept on writing for magazines after her only child was born in 1928. Bruce joined the staff of the *Saturday Evening Post*, then run on authoritarian lines by George Horace Lorimer.

We know exactly how Bruce and Beatrice came to coedit the *Ladies Home Journal* because they have set it all out in a joint autobiography, *American Story*, published in 1968. Their book, like the magazine they published, exalts the differences between men and women, and is written in alternate chapters, first by him and then by her.

According to Bruce, whose chapter covers the event, the idea of "adding Beatrice" as coequal coeditor occurred to The Boss "directly after a *Saturday Evening Post* party at which Beatrice had not only looked very pretty in a wine velvet evening gown (copied by her mother from one worn by Lady Abdy in *Vogue*) but had also (deliberately) flattered the Old Man" (that is, Lorimer). The deliberate flattery, he hastens to explain, was by way of reaffirming her "honest admiration" for Lorimer following one of their not-infrequent political arguments in which Beatrice had defended Walter Lippmann, a liberal columnist turned conservative, whom George Lorimer apparently regarded as a dangerous radical.

"Of course he knew her qualifications as writer and editor

were sound," husband Bruce continued. "But, I have always felt that the conversation that evening had persuaded him of her very womanly nature—valuable assistance in editing a woman's magazine."

Beatrice needed persuading. "She didn't care to be a big executive," Bruce wrote. "She didn't fancy long commuting days away from home and child—our daughter was not quite eight. Beatrice's schedule was arranged so she could drive Sesaly to Miss Fine's school in Princeton, spend the morning writing in the University library, pick up Sesaly again and take her home to lunch."

The account of the discussion in the Gould household is a revealing exposition of the guilt the *Journal* was to stimulate in naturally enterprising women.

"If I could have chosen my own pattern, I would have stayed at home until our daughter was older," Beatrice wrote. "But . . . it was then that opportunity offered, *that my husband needed me*" (italics supplied).

Bruce reports the compromise. "Beatrice finally said she would go along with Mr. Lorimer's idea provided she need appear at the office only three days a week, working the rest of the time at home." So it was arranged, with Beatrice getting $5,000 and Bruce $20,000 a year starting in July, 1935. Lorimer called the *Journal* staff together and announced that the husband-and-wife team would have equal billing at the head of the masthead, adding a clear but hasty aside, "and, Bruce, don't forget—you're the Boss!" Beatrice didn't go to really important editorial conferences attended by Lorimer, but waited to get the word from Bruce.

It worked. From 1935 to their retirement in 1962, the Goulds used themselves as role models for the ideal marriage which they never tired of declaring was a "woman's business." They developed the *Journal* into the most profitable of the Curtis magazines, one of the most profitable magazines, as a matter of fact, of all time. In 1940, a cover line boasted: "The *Journal* now has the largest paid circulation of any magazine in the world."

It is tempting to wonder what Sarah Hale would have thought of Beatrice, who a century later worked only a few blocks away from the site of *Godey's Lady's Book* in Philadelphia. Sarah would have been enchanted with the *Journal* motto, "Never underestimate the power of a woman." She would have approved of Beatrice's crusades for hot school lunches, and better medical care for childbirth. Sarah was so sensible a woman that she might even have overcome her prudery to campaign, as Beatrice did, for the eradication of venereal disease, if a remedy had been discovered in her time.

The two were alike in many ways. They both sincerely believed that women were nobler than men. Both may have fantasized themselves as American Queen Victorias. Sarah praised the English monarch for setting an example of womanly virtue, and ordered extensive coverage in *Godey's* when Victoria ascended the throne. Beatrice was franker about it, unaffectedly admitting that she felt "great kinship with Queen Victoria, who found her true self in marriage rather than in the responsibilities and rewards of her position." Both Sarah and Beatrice won White House support for their projects; Beatrice by personal visits and through her most famous *Journal* contributor, Eleanor Roosevelt.

There was one critical difference between the situation of the two editors. *Godey's* was supported entirely by subscriptions. What Sarah would not have understood was that the *Journal* slogan was an appeal not only to readers, but to advertisers, too. Sarah thought of herself as a model of noble womanhood. Unwittingly, perhaps, Beatrice was made a symbol of the Mrs. Consumer advertisers hoped to sell.

A cartoon prepared for *Journal* advertisers in 1945 cast Beatrice in this role. The first frame showed a glum male executive sitting alone in front of a sales chart going steadily down; the second showed a male executive and a female executive at adjoining desks in happy conversation in front of a chart going steadily up. The caption amended the famous *Journal* motto to include the male sex: "Never underestimate the power of a . . . woman and a man!"

22

WORD WOMEN
Sylvia Porter,
Mary Wells Lawrence,
Katharine Graham

Words have been the favorite weapon of women in winning access to public arenas. The word business has been their best-traveled road to money and power since the days when colonial women were printers and publishers, and it has continued to offer them opportunity in an economy increasingly dependent on information.

Women have used their favorite weapon in many different ways. Words were used by the social reformers, both in spreading their causes and in making the money to support them through their crusades. Emma Willard and Catharine Beecher promoted the cause of women's education by writing about it, and they made more money on their books than through their schools.

Women who managed to enter traditionally male occupations discovered that they could accomplish more by writing than in any other way. Instead of exercising the right to practice law which Myra Bradwell helped to establish for all women, she founded the influential law journal, the *Chicago*

Legal News. Mary Parker Follett was a writer on personnel practices and a lecturer to business groups rather than a management consultant or a personnel director employed directly by a bureaucracy.

Advertising and promotional literature were the secret of the success of Lydia Pinkham's Vegetable Compound and Harriet Hubbard Ayer's cosmetics. Mary Seymour founded the *Business Woman's Journal* very soon after she opened the first school to teach women typing. Maggie Lena Walker held and increased the membership of The Independent Order of St. Luke's, the base of her insurance organization, by publishing the *St. Luke's Herald.*

It is easy to think of reasons why women have been so continuously attracted to the word business. As Sarah Hale observed a long time ago, a writer needs no formal, specific schooling, and in addition, any attempt to restrict entry by licensing regulations would violate constitutional guarantees of the freedom of the press.

The word business requires little capital, an attraction of special importance to women without money of their own. From an economic point of view, writing is the intellectual equivalent of the free land of the West: both demand little investment beyond intensive labor. And it has always been something a woman could do at home. It was even respectable for a True Woman to cultivate herself by writing poetry, the way she might take up fancy embroidery, providing, of course, that she didn't make money at it. And if she did want to make money, or say something to the world, she could do it in secret. Sarah Hale was one of the first editors in America to print the full names of women authors, but for many years after, women writers used pseudonyms or initials to conceal their sex.

The business of words, to which women have always been attracted for reasons of their own, has steadily become more powerful and pervasive. Business and government are no longer run by people who talk to each other face to face without telling anybody else what is going on. So many people are involved in the large-scale organizations of the 1970s that increasing numbers of words on paper are needed to glue them together. Drafting, processing, and transmitting all these words have created new occupations, all of which offer opportunities for women. Women write technical manuals. They edit company publications. They preside over the keeping of records. They write the advertising copy that sells the company's products, and the promotion copy that tells the public what the company wants the public to know.

Billions of words spoken on television and clattering out of the teletype machines in hundreds of newspaper offices proclaim business and government policies. The production and distribution of news has become a giant industry in itself, and women who have made their way in journalism have gained access to power they could not have acquired in any other way—even in the male stronghold of money itself.

Analyzing how money is made is an even more sacredly male province than making it. "We have never hired a woman in the financial department, and we never will," the Associated Press told Sylvia Porter (1913–) when she applied for a job as a financial reporter in 1935. Nine years later, in 1944, the Associated Press hired Dorothy Carew as a financial editor. In 1976, Sylvia Porter reached 40 million newspapers through her column "Your Money's Worth."

Sylvia Porter is one of the few self-made women who have reached the top of a man's field in direct competition with men. In the taxonomy of successful women, she is not a "family woman" who inherited or worked in the shelter of an established enterprise. She is not a "woman's woman," supervising or selling to women. She is not a "token woman" put in for show, or a "gimmick woman" attracting profitable attention by her oddity value. She is a pure and simple talent bargain who made it with her brain and her willingness to work nonstop, all day long, day in and day out for years.

She had unusual encouragement from her mother, who had always regretted the career she might have had if she had not married. Sylvia has so distinct a recollection of her mother saying "I want you to have a career" that she thinks her mother must have started saying it to her while she was still in the cradle. "I'm my mother's daughter," she says.

Sylvia's father was a physician in Brooklyn who dropped dead of a heart attack when Sylvia was 12 years old. Like

many other widows, Rose Feldman was confronted with the
need—and to some extent, the opportunity—to start the career she had always wanted. After trying various lines of
work, she opened up a millinery business.

Sylvia reacted by racing through school so that she could
help her mother as soon as possible. In those days, public
schools promoted bright students to the level of their
achievement, regardless of age. Sylvia went directly from the
sixth grade to high school, which she negotiated in three and
a half years. When Cornell University refused to give her a
scholarship because she was only 16, she went to tuition-free
Hunter College in New York, and lived at home.

Sylvia had been at Hunter only a month when the Great
Crash of October, 1929, wiped out her mother's nest egg of
$30,000, most of it in Cities Service stock. There was no
money to pay the mortgage on their Brooklyn home. Like
many other families in the same boat, the Feldmans simply
walked away from the house and let the bank take it.

Where could all that money have gone? To find out, Sylvia
switched from English to economics, and systematically competed for every money prize open to her. In 1931, she married Reed Porter, a young statistician who worked in a bank,
and a year later she was graduated from Hunter magna cum
laude and was elected to Phi Beta Kappa.

It was the Phi Beta Kappa key jangling on a chain around
her neck that got her hired in the dismal job market of that
year. She had seen a notice about the opening of a new
investment counseling firm in the newspaper, and hurried to
the new office to see if they had a job. Arthur W. Glass, the
boss, needed no help, but the swinging key caught his interest and he hired her, duties unspecified, at $15 a week.

The duties turned out to be varied, including much talk
about the perilous state of the economy. Once Arthur sent
Sylvia to Bermuda with $175,000 in gold coins to be ready if
the U.S. went off the gold standard. When she received his
cable saying THE EXPECTED HAS HAPPENED, she converted
the gold into British pounds, converted the pounds into U.S.
bonds, and returned to the U.S. with $85,000 more than she
had taken out of the country.

The Depression was a hard school for beginners, but it

discouraged the noncompetitive and so conferred a comparative advantage to those with Sylvia's drive. She soon discovered, as many women had done before her, that the establishment would let a woman *write* about things they wouldn't let her *do*, providing, of course, that she did it anonymously and for less money than a man could make. Sylvia didn't mind, because writing was what she wanted most to do.

She wrote for financial magazines and looked around for a corner of financial reporting she could call her own. No one was regularly reporting the market for government bonds into which she had ventured for Arthur Glass, so in 1935 she started writing a column on the bond market for the *American Banker*. And she profited from her own words. With help from her husband's statistical charts, she managed to double the small capital she herself had to invest, a neat trick during the 1930s.

While she was writing the bond column she was also freelancing, at space rates, for the financial department of the *New York Post*. She landed a permanent job on the *Post* the hard way. In an economy drive, the *Post* fired the entire financial department one day in August, 1938, at noon. At four P.M. Sylvia was in the office of editor-in-chief Harry Saylor suggesting that she write a column to be called "Financial Post Marks." He agreed to give it a one-week trial providing she would also do the work of all the men who had been fired.

The column succeeded so well that the *Post* later rewarded Sylvia with a by-line of sorts by changing its title to "S. F. Porter Says." Bushels of mail arrived for Mr. S. F. Porter, and Sylvia soon became too good a secret to keep. "The time has come for us to make capital of the fact that S. F. Porter is a woman," *Post* editor T. O. Thackrey wrote in 1942. The unveiling of Sylvia Porter with an unequivocally feminine picture tapped an unexpected new source of income for her: lecturing to audiences of male business leaders curious to see what kind of woman would write about money.

Meanwhile, she had divorced Reed Porter shortly before he joined the Navy in 1941. Two years later she married G.

Sumner Collins, later General Promotion Manager of all Hearst newspapers, but it was not until 1950, when Sylvia was 37 and well established as a columnist, that their daughter Cris Sarah Collins arrived. The event did not delay a single one of the daily columns Sylvia continued to turn out, rain or shine, for a growing number of newspapers all over the country.

Sylvia's influence steadily increased. The affluent postwar years were the right time for a column addressed to the millions who had never before had money to invest. She explained economic news in plain words anyone could understand. In her column, the "discount rate" became the "basic borrowing rate." "Increasing productivity" became "a bigger output per manhour." She made the powerful second person singular her trademark. She talked about *you*, and *your* money.

Main Street ate it up. In 1960, when Sylvia Porter recommended a pamphlet, 17,000 people wrote in to the New York Stock Exchange for it. Wall Streeters liked to say that they didn't read her, but watched her as an influence on the market. Politicians respected her clout. In late 1963 President Lyndon Johnson invited her to the LBJ ranch in Texas to tell him what she thought of the Kennedy budget he had inherited. She told him in private, and after the budget was published, blasted it publicly as inflationary in her column, too.

"I've always been independent," she says, "and I don't see how it conflicts with femininity."

She tackled every economic issue from the consumer's point of view. In *Sylvia Porter's Money Book*, published in 1975, she filled more than 1000 pages with the no-nonsense money advice she had been dispensing five days a week for 29 years. The "money book's" subtitle promised to tell how to earn it, spend it, save it, invest it, borrow it, and use it to better your life. At an original price of $12.50, it was the book bargain of the year.

On the road to national recognition, Sylvia has had to deal with all the problems enterprising women have when they succeed in a man's field. Take, for instance, the minor but symbolic problem of names. Sylvia Porter was so well known when she divorced Porter that she kept his name. Later, she was sorry, but it was too late to change. And like many another famous woman, there was a flip-flop on sexual identification, from concealment to the exploitation that comes with success. While she was still signing her name with initials, Sylvia attacked Secretary of the Treasury Henry Morgenthau for his "lapse into disharmony with the Government bond market" every summer. "Is it obstinacy, stupidity, or sheer ill advice?" she queried in a freelance article in the *American Banker.* When Secretary Morgenthau demanded an interview with the author, the embarrassed editors managed to draft a letter of refusal without using pronouns. Later on, Secretary Morganthau wooed the well-known Sylvia Porter with presents of roses.

Enterprising women in the public eye have had to deal with curiosity about details of their personal lives irrelevant to what they are intent on saying or doing. News reporters feel constrained to satisfy this curiosity, if necessary by fiction. Sylvia has been a public figure long enough to have experienced a number of conflicting versions. Early accounts, for instance, ascribe her financial career to the influence of her banker husband, while more recent profiles emphasize her mother's losses in the stock-market crash.

The contradictions are an interesting study in the changing stereotypes of journalism. In pre-liberation 1960, *Time* Magazine reported that "husband Sumner, 56, has learned from experience that it is wise to lose some of the arguments" with a wife who "dominates her household without even pretending an interest in domesticity." In a 1975 newspaper article headed "A Friend's View," Phyllis Battelle described her as "intensely feminine in her relationship with Sumner" who "appears to be the number-one boss," and revealed that she was on the verge of taking cooking lessons when President Ford persuaded her to chair a Citizens Action Committee to publicize measures that individuals could take to combat inflation.

Enterprising women may shrug off this treatment, but eventually they have to adopt a policy for dealing with it. Some have withdrawn into pathological secrecy: Susan King was so publicity shy that little is known about her. Others have fabricated a commercially desirable public image: Miriam Leslie exploited intimate domestic details to attract attention.

Sylvia Porter has played it straight. She has tried to protect herself and her family from the attempts of reporters to mythologize her without projecting a counter-myth of her own making. She has preserved this admirable sanity because she has not been enticed by the opportunity to convert the power she exercises through her words into more direct forms of power.

She has refused all federal appointments, ostensibly because she doesn't want to get involved with politics, but it is quite likely that she really believes the excuse she gives when she's asked: "You can take a leave of absence from a corporation or a university and go back. But you cannot take a leave from a column; many people will come in and fill the vacuum. There will be nothing for me to return to."

Sylvia Porter probably earns as much money as anyone can make with a typewriter. To win the highest rewards in the word industry, however, it is necessary to leave the typewriter behind. One who succeeded in breaking loose has been called the "bright young witch" of Madison Avenue, and in the 1970s she was earning more money than any other man or woman in advertising. In 1974, Mary Wells Lawrence (1928–) received total compensation of $440,595 for her services as president of Wells, Rich, Greene, Inc., the advertising agency she founded.

Although she has four overworked secretaries, Mary keeps her manual typewriter handy in her glamorous office and she knows how to use it. She entered advertising by writing retail-store copy, but unlike earlier women successes, she did not move up by convincing male bosses that they really ought to pay more attention to "the woman's point of view." Mary Wells made no pretense of either being, or especially empathizing with, "Mrs. Consumer." Instead, she headed straight for the heart of the business: account strategy, account selling, and financing; and very soon—when she was only 37—she established her own agency. Wells, Rich,

Greene had a food account and a cosmetic account or two, but its mainstays were the "hard" profitable accounts dominated by men: liquor, cigarettes, airlines, automobiles, drugs, soft drinks. Mary Wells sold razor blades. Mary Wells sold the New York State Lottery. And the year after she went into business, Mary Wells went public and sold some of the stock of Wells, Rich, Greene at a tidy profit of several million dollars.

Mary Lawrence has said that she "concentrated on seeing that I never had to spend my life in the kitchen." Her father, Waldemar Berg, was a furniture salesman in Youngstown, Ohio, and her mother was determined that their only child should have every advantage. From the age of five, Mary was swamped with lessons in elocution, dancing, singing, and music.

Like Sylvia Porter's mother, Mrs. Berg prodded her daughter to achieve. "I was taught to think you can always do anything you want to do if you work hard enough," she says of her childhood. "My mother really pushed me into performing. I didn't have any big allowance. When there were contests, I was expected to enter them."

At 18 she went to New York to study acting at the Neighborhood Playhouse. The experience convinced her that she didn't want to go on the stage, but her theatrical training has helped in presentations to clients, which are organized like dramatic productions. And Mary's talent for dramatizing herself made her a super-saleswoman. According to reporter Eugenia Sheppard, her "soft, thrilling voice makes the maddest ideas seem perfectly possible."

Aside from drama training, her only other formal education was two years at the Carnegie Institute of Technology in Pittsburgh, where she met and married Burt Wells, an industrial design student who later headed his own art services agency in New York. They divorced, remarried and adopted two children, and were divorced a second time.

Mary's first job was writing ads for bargain basement merchandise in McKelvey's department store in Youngstown during the summer. In 1950 she and Burt moved to New York where she got a job in the advertising department of Macy's and moved up to be its fashion advertising director. She worked briefly thereafter at a number of agencies, including McCann-Erickson.

She went to Doyle, Dane, Bernbach in 1957, when it was a "hot" agency creating jazzy campaigns for Volkswagen Beetles and Avis rental cars. She did her stint there writing copy on food products such as a new line of casserole meals for General Mills, and in little more than a year had become associate copy chief. Then her career took off. By 1964, when she was 35, she was a vice president earning $40,000 a year —and ambitious to make more.

Marion Harper, the reigning wizard of Madison Avenue, offered her $60,000 to come to Interpublic, the new cluster of advertising enterprises he was founding. There she joined Jack Tinker and Partners, the elite think-tank of the cluster, set up to solve special problems. Three years later, when Harper did not make her president of Tinker, she left to become president of her own shop, taking two Tinker associates and the Braniff Airlines account with her.

Mary Wells created an image of instant success that attracted clients. She persuaded Harding Lawrence, president of Braniff Airlines, to paint the planes pastel colors and to dress the stewardesses in costumes designed by Pucci. The industry jeered, but the "Easter-egg airline" increased sales 41 percent and profits 114 percent.

When Mary Wells and Harding Lawrence were married in 1967, some 50 guests flew the Atlantic to attend the ceremony in a Paris town hall. The marriage created an obvious conflict of interest. Mary was spending $7.5 million a year of the money of a public company headed by her husband. She resolved the conflict by resigning the Braniff account in order to take on TWA, with an advertising budget of $22 million. Braniff could not object because the airlines fly different routes.

These events raised a few eyebrows on Madison Avenue, but they served only to boom the stock of Wells, Rich, Greene, which Mary had offered to the public in 1968. Going public was a smart financial move. By selling some of her stock in 1968 when the market was high and buying more of it back in 1974 when the market was low, she made $3 million and increased her stock interest in the firm at the same time.

Personal style pays off in the Madison Avenue competition for clients. After Mary left Doyle, Dane, Bernbach, Ned Doyle described her as a "quite beautiful" advertising woman, and added, "Most of 'em look like haunted houses." The Mary Lawrence touch may be sexy—she takes pains to be a stunning ash blond—but she is forthrightly aggressive. She admits to a "staggering lack of modesty" which makes it easy for competitors to gossip about her. She inspires cracks: critics have called her "Bloody Mary," and "a tough broad," and said that "if there's anything that Mary has got, it's cupidity."

When Dick Rich resigned as copy chief of the firm, he said, "The only critical thing I would say about her is that this country's total money supply is $92 billion and Mary will never get it all."

Money has a symbolic value to Mary Lawrence. She always drove hard bargains with the agencies employing her, and she expects her own employees to justify their salaries. "Wells, Rich, Greene is not a home for people," she says. "It is an opportunity. . . . We like people who are anxious to make money and who are hungry for money and who appreciate money, because it does tend to give you a certain drive." She pays her employees well, and many of them have profited from the agency's stock.

Mary Wells Lawrence shocks some of the men on Madison Avenue. They are accustomed to women who stay at their typewriters and take some of their pay in the fun of playing with words. Mary has seen that money is the name of the game and she insists on playing it to win.

Mary Wells Lawrence is probably the highest-paid woman in any branch of the word business, but she is not the most powerful. That honor goes to a woman who spent the first 46 years of her life as a housewife and sometimes acts as if power were an uncongenial burden thrust upon her.

Katharine Meyer Graham (1917–) is the daughter of Eugene Meyer, a self-made millionaire who was once chairman of the Federal Reserve Board. When the *Washington Post* was auctioned in 1933, Meyer was the mysterious stranger who bid it in for a bargain $825,000. Agnes Meyer, his wife, was an author and art collector, a Republican conservative and a classic Roosevelt hater. Indefatigable in cultural pursuits, Agnes Meyer expected her children to be as accomplished and active as she was.

As a young woman, Katharine feared she would never be able to live up to the standards of her family. During and after her college years, she worked as a reporter on the *San Francisco News* as well as on her father's *Washington Post.* In 1940 she retired, without regrets, to marry Phil Graham, a young lawyer, and they had four children.

After the war, Eugene Meyer persuaded Graham to join the *Post* as publisher, and in 1948, he sold the voting stock of the paper to the Grahams on their promise to continue its tradition of "virile, strong, and independent concern for the general welfare." Meyer and Graham were a good business team, and they set out to acquire properties. They bought the Washington *Times Herald, Newsweek* Magazine, radio and television stations, and a news service.

Then the catastrophe struck which jolted Katharine out of her comfortable life as a Washington matron. Phil Graham suffered increasingly more serious manic-depressive cycles. In 1963 he shot himself to death, leaving Katharine a publishing empire worth hundreds of millions of dollars. She could have sold it, but she had promised her father that she would maintain the *Post*'s tradition of public service. Someone had to take Phil Graham's place, and Katharine nominated herself.

Anecdotes abound about her shyness: how she made her first appearance in the newsroom, "a shaky little doe coming in on wobbly legs out of the forest"; how she used her parties and social connections to gather news for the paper; and how she was a good listener at news conferences, and encouraged the newsmen, never ordering, but always supporting.

The *Post* thrived under Katharine's management. James Reston, an editor of the *New York Times* and former chief of its Washington bureau, thought it became "an immensely better paper than it was when she took it over." Word spread that Katharine was becoming a power, but she resisted the compliment. "I think it's luck, or it's Fritz," she once said, referring to Frederick Beebe, who was hired by the Grahams to be chairman of the board before Phil's death.

She worked hard to escape notice, ducking interviewers, and using her knowledge of journalism to keep herself out of the papers. People in Washington knew about her, but she was not a national figure.

She gave others the credit, but she took the risks herself. It was her decision, in 1971, to publish the controversial Pentagon Papers and thus expose the *Post* to reprisals, if not court action, for printing classified material illegally "leaked" or stolen from a government office.

Then came the Watergate scandal. It broke as a local story in the *Post*—a local story that only an alert newsroom would have pursued. Katharine did not interfere or direct, but she followed the story every day. "My role was to make sure we were being fair and we were being factual and we were being accurate," she says. "I had to ask every question I could think of because the reputation of the paper was clearly at stake." An editor who recalls her husband's editorial style thinks hers was better. "Phil never had a Watergate, and if he had, he wouldn't have handled it as sagely. He was more brilliant but not as detached, too politically involved. I seriously doubt he could have made the claim, as Katharine has every legitimate right to do, of letting the journalistic chips, if you'll forgive the cliché, fall where they may."

Katharine did not flinch when word spread that John Mitchell had told *Post* reporter Carl Bernstein, "Katie Graham's gonna get her tit caught in a big fat wringer if that's published." A dentist sent her a little gold charm he had fashioned demonstrating the threatened punishment. Katharine wore it proudly into her newsroom.

Katharine Graham invites comparison with the Revolutionary printer Mary Goddard, another woman in the word business who was on the scene when American history was being made. Both exemplify all of the unusual circumstances that we have found characteristic of enterprising women.

Katharine Graham had an unusually thorough education

supervised by her mother, a woman of exceptional cultivation. Mary Goddard's mother was a women of extraordinary
culture, too. Both mothers provided their daughters models
of achievement beyond the usual pursuits of women.

Katharine Graham assumed management of the *Post* to
maintain its tradition when her husband died. Mary Goddard
took charge to backstop her brother. Neither woman would
have started these enterprises on her own.

Katharine Graham worked behind the scenes, through
others. She avoided personal confrontations. So did Mary
Goddard.

Both women publishers became more assertive personally
as they grew older and more experienced in exercising authority. The reader may recall that late in her career, Mary
Goddard vigorously protested her dismissal as postmistress of
Baltimore by soliciting signatures from citizens to a petition
on her behalf. Kay Graham has become noticeably more
feminist. In 1970, for instance, she refused to attend the all-
male Gridiron Club dinner because women less important
than herself were not invited on the same basis as men. She
had quietly contributed $20,000 to help found *Ms* Magazine,
but it was not until a few years later that she spoke on behalf
of the magazine in public.

Kay Graham is personally modest. Self-deprecation is too
old a habit to kick. She credits the unraveling of Watergate
to her staff, to the press in general, to the courts, to Congress
—to anyone but herself. But it is increasingly difficult even
for her to maintain that she deserves no personal credit for
what she has done because she fell into her position, as she
once put it, "by matrimony and patrimony." Women who
inherit large-scale enterprises do not usually undertake to
run them personally. For the brilliant performance of the
Washington Post, Katharine Graham must take some credit
herself.

23

RISING EXPECTATIONS
Jayne Baker Spain,
Eleanor Holmes Norton

In the years since World War II, the American economy has expanded by taking into the mainstream some of the people ignored by the Founding Fathers and left behind by the Industrial Revolution: the chronically poor whites, the marginal farmers, blacks, individuals suffering from handicaps of one kind or another, and that half of the population that was born female.

These were the people women had always been trying to help, so it was natural to find them concerned with the relative deprivation of those who were left out of the affluence most Americans were enjoying. For some women, social concern was also good business.

Defense industries had shown that blacks and women and older people could do jobs previously closed to them, and many companies had made good use of the physically handicapped, too. These wartime successes encouraged more ambitious experiments after the war. One of the most successful was undertaken by a woman who was so involved in her volunteer work with handicapped children that she was thinking of becoming a physician when she inherited her family's conveyor-belt company.

Jayne Baker Spain (1927–) wasn't groomed to run a business, but her father had always told her that she could do anything she set herself to do. A few years after she was graduated from college, deaths in the family left her sole owner of a substantial majority of the stock of Alvey-Ferguson, an international company which engineered and manufactured conveyor-systems.

There were many attractive offers to purchase her controlling interest. The materials-handling industry was growing, and Alvey-Ferguson had been founded on the original patents for gravity conveyors from which power conveyors evolved. These are the endless moving belts on which groceries ride out of the supermarkets to loading platforms, mail sacks move around post offices, and commercial baked goods march from oven to freezer. But, if she sold it, what would happen to all the loyal people in the company who had given their lives to it, many no longer young?

She put it up to the employees. "Shall *we* run the company, or shall *I* sell it?" There could, of course, be only one answer, so "we ran it." A year later she married John Spain, a young lawyer, and warned him he was marrying a company as well. Another year later, when their first child was born, she was deep in the intricacies of conveyors.

Because Alvey-Ferguson was her own company, she felt she could take the financial risk of training blind workers to do the assembling of the 450 little parts that went into the finished product.

She had the Cincinnati Association for the Blind work out a system for teaching the work. Then she herself learned the way the blind workers were taught and personally taught others. Eventually, one out of every ten workers in the company had some handicap. There were, among others, blind workers on the regular assembly line, physically handicapped people working at drawing boards, and workers with various disabilities doing other jobs. Profits could have plummeted, but they didn't.

The post World War II expansion transformed the materials-handling industry. Conveyors were needed in all manufacturing processes to move war supplies around factories, and warehouses and into and out of ships. Then came Korea. Labor was scarce. Orders were big. Jayne's handicapped workers were indispensable. "One of the advantages of a family-owned business is that you can build deep, trusting relationships with your people," Jayne says of that wartime period. "When news of a big order hits, you can feel it ripple through the plant."

Morale at Alvey-Ferguson was so good that Jayne found herself lecturing all over the country on the virtues of utilizing the talents of the handicapped. After the war, at the invitation of the U.S. government, she took her demonstration overseas to prove that American capitalism was not heartless. At trade fairs in Algiers, Greece, Yugoslavia, Czechoslovakia, Hungary, and Poland, she exhibited Alvey-Ferguson wheel conveyors being assembled by local blind workers. For every country she personally learned enough of the language to train a dozen blind nationals to do the work. And, it was with considerable relish that she explained to her Communist hosts that she employed handicapped workers because it was good business.

It is hard to evaluate from the balance sheet all that the handicapped workers accomplished for Alvey-Ferguson but there were obvious tangible gains: Their absentee rate was negligible. They came to work on time every day, rain, snow, or shine. They did not jump from job to job but stayed so long on the job that training costs were lowered. They had no accidents, as they were extremely safety conscious, so insurance rates came down. They were so proud to be productive members of society that the quality and the quantity of their work were excellent, and, says Jayne, their cheerful outlook, despite their physical handicaps, raised the morale of all employees. They enabled Alvey-Ferguson to attract as well as hold a loyal work force.

There was another, less obvious payoff. The opportunity to try a risky experiment with her own company enabled her to demonstrate that traditional personnel practices excluded whole classes of people who were quite capable of skilled work. The demonstration was important during the labor shortages of World War II, and it remained important during the equal opportunity movement of the 1970s. In 1966, Jayne Baker Spain sold Alvey-Ferguson to Litton Industries, but only on terms that protected the employment of the workers. She remained as a Litton Division President. In 1970, she became a director of Litton Industries, and in 1971 became vice-chairman of the U.S. Civil Service Commission, charged with getting more women and handicapped people into high-level government jobs. The assignment was a logical outgrowth of her lifelong interests, as was her 1976 appointment as Gulf Oil's Public Affairs Vice President.

Most employers, however, were not interested in welfare experiments. They continued to prefer young white males as employees, and as these moved ahead to higher standards of living, the excluded lagged farther and farther behind. Disappointment was keenest among the newly awakened blacks, the chronically poor whites, and eventually women.

The blacks were the first to protest and to win laws prohibiting discrimination in employment. Women followed suit. The National Federation of Business and Professional Women's Clubs had long campaigned for equal employment opportunity laws, and they were joined by activist organizations of the new movement for sex equality.

The work of enforcing these laws became an attractive new career for women. It was a logical way for enforcement agencies to practice what they were preaching. One of the ablest practitioners of the profession has been a lawyer who represents three of the groups protected by the new laws.

Eleanor Holmes Norton (1937–) is young, black, and female. She was just 32 years old when Mayor John V. Lindsay appointed her Commissioner of Human Rights of New York City in 1970. She was also pregnant. Many organizations would have refused to consider her for the $35,000 post, but as a token she was ideal. At her first press conference, Eleanor made it clear that she was not going to favor any of her client groups over another. "As Commissioner, I will attempt to see that no man is judged by the irrational criteria of race, religion, or national origin. And I assure you I use the word 'man' in the generic sense, for I mean to see that the principle of nondiscrimination becomes a reality for women as well."

As Commissioner of Human Rights, Eleanor had unusual powers. She could conduct investigations, hold hearings, subpoena witnesses, and award damages to complainants, even for pain and suffering.

One of her first actions was to force the 21 Club to serve women on an equal basis with men, and to rule that the Biltmore Hotel had to stop excluding women from its Men's Bar and had to stop *calling* it a Men's Bar as well.

She secured state laws widening job and educational opportunities, a minimum wage law for domestic servants, and the nation's strictest law against real estate practices that lead to residential segregation of the races.

Eleanor worked to make the City of New York itself a model employer. She kept a sharp watch on sex discrimination in city employment, broadened maternity-leave policies, and set up an affirmative action program.

With funds provided by the Federal Equal Employment Opportunity Commission, she studied company personnel systems.

Eleanor's achievements are a logical outgrowth of her whole life. Her father was a civil servant in the housing department of the District of Columbia who studied law at night and would have become a practising lawyer if he had thought that a black lawyer could make a living at it. Her mother was a schoolteacher, a job carrying high prestige in the black community of Washington, D.C., in those days.

Eleanor is the oldest of three Holmes daughters. According to family tradition, her father always wanted a son, and was dismayed when he learned that his third child was another girl. He transferred his ambitions for an achieving son to his girls, Eleanor in particular. Eleanor had a grandmother living nearby who watched her progress in school on a daily basis too. Eleanor went to Dunbar High School, for years the only college preparatory school attended by blacks in Washington, and she graduated the year the city's other schools were legally desegregated.

Although Eleanor would be the last to recommend segregation, Dunbar allowed her to grow up in a nonhostile community of self-selected, academically oriented blacks, most of whom went on to liberal arts colleges. Eleanor chose Antioch College because she thought its work-study program would give her a wider experience of the world than the Ivy League colleges attended by her classmates.

She decided to be a lawyer in order to work in the civil rights movement. She graduated from Yale Law School in 1964 and moved on to a staff job with the American Civil Liberties Union in New York, where she became a First Amendment specialist.

During her five years on the legal staff of the ACLU, Eleanor accepted assignments involving the defense of white supremacists denied freedom of speech or assembly. One of her first cases came to the ACLU from the National States' Rights Party on the Eastern Shore of Maryland. This racist group was enjoined from holding a meeting by local authorities who thought it likely that their derogation of Jews and blacks would provoke violent reprisal from civil-rights advocates.

When the Maryland courts upheld the injunction, Eleanor took the case to the Supreme Court of the United States, argued personally for the right of the segregationists to hold a meeting, and won. While not the first black woman to argue before the Supreme Court, she was still in her twenties, and easily the youngest.

Her most celebrated case was in defense of George Wallace when he was campaigning for the presidency. In 1968, Mayor Lindsay refused to grant Wallace permission to hold a rally in Shea Stadium, fearing, perhaps, that his segregationist views were so unpopular that his appearance would be a threat to civil order in New York City.

Wallace took the problem to the ACLU.

"We ought to assign him Eleanor," the ACLU director joked. However odd the assignment may have seemed, Eleanor took the suggestion seriously. She wanted the case because it involved her field, the First Amendment, and she won it.

Eleanor Holmes Norton is a symbol of the rising aspirations of women and a model of the professional life young women contemporaries find most attractive.

Her two young children were born during a period of intense career involvment. She is a lawyer engaged in helping underprivileged people. She is married to a lawyer who shares her goals, but they have separate careers. And instead of doing this work on a volunteer basis as women have always done, she is getting the money and the credit she deserves.

EPILOGUE

Two hundred years after Mary Goddard printed the Declaration of Independence, enterprising women had indeed come a long way from their counterparts of the Revolutionary era, but they were not yet displacing men at the highest policy-making levels. In 1973, *Fortune* Magazine checked the names of the three highest-paid officers of the 1000 biggest industrial companies on its list, plus the 50 largest in six nonindustrial fields. Among these 6500 top dogs in American business, only 11 were women, and one of them appeared to be a nonworking figurehead. In business, at least, women are still where they've always been—at the bottom.

They are at the bottom, however, in proportions unprecedented at any earlier period of American economic history. Among those in the entry jobs on the lowest rung of the occupational ladders in the 1970s were three fourths of the women 20 to 24 years old. In 1944, the biggest war production year, only 46 percent of this age group were working for wages.

The 20- to 24-year-olds are the key to the future. They are at the peak childbearing age and these are also the years during which serious careers are launched. Whether and how many women appear in future boardrooms depends on how many of them stay to climb the occupational ladder rather than drop out or mark time as so many of them have been content to do in the past.

We have learned something about enterprising women while writing and researching this book, and what we have learned holds hope that there will be more female faces at the top when this cohort of 20- to 24-year-old women comes of boardroom age. The hope lies in cultural and demographic changes which have begun to increase the numbers and proportion of women whose lives fit a pattern that seems to have made enterprise possible in the past.

With few exceptions, enterprising women have almost always had to have an education equal to the best available to the men of their time. For almost a century after the Revolution, the only way for a woman to get such an education was to be born into a family of educated men. The proportion of enterprising women rose noticeably in the second half of the nineteenth century after the first women college graduates set out to use their education.

Much more recently, women have finally won admission to the most prestigious undergraduate and graduate schools that provide them with credentials for the most desirable posts.

In addition, more women now have access to the higher education that many of them feel is necessary to convince employers of their competence.

The women we found enterprising in the past were lucky in having parents, husbands, or mentors who supported their interests on a personal basis, and encouraged them to achieve. Many observers noticed a decline in the number of achievers during the years when the Cult of True Womanhood pictured women as clinging vines. In the 1970s, a woman who does not have personal support can find encouragement from the culture. Television programs, newspaper stories, and the textbooks used in schools carry the message of equal opportunity. Feminists of 1976 have a right to be impatient with the lip service accorded to this equal opportunity by many employers, but ideas do have consequences. We found, for instance, that a surprising proportion of enterprising women had Quaker parents or sponsors. A majority of the American population now agree with the Quaker view of sex equality.

In earlier times, when women were almost continuously exposed to pregnancy, most of the enterprising women we found happened to be child- and/or husband-free during the years they began their careers. Some were unmarried by design, but in most cases they were liberated from domestic responsibilities by circumstances beyond their control. But this too has changed. Women of the 1970s can control their reproductive lives, and many of them plan their pregnancies around their careers. The American population of the 1960s and 1970s is one of the first in which all classes of women have access to reliable contraception and a majority have the means to protect themselves against unwanted childbearing.

Finally, we noticed that women in the past seemed to require the incentive of a family crisis to spur them to enterprise beyond the normal pursuits of women. Very frequently this crisis was the death or absence of a husband, father, or brother. This not only made it essential that they earn their own keep, but often it meant taking over the enterprise that had been run by the man of the family.

Women who got their start through a family business account for a substantial portion of every list of enterprising women in every historical period. Seven of "Ten Most Important Women in Big Business" chosen by *Fortune* in April, 1973, were in family businesses. Thirty-eight years earlier, in 1935, *Fortune* had looked for important women in business and found 16 worthy of mention. Of these, six profited by family connections.

More important than the statistics is the change in *Fortune's* attitude. In 1935, *Fortune* made the patronizing suggestion that women really couldn't succeed without the crutch of help from home. In 1973, chastened no doubt by some consciousness raising from its preponderantly female research staff, *Fortune* wondered how many potential women managers were being held back simply because they did *not* have a family connection behind them.

But in the 1970s an increasing proportion of young women expect to support themselves whether married or single, so their incentives are similar to those of males and do not depend on the accident of disaster.

Those who inherit family businesses in the future will perhaps have already established careers of their own, and the family business will not be the only business open to them.

In the past, too much enterprise, male as well as female, has been undertaken out of desperation. In the 1970s more people are free to choose the kind of work they do, or none at all if that's what they want. We can only hope that in the next two hundred years more enterprising women and men will found their careers not on necessity, but on their own free choice.

NOTES

PROLOGUE

"The role of women in American history has long been ignored," writes Gerda Lerner in *The Woman in American History* (Addison-Wesley Publishing Company, Menlo Park, Ca., 1971). Most of the few women included in economic histories are mentioned not as participants but as writers—for instance, Ida Tarbell, Helen M. Lynd, Margaret Myers, and Mary Beard. In this category are all six women listed in the index of *The Dynamics of the American Economy* by Charles H. Hession, S. M. Miller and Curwen Stoddart (Alfred A. Knopf, New York, 1956). Elizabeth of England and Eliza Lucas (or Eliza Pinckney under her maiden name) are the only women other than writers indexed in *American Economic History* by Harold Underwood Faulkner (Harper & Brothers, New York, 1938 and many other editions).

The most useful of many reference works consulted has been *Notable American Women, 1607–1950,* edited by Edward T. James, Janet Wilson James, and Paul S. Boyer (The Belknap Press of Harvard University Press, Cambridge, Mass., 1971). Authors of most of the 1359 biographies are recognized authorities on their subjects, and a bibliography is included for each woman. Women alive in 1950 are excluded. There are lists of the biographies by fields, permitting comparisons of many kinds. This work is abbreviated to *NAW* in later notes.

1. THE DECLARATION OF INDEPENDENCE: *Mary Goddard and the Early Printers*

Professor Ward L. Miner of Youngstown State University is our principal source on Mary Goddard. He wrote her *NAW* biography after writing *William Goddard, Newspaperman* (Duke University Press, Durham, N.C., 1962). Mrs. C. Oliver Iselin, a descendant of William Goddard, has given the only known picture of Mary, an engraving in an almanac she published in 1783, to the John Carter Brown Library, Brown University. With the permission of that library, the Enoch Pratt Free Library of Baltimore made us a copy from a negative in their picture collection.

Information on the Goddards is also found in Isaiah Thomas's *The History of Printing in America* (Joel Munsell, Albany, N.Y., 1874); John Tebbel's *A History of Book Publishing in the United States* (R. R. Bowker, New York, 1972); and Lawrence C. Wroth's *History of Printing in Colonial Maryland* (Williams & Wilkins, Baltimore, 1922). An article in the *Baltimore Evening Sun* of May 15, 1933, recalled Mary's disputes with the postal authorities. There are accounts of William Goddard's postal pioneering in Carl H. Scheele's *A Short History of the Mail Service* (Smithsonian Institution, Washington, D.C., 1970), and in Gerald Cullinan's *The United States Postal Service* (Praeger Publishers, New York, 1973). An excellent account of early women printers is given by Elisabeth Anthony Dexter in her *Colonial Women of Affairs* (Houghton Mifflin, Boston, 1924).

A legend persists in Baltimore that George Washington reappointed Mary postmistress and that she served from 1793 to 1799. This information was printed in *A Brief History of the Baltimore Post Office from 1753 to 1930* compiled by Ernest Green, assistant postmaster (Baltimore, Md., Post Office, 1930), and was repeated in 1975 Bicentennial publicity of the Baltimore Philatelic Society.

However, a recheck of official records by Arthur Hecht, in charge of postal history at the National Archives, shows Alexander Furbish as Baltimore postmaster from 1790 to 1800.

2. FAMILY BUSINESS: *Nantucket Women, Eliza Pinckney, Abigail Adams, Sarah Astor*

The quotation from Hector Crevecoeur appears in Oscar Handlin's *This Was America* (Harper & Row, New York, 1964, pp. 55–59; a reprint of a 1949 Harvard University Press book), which also contains other impressions of Nantucket. Nantucket women are reported in *Women of the Sea* by Edward Rowe Snow (Dodd, Mead & Co., New York, 1962), and *Career Women of America, 1776–1840* by Elisabeth Anthony Dexter (Marshall Jones Co., Francestown, N.H., 1950). Dexter's son, Lewis Anthony Dexter, now on the Johns Hopkins University political science faculty, supplied additional information.

Much about life on the Lucas and Pinckney plantations is found in *The Letterbook of Eliza Lucas Pinckney, 1737–1762*, edited by a member of the family, Elise Pinckney, and published by the University of North Carolina Press in 1972. Elise Pinckney also wrote Eliza's *NAW* biography. Elisabeth Dexter's *Colonial Women of Affairs* also includes Eliza (pp. 119–125).

Her own letters speak best for Abigail Adams. Collections include those by Charles Francis Adams (*Letters of Mrs. Adams with an Introductory Memoir*, Little Brown and Company, Boston, 1840) and by Stewart Mitchell (*New Letters of Abigail Adams*, Houghton Mifflin, Boston, 1947). L. H. Butterfield, an editor of the *Adams Family Correspondence* (Harvard University Press, Cambridge, 1973), wrote Abigail's *NAW* biography. Another is Janet Whitney's *Abigail Adams* (Little Brown and Company, Boston, 1949).

Practically all chronicles of the Astor family praise Sarah's help in her husband's career. Among the more recent are Lucy Kavaler's *The Astors: A Family Chronicle of Pomp and Power* (Dodd, Mead & Co., New York, 1966) and James L. Stokesbury's article, "John Jacob Astor," in *American History Illustrated* (October, 1971). The most detailed account of their business affairs is Kenneth Wiggins Porter's *John Jacob Astor, Business Man* (Harvard University Press, Cambridge, 1931).

3. COMMUNITY BUILDERS: *Women of the Frontier*

Principal sources are *A Woman's Story of Pioneer Illinois* by Christiana Holmes Tillson, edited by Milo Milton Quaife (R. R. Donnelly & Sons, Chicago, 1919); *Grandmother Brown's Hundred Years, 1827–1927* by Harriet Connor Brown (Little, Brown and Co., Boston, 1929); *Westward the Women* by Nancy Wilson Ross (Alfred A. Knopf, New York, 1933); *The Sod-House Frontier, 1854–1890* by Everett Newton Dick (D. Appleton, New York, 1937); and "Women's Role in the American West" and other articles by T. A. Larson in *Montana, the Magazine of Western History* (July, 1974).

For details of the Mercer ventures, see "The Story of the Mercer Expeditions" by Flora A. P. Engle, in the *Washington Historical Quarterly* (October, 1915), *Mercer's Belles: The Journal of a Reporter* by Roger Conant, edited by Linna Deutsch (University of Washington Press, Seattle, 1960).

4. THE INDUSTRIAL REVOLUTION: *Rebecca Lukens*

Madeleine Bettina Stern, who is a dealer in rare books as well as an author, wrote the *NAW* biography of Rebecca Lukens and devoted a chapter to her in *We The Women: Career Firsts of Nineteenth Century America* (Schulte, New York, 1963). The latter has a lengthy bibliography. There also are accounts of Rebecca in the *Directory of American Biography* and in *The Canning Clan* by Earl Chapin May (Macmillan Co., New York, 1937).

There is persistent legend that Catherine Greene (widow of Gen. Nathanael Greene), not Eli Whitney, invented the cotton gin. "The invention of the cotton-gin . . . was due to a woman, Mrs. Greene, though the work was done and the patent taken out by Eli Whitney," wrote Phebe A. Hanaford, for example, in *Daughters of America* (True & Co., Augusta, Me., 1882, p. 623). Catherine called Whitney's attention to the problem, and he was a guest at her plantation when he made his first gin; later, she backed him financially; but technically the invention was his. "There seems to be no basis for the legend which later credited her with . . . one of the basic principles," concludes Constance McLaughlin Green in her *NAW* biography of Catherine.

5. THE VOCATION OF WOMANHOOD: *Sarah Hale*

Barbara Welter explained the concepts of "The Cult of True Womanhood, 1820–1860" (*American Quarterly*, Summer, 1966, pp. 151–174), listing its cardinal virtues as "piety, purity, submissiveness and domesticity."

Most quotations from Sarah Hale are from her monthly column, "The Editor's Table," in *Godey's Lady's Book* (especially December, 1850). Paul S. Boyer wrote her *NAW* biography. Other biographies include: *The Lady of Godey's* by Ruth E. Finley (J. B. Lippincott Co., Philadelphia, 1931), and *Sarah Josepha Hale and "Godey's Lady's Book"* by Isabelle Webb Entrikin (Lancaster Press, Philadelphia, 1946). There are chapters on her in *Bold Women* by Helen Beal Woodward (Farrar, Straus and Young, New York, 1953), and *Forgotten Ladies* by Richardson Wright (J. B. Lippincott Co., Philadelphia, 1928). Ray W. Sherman, in "A Toast! To Sarah" (*National Business Woman*, November, 1958), recounts her campaign for Thanksgiving observance. James P. Wood, in *Magazines in the United States* (Ronald Press, New York, 1956), credits her with being the first editor of an important magazine to pay writers systematically.

6. TEACHERS: *Catharine Beecher*

A recent appraisal is Joan N. Burstyn's "Catharine Beecher and the Education of American Women" (*New England Quarterly*, September, 1974, pp. 386–403). Barbara M. Cross wrote the *NAW* biography. See also *Pioneers of Women's Education in the United States* by Willystine Goodsell (McGraw-Hill, New York, 1931); *Catharine Esther Beecher, Pioneer Educator* by Mae Elizabeth Harveson (privately printed, Philadelphia, 1932); *Catharine Beecher: A Study in American Domesticity* by Kathryn Kish Sklar (Yale University Press, New Haven, 1973); *Saints, Sinners and Beechers* by Lyman Beecher Stowe (Ivor Nicholson and Watson, London, 1935); *These*

Were the Women, U.S.A.: 1776-1860 by Mary Ormsbee Whitton (Hastings House, New York, 1954).

7. FASHIONS FOR EVERYONE: *Ellen Demorest, Margaret LaForge*

The basic book on the Demorests is *Crusades and Crinolines* by Ishbel Ross (Harper & Row, New York, 1963), researched from family papers and complete files of their publications. Ms. Ross wrote the *NAW* biography of Ellen Demorest. Histories of magazines by Frank Luther Mott and others also report the Demorests' ventures.

For more details on Margaret LaForge, see *America's First Lady Boss—A Wisp of a Girl, Macy's and Romance* by Curtiss S. Johnson (Silvermine Publishers, Norwalk, Conn., 1965). Paul Goodman wrote her *NAW* biography. See also Ralph M. Hower's *History of Macy's of New York, 1858-1919* (Harvard University Press, Cambridge, Mass., 1946), and *The Great Merchants* by Tom Mahoney and Leonard Sloane (Harper & Row, New York, 1974).

8. MONEY MAKERS: *Margaret Haughery, Susan King*

For the material on Margaret Haughery, we are indebted to Sister M. Catharine Joseph Haughey, C.I.M., of Immaculata College, Immaculata, Pa. She wrote "A Candle Lighted: A Capsule Biography of Margaret Gaffney Haughery (1813-1882)," in *American Catholic Historical Society Records* (Philadelphia, June, 1953, pp. 112-130), and the *NAW* biography. See also "Margaret of New Orleans," by Emily Wangard Thomann, in *The Catholic World* (April, 1936, pp. 50-56) and "This Is Margaret," by Violet Alleyn Storey, in *Independent Woman* (January, 1956, p. 9). Her name, pronounced Haw-ry, also is found spelled Haughey, Haugherty, Hoey.

Ishbel Ross kindly amplified in a personal communication what she wrote about Susan King in *Crusades and Crinolines.* Her sources were the New York press and Demorest publications.

9. THE CIVIL WAR: *Mary Ann Bickerdyke, Annie Wittenmyer, Dorothea Dix, Clara Barton*

Among the more recent of many volumes on women in the Civil War are *Bonnet Brigades* by Mary Elizabeth Massey (Alfred A. Knopf, New York, 1966); *Noble Women of the North* by Sylvia G.L. Dannett (Thomas Yoseloff, New York, 1959); and *Lincoln's Daughters of Mercy* by Marjorie Barstow Greenbie (G. P. Putnam's Sons, New York, 1944).

Early works include *Women of the War* by Frank Moore (S. S. Scranton & Co., Hartford, 1866); *My Story of the War* by Mary A. Livermore (A. D. Worthington, Hartford, 1887); and *Under the Guns* by Annie Wittenmyer (E. B. Stillings & Co., Boston, 1895).

Louisa May Alcott's hospital journal can be found in *Louisa May Alcott, Her Life, Letters and Journals*, edited by Ednah D. Cheney (Little, Brown and Company, Boston, 1930, pp. 115–119). Louisa's book *Hospital Sketches* (James Redpath, Boston, 1863) is a much modified version of the journals, with names deleted and the hospital called "Hurlyburly House."

The best account of the United States Sanitary Commission is *Lincoln's Fifth Wheel* by William Quentin Maxwell (Longmans, Green & Co., New York, 1956). In approving the commission, Lincoln said he feared it might become "a fifth wheel to the coach." There is a full-length biography of Mother Bickerdyke: *Cyclone in Calico* by Nina Brown Baker (Little, Brown and Company, Boston, 1952). The best source on Dorothea Dix is *Forgotten Samaritan* by Helen E. Marshall (University of North Carolina Press, Chapel Hill, 1937). For Confederate medical affairs, see *Doctors in Gray* by H. H. Cunningham (Louisiana State University, Baton Rouge, 1958).

Most readable of the many biographies of Clara Barton is *The Angel of the Battlefield* by Ishbel Ross (Harper & Brothers, New York, 1956). Mabel Boardman, who after a bitter squabble succeeded Clara as leader of the American Red Cross (though refusing the title of president), accused her of exaggerating her war achievements and took the extraordinary step of asking electors of the Hall of Fame for Great Americans not to vote for Clara when she became eligible for that honor. And the "angel of the battlefield" was not elected.

10. RECONSTRUCTION: *Frances Leigh*

Our major source is *Ten Years on a Georgia Plantation Since the War* by Frances Butler Leigh (Richard Bentley and Son, London, 1883). See also H. L. Kleinfield's *NAW* biography of Frances' mother, Frances Anne Kemble; and C. Mildred Thompson's *Reconstruction in Georgia* (Columbia University Press, New York, 1915).

11. THE PROFESSIONALS: *Myra Bradwell, Lucy Taylor,*
Elizabeth Blackwell

The *NAW* biography by Dorothy Thomas is the only easily available account of Myra Bradwell's life. See also George W. Gale's article, "Myra Bradwell: The First Woman Lawyer" (*American Bar Associ-*

ation Journal, December, 1953, pp. 1080–83, 1120–21). Nancy P. Johnson, University of Chicago Law School librarian, supplied copies of the *Chicago Legal News* reporting Myra's death from cancer and reviewing her career.

Madeleine Bettina Stern chronicled Lucy Hobbs Taylor for *NAW* and also in her book *We the Women.* See also articles by Ralph W. Edwards ("The First Woman Dentist—Lucy Hobbs Taylor, D.D.S. (1833–1910)," *Bulletin of the History of Medicine* 25:3, May–June 1951) and by Elizabeth Neber King ("Women in Dentistry," in *The Washington University Dental Journal,* August–November 1945). The 1870 census counted 24 women dentists. There were 61 in 1880 and 337 in 1890.

Elizabeth Blackwell's own addresses and autobiography are the primary sources on her life. She wrote her autobiography, *Pioneer Work in Opening the Medical Profession to Women,* at the suggestion of her adopted daughter, Katharine Barry. In the Vassar College Library copy, the Longmans imprint is covered by a label that reads "Published by K. Barry, Exmouth Place, Hastings, 1895." This was reprinted by E. P. Dutton (New York, Everyman's Library, 1914) with a bibliography of Dr. Blackwell's writings, a foreword by M. G. Fawcett, and a supplementary chapter by Robert Cochrane covering the last years of her life.

The principal biographies are *Child of Destiny* by Ishbel Ross (Harper & Brothers, New York, 1949), and *Lone Woman* by Dorothy Clarke Wilson (Little, Brown and Company, Boston, 1970). The family is reported by Elinor Rice Hays in *Those Extraordinary Blackwells* (Harcourt, Brace and World, New York, 1967).

Hobart College, successor to the institution which Dr. Blackwell attended, named its first women's dormitory Blackwell House. Since 1958, Hobart and William Smith Colleges have given an annual Elizabeth Blackwell Award, a gold medal bearing her portrait, to a woman whose life exemplifies her "unselfish devotion, sense of dedication, and reverence for life." An 18-cent U. S. postage stamp pictured her in 1974.

While Dr. Blackwell lived to see many medical schools open their doors to women, it was not until 1945 that the Harvard Medical School admitted women, and the Jefferson Medical School in Philadelphia was all-male until 1960. While increasing steadily in numbers, the proportion of physicians who are women continues to be less in the United States than in many countries—notably Russia, where a majority of physicians are women.

12. CONFIDENCE BUILDERS: *Mary Baker Eddy, Lydia Pinkham, Harriet Hubbard Ayer, C. J. Walker*

Ann Douglas Wood, who teaches a course on Women in America, 1820–1920, at Princeton University, has documented thoroughly women's illnesses of this period. See her article, " 'The Fashionable Diseases': Women's Complaints and Their Treatment in Nineteenth-Century America," *Journal of Interdisciplinary History* 4:1 (summer 1973), pp. 25–52. This is reprinted conveniently in *Clio's Consciousness Raised*, edited by Mary S. Hartman and Lois Banner (Harper & Row, New York, 1974).

Reflecting her importance, the complexity of her career, and the availability of material, Sydney E. Ahlstrom's 7000-word account of Mary Baker Eddy is the longest of the 1359 biographies in *NAW*. (Dr. Ahlstrom is professor of American history and modern church history at Yale University.) Full-length biographies include: *The Life of Mary Baker Eddy*, by Sybil Wilbur, and *Mary Baker Eddy: A Life Size Portrait*, by Lyman P. Powell (Christian Science Publishing Society, Boston, 1907 and 1930); *Mary Baker Eddy: The Years of Discovery* by Robert Peel (Holt, Rinehart and Winston, New York, 1966); and *Mrs. Eddy: The Biography of a Virginal Mind* by Edwin Franden Dakin (Charles Scribner's Sons, New York, 1929). Dr. Ahlstrom calls Dakin's book "bitter and opinionated but based on considerable research."

In William Dana Orcutt's *Mary Baker Eddy and Her Books*, (Christian Science Publishing Society, Boston, 1950), a non-Scientist who printed her books lauds her business acumen, saying: "Mrs. Eddy was a great executive and would have been great in any vocation." *Battle for Heaven*, a play by Michael O'Shaughnessy and Randolf Carter dramatizing her triumphs at 86, was presented for the first time in 1969 at Elizabeth Seton College.

For material on Lydia Pinkham we are much indebted to Sarah Stage, assistant professor of history at Williams College. She wrote her Ph.D. dissertation on Lydia and studied her papers in the Schlesinger Library at Radcliffe. Dr. James Harvey Young, professor of history at Emory University, wrote Lydia's *NAW* biography.

See also *Life and Times of Lydia Pinkham* by Robert Collyer Washburn (G. P. Putnam's Sons, New York, 1931); *Lydia Pinkham Is Her Name* by Jean Burton (Farrar, Strauss and Giroux, New York, 1949); and *Lydia E. Pinkham* by Elbert Hubbard (Roycrofters, East Aurora, New York, 1915).

Our principal sources on Harriet Hubbard Ayer were *The Three*

Lives of Harriet Hubbard Ayer by Margaret Hubbard Ayer and Isabella Taves (J. B. Lippincott Company, Philadelphia, 1957) and the *NAW* biography by Bernard A. Weisberger. Harriet's 1899 book on "the laws of health and beauty" was reprinted in 1975 by Arno Press, New York.

Walter Fisher wrote Madame Walker's *NAW* biography. See also *New World A-Coming* by Roi Ottley (Houghton Mifflin, Boston, 1943, pp. 170–77); "Madame C. J. Walker, Pioneer Big Business-woman of America" by George S. Schuyler (*The Messenger*, August, 1924, pp. 251–66); and two articles in *Ebony:* "Madam Walker" (January, 1949, pp. 62–66) and "Ebony Hall of Fame: First Person Named by Readers is Madame C. J. Walker" (February, 1956, p. 25).

13. INSTITUTION BUILDERS: *Henrietta King, Eliza Nicholson*

King Ranch stationery for 40 years listed "Mrs. J. M. King, Proprietor." The best source on Henrietta King is *The King Ranch* by Tom Lea (Little, Brown and Company, Boston, 1957), a scholarly two-volume history written with the help of ranch records following the ranch's centennial. *Fortune* gave a detailed account of the ranch in the years immediately following Henrietta's death in "The World's Biggest Ranch" (December, 1933). Charles J. V. Murphy reported the overseas operations in two *Fortune* articles: "The Fabulous House of Kleburg" (June, 1969) and "The King Ranch South of the Border" (July, 1969). A firsthand account of an earlier period is given in Frank Goodwin's *Life on the King Ranch* (Thomas Y. Crowell, New York, 1951).

The most recent and most objective account of Eliza Jane Nicholson is that of William G. Weigand in *NAW*. The most detailed is the highly sentimentalized *Pearl Rivers* by James H. Harrison (Tulane University Press, New Orleans, 1932). Her considerable part in the success of the *Picayune* is acknowledged by Thomas E. Dabney in *One Hundred Great Years, The Story of the Times-Picayune from Its Founding to 1940* (Louisiana State University, Baton Rouge, 1944).

14. WOMEN IN THE OFFICE: *Mary Seymour, Katharine Gibbs*

We are indebted to Robert W. Lovett, Curator of Manuscripts and Archives, Baker Library, Harvard University, for help on Mary Seymour. He wrote her *NAW* biography and shared his research, including a letter from Robert W. Hill, Keeper of Manuscripts, The New York Public Library, which says that Mary seems "to have vanished without trace of personal effects."

Her business affairs were documented in the *Business Woman's Journal* and the *American Woman's Magazine* (photocopies of which were supplied to us by the Kansas State Historical Society). Additional information came from her obituary in the March 22, 1893, issue of the *New York Times* and from *American Women* by Frances E. Willard and Mary A. Livermore (Mast Crowell and Kirkpatrick, New York, 1893, vol. 1).

Commercial Work and Training for Girls by Jeannette Eaton and Bertha M. Stevens (Macmillan, New York, 1915) has more information on women's conquest of office work; Richard N. Current's *The Typewriter and the Men Who Made It* (Urbana Illinois Press, 1954) and Bruce Bliven, Jr.'s *The Wonderful Writing Machine* (Random House, New York, 1954) document the story of the typewriter from its earliest beginnings.

The quote detailing the advantages of having women clerks ran in *Cosmopolitan* magazine and was reprinted in *What America Owes to Women: The National Exposition Souvenir*, edited by Lydia Hoyt Farmer (Charles Wells Moulton, Buffalo, 1893), in a selection titled "Women Clerks in New York" by Marquise Clara Lanza. The quotations from S. S. Packard are from a book published by the *New York Tribune: Occupations of Women and Their Compensation* (New York, 1898).

Miss Barbara Lyon, the Alumni Secretary of the Katharine Gibbs School in New York, supplied biographical material on Katharine. Most of the records of the school, which were stored at the Cape Cod home of Gordon Gibbs, Katharine's son and long the president of the schools, were destroyed in the hurricane of 1954. Information also came from an article in the *Providence Sunday Journal* of March 23, 1969 ("45,000 Girls Are Glad Katie Sold Her Jewels," by Phyllis Meras), which was based on interviews with Gordon Gibbs and Blanche Lorraine Gibbs, Gordon's wife and one-time secretary to Katharine, and at that time president of the enterprise. Since then, the schools have been sold to The Macmillan Company. Other sources included two articles in *The Gibsonian*: "In Appreciation of Mrs. Katharine M. Gibbs" (November, 1934), and "Beginnings," from the first issue (January, 1929).

15. SEX WOMEN: *Miriam Leslie, the Everleighs*

Excellent accounts of Miriam Leslie are to be found in *Charmers & Cranks* by Ishbel Ross (Harper & Row, New York, 1965) and *Purple Passage: The Life of Mrs. Frank Leslie* by Madeleine Bettina Stern (University of Oklahoma Press, Norman, 1953). Ms. Stern also wrote the *NAW* biography. The New York Public Library and the Library of Congress have collections of Miriam's letters.

Our account of names, dates, and origins of the Everleigh sisters differs from the accounts found in most other sources and is based on two documents unavailable earlier: the death certificate of Minna, who died in New York's Park West Hospital on September 16, 1948, and the obituary of Aida published on January 4, 1960, by the *Daily Progress* of Charlottesville, Virginia, the day after her death there.

Charles Washburn, who knew the Everleigh Club as a young *Tribune* reporter and became friendly with the sisters, wrote *Come Into My Parlor: A Biography of the Aristocratic Everleigh Sisters of Chicago* (Knickerbocker Publishing Co., New York, 1934). In this book he withheld their names because their brother was alive and shifted their background to Kentucky.

Herbert Asbury described the club in *Gem of the Prairie* (Alfred A. Knopf, New York, 1940). Edgar Lee Masters, the poet, recalled its attractions in the April, 1944, issue of *Town & Country*. M. M. Musselman revealed the sisters' automobile connections in *Get a Horse: The Story of the Automobile in America* (J. B. Lippincott Company, Philadelphia, 1950).

Herman Kogan wrote of the sisters (in collaboration with Lloyd Wendt) in *Lords of the Levee: The Story of Bathhouse John and Hinky Dink* (Bobbs-Merrill, Indianapolis, 1943) and also for *NAW*, which kept within its 1950 cutoff rule by listing the entry in Minna's name though the article also dealt with Aida, who lived until 1960.

16. PROFESSIONALIZING HOUSEWORK: *Ellen Richards, Fannie Farmer, Alice Lakey*

Our principal sources on Ellen Richards were *Ellen Swallow: The Woman Who Founded Ecology* by Robert Clarke (Follett Publishing Co., Chicago, 1973); *The Life of Ellen H. Richards* by Caroline L. Hunt (Whitcomb & Barrows, Boston, 1912); *His Mark* by Robert Hallowell T. Richards (Little, Brown and Company, Boston, 1936); and Madeleine Bettina Stern's *We the Women.* Janet Wilson James wrote Ellen's *NAW* biography. The Vassar College Library has a collection of her papers.

For more on Fannie Farmer, see the *Dictionary of American Biography* and Elizabeth Bancroft Schlesinger's *NAW* biography, as well as "Fannie Farmer and Her Cookbook," by Zulma Steele (*American Mercury*, July, 1944), and "Fannie Merritt Farmer: An Appreciation," by Mary Bronson Hartt (*Woman's Home Companion*, December, 1915).

Helen T. Finneran's *NAW* biography of Alice Lakey is the only easily available account. For material on her pure food activities, see Oscar E. Anderson, Jr.'s *The Health of a Nation: Harvey W. Wiley and the Fight for Pure Food* (University of Chicago Press, 1958).

17. THE INNOVATORS: *Maggie Walker, Kate Gleason*

Many biographical sketches are available on Maggie Walker, including a somewhat flowery account by a schoolmate of hers, *Maggie L. Walker and the Independent Order of Saint Luke*, by Wendell L. Dabney (Dabney Publishing Company, Cincinnati, 1927). Other good sources are Lily Hammond's *In the Vanguard of a Race* (Council of Women for Home Missions and Missionary Education Movement of the United States and Canada, New York, 1922), and *Women Builders* by Sadie Iola Daniel (The Association Publishers, Inc., Washington, D.C., 1931). Ms. Daniel also wrote the *NAW* biography.

Background information on the social climate following the Civil War and on black fraternal orders and insurance companies in the 1880s was obtained from Norman Hodges, professor of history at Vassar College, as well as from August Meier's book, *Negro Thought in America, 1880–1915* (University of Michigan Press, Ann Arbor, 1963).

Timothy Wheeler of the *Richmond Times-Dispatch* researched the Independent Order of St. Luke's and the St. Luke's Bank and Trust Company for us, supplying Maggie Walker's obituary from the Richmond newspaper of December 16, 1934.

We were greatly assisted in researching the life of Kate Gleason by Shirley Iversen, Local History Division Librarian at the Rochester Public Library, and by Nancy E. MacKenzie at Gleason Works, who supplied other articles as well as a photograph of Kate.

Much of the personal information about Kate comes from an article in the October, 1928, issue of *American Magazine:* "Kate Gleason's Adventures in a Man's Job," by Helen Christine Bennet. Her East Rochester project Concrest is described in "How a Woman Builds Houses to Sell at a Profit for $4,000," published in *Concrete* (January, 1921), and written by Kate herself.

18. HELPERS: *Mary Follett, Josephine Roche, Mary Richmond*

Sources on Mary Follett include: *Dynamic Administration: The Collected Papers of Mary Parker Follett*, edited by Henry C. Metcalf and L. Urick (Harper and Brothers, New York, 1941); "Mary Parker Follett: An Appreciation," by Richard C. Cabot (*Radcliffe Quar-*

terly, April 1, 1934); the *NAW* biography by Dawn C. Crawford; and Peter F. Drucker's *Management: Tasks, Responsibilities, Practices* (Harper & Row, New York, 1974).

Articles on Josephine Roche include "Women in Business," in *Fortune* (September, 1935); "Miss Roche Receives the National Achievement Award," in the *Elevsis of Chi Omega* (September, 1935); the entry in *Current Biography*, 1941; "A Union Angel," in *Business Week* (June 17, 1944); "Battler for Miners," in *Business Week* (April 8, 1967); and an interview by Nicholas Von Hoffman in the *Washington Post* (November 24, 1972). See also *Miners and Management* by Mary Van Kleeck (Russell Sage Foundation, 1934). Vassar College and the Franklin D. Roosevelt Library have some of her papers.

We are indebted to Prof. Muriel W. Pumphrey, Department of Sociology and Anthropology, University of Missouri at St. Louis, author of the *NAW* biography of Mary Richmond, for suggestions and additional material, including her *Social Casework* articles, "Mary A. Richmond—The Practitioner" and "The First Step—Mary Richmond's Earliest Professional Reading" (June, 1957). See also Margaret Rich's "Mary E. Richmond—Social Worker," also in *Social Casework* (November, 1952) and *The Heritage of American Social Work* edited by Muriel Pumphrey (Columbia University Press, New York, 1961).

19. FASHIONS FOR EVERYONE II: *Ida Rosenthal, Nell Donnelly*

For material on Ida Rosenthal, we are obliged to her daughter, Beatrice Coleman, to Ellis Rosenthal, and to Lynn Goldfarb of Maidenform. Published references include *The Economy of Cities* by Jane Jacobs (Vintage Books, Random House, New York, 1970, pp. 11–12, 56–57, 191); "Her Half-Billion-Dollar Shape," by Pete Martin (*Saturday Evening Post*, October 15, 1949); "Maidenform's Mrs. R.," in *Fortune* (July, 1950); "I Dreamed I Was A Tycoon," in *Time* (October 24, 1960); "Our Town's Leading Business Women," by Judy Michaelson (*New York Post*, September 6, 1963); and Ida's obituary in the *New York Times* of March 30, 1973.

We are indebted to Nell Donnelly herself for some of the information about her life. Published sources include articles in *Fortune* (September, 1935); *Time* (December 28, 1931, and December 25, 1933); the *Kansas City Journal-Post* (February 2, 1930); the *Kansas City Star* (September 8, 1934; November 14, 1937; October 8, 1939; January 4, 1948); and the *Kansas City Times* (July 2, 1932; June 12,

1946; January 8, 1971). Peggy Smith of the Missouri Valley Room of the Kansas City Public Library supplied the newspaper articles.

20. WORLD WAR II: *Olive Ann Beech, Tillie Lewis*

Accounts of Beechcraft's soaring progress under O. A. Beech are to be found in *The History of Beech* by William H. McDaniel (McCormick-Armstrong Co., Inc. Wichita, 1971). Articles on her include "The Ten Highest-ranking Women in Big Business," by Wyndham Robertson, (*Fortune*, April, 1973) and "Danger: Boss Lady at Work," by Peter Wyden, (*Saturday Evening Post*, August 8, 1959). Her many activities include the National Federation of Business and Professional Women, of which she has been a director.

Tillie Lewis, with whom we had a long interview in New York, is also discussed by Wyndham Robertson in the *Fortune* article listed above. Other articles about her include "Tillie of the Valley," by Ruth Winter (*San Francisco Sunday Examiner & Chronicle*, January 6, 1974); "Tillie of the Valley," by Dorothy Walworth (*Reader's Digest*, August, 1952); and "New Wealth for Their Valley," by Alilea Haywood (*Independent Woman*, June, 1952).

21. THE VOCATION OF WOMANHOOD II: *Beatrice Gould*

The quotations are from *What Makes Women Buy* by Janet Wolff (McGraw-Hill Book Co., New York, 1958). Other references are *Macy's, Gimbels, and Me* by Bernice Fitz-Gibbon (Simon and Schuster, New York, 1967); *George Horace Lorimer and the Saturday Evening Post* by John W. Tebbel (Doubleday, Garden City, 1948, pp. 212–13); *Magazines in the Twentieth Century* by Theodore Peterson (University of Illinois Press, Urbana, 1956, pp. 175–78); and *American Story* by Bruce Gould and Beatrice Blackmar Gould (Harper & Row, New York, 1968).

22. WORD WOMEN: *Sylvia Porter, Mary Wells Lawrence, Katharine Graham*

"Authors" is the biggest of all categories into which the 1359 women in *NAW* are sorted. At least a third of those classed as "entrepreneurs" were involved in publishing, writing or editing. Classifications include "newspaperwomen" and "literary scholars."

Sylvia Porter was the subject of a *Time* cover article, "Sylvia and You" (November 28, 1960, pp. 46–52). More recent accounts include "Woman in the News," by Fern Marja Eckman (*New York Post*, October 4, 1974); "Economic Summiteer Sylvia Porter," by Diane

K. Shah (*National Observer*, October 12, 1974); "The President's Reluctant Analyst," by Marlene Cimons (*Los Angeles Times*, October 29, 1974); and "Sylvia Porter," by John F. Baker (*Publishers Weekly*, June 2, 1975). We also gathered material during a pleasant talk with her.

Accounts of Mary Wells Lawrence include: "As the World Turns on Madison Avenue," by Carol J. Loomis (*Fortune*, December, 1968); "The Best Paid Woman in America," by Kate Lloyd (*Vogue*, February 15, 1972); and "America's Corporate Sweethearts," by Marylin Bender (*New York Times*, January 20, 1974).

Some of our information on Katharine Graham came from correspondence with her. Articles about her include "Katharine Graham," by Jean Stafford (*Vogue*, December, 1973); "Katharine Graham, the Power that Didn't Corrupt," by Jane Howard, and "Kay Meyer Goes to College," by Laura Bergquist (both in *Ms*, October, 1974); and "Katharine Graham," by Clare Crawford (*Family Circle*, February, 1975).

Two years before Watergate, Donald Robinson included Katharine Graham in his book, *The 100 Most Important People in the World Today* (G.P. Putnam's Sons, New York, 1970, pp. 175–78). Other women in the volume are Indira Gandhi, Golda Meir, Margaret Mead, the anthropologist; and Gwendolyn Brooks, first black to win the Pulitzer Prize for poetry.

23. RISING EXPECTATIONS: *Jayne Baker Spain, Eleanor Holmes Norton*

Most of our material on these interesting and important women came directly from them. Earlier articles on Spain include: "The Spectacle That Astonished Salonica," by Don Wharton (The *Rotarian* and *Reader's Digest*, September 1963); "Jayne Spain: Conveyor of Help," by Gloria Anderson (*Cincinnati Enquirer Magazine*, October 11, 1970); and "Vice Chairman Jayne Baker Spain," by Mary Robbins (*New Woman*, December 1971). *Vital Speeches of the Day* for April 1, 1971, reprinted her U.S. Air Force Academy address, "A Woman Could be President."

Articles on Eleanor Holmes Norton include: "Eleanor Holmes Norton: Constitutional Lawyer," by Caroline Mahoney (*New Woman*, September, 1971); "Defender of Unpopular Causes," in *Ebony* (January, 1969); "She Fights Bias," by May Okon (*New York Sunday News*, November 29, 1970); and *"I Hope I'm Not a Token,"* by Claudia Dreifus (*McCalls*, October 1971). Ms. Norton is one of ten women profiled in *Women Today* by Greta Walker (Hawthorn Books, New York, 1975).

INDEX